RECOLONIZATION
GATT, the Uruguay Round & the Third World

Chakravarthi Raghavan

Foreword by
Julius Nyerere

Zed Books Ltd.
London and New Jersey

Third World Network
Penang, Malaysia

Recolonization is published by Zed Book Ltd.
57 Caledonian Road, London N1 9BU, UK and 171 First Avenue,
Atlantic Highlands, New Jersey 07716, USA, and by
Third World Network, 87, Cantonment Road, 10250 Penang, Malaysia.

Copyright © Third World Network 1990.

Printed by Jutaprint
54, Kajang Road, 10150 Penang, Malaysia.

British Library Cataloguing in Publication Data

Raghavan, Chakravarthi
    Recolonization: GATT, the Uruguay Round & the
    Third World.
    1. Foreign trade. Treaties: General Agreement on
    Tariffs and Trade. Uruguay Round: (Negotiation).
    Negotiations
    I. Title
    382.92

    ISBN 0-86232-966-3
    ISBN 0-86232-967-1 pbk

CONTENTS

To Kalyani and Artie

LIST OF TABLES

GLOSSARY

A glossary of some abbreviations, acronyms, and technical words used in the GATT and in the Uruguay Round, and in this book.

ACP: African, Caribbean and Pacific (Group of States in the Lome Agreement with EEC).

AMS: Aggregate Measure of Support - a formula to measure the level of government support for agriculture by commodity sectors of total agriculture. It involves aggregating budget payments and determining the 'price gap' between world and domestic prices. There are several variants of this being used by different participants in the agricultural trade negotiations, and are aimed at defining and focussing the measurement according to the different rules and concepts envisaged for the negotiations.

PSE: Producer Subsidy Equivalent, an OECD term for a broad measure of support to the income of producers arising from government intervention in production and trade.

ASEAN: Association of South East Asian Nations, whose GATT members are Indonesia, Malaysia, Philippines, Singapore and Thailand.

bindings: Tariffs which are frozen or fixed in GATT schedules and cannot be increased without the negotiation of compensation elsewhere.

BOP: Balance of payments.

CAP: Common Agricultural Policy (of the EEC).

Cairns Group: So-called non-subsidising agricultural exporters, named after the town in Australia where they first met. Members are Argentina, Australia, Brazil, Canada, Chile, Colombia, Hungary, Indonesia, Malaysia, New Zealand, Philippines, Thailand and Uruguay.

CCCN: Customs Cooperation Council Nomenclature (of tariff classifications).

contracting party (cp): government signatory to and applying the General Agreement on Tariffs and Trade. Spelt in lower case, it is used generically for country (and in plural for countries) signatory to the GATT.

Contracting Party (CP): A country signatory to the GATT, and in its plural form to signify one or more of them. Their annual meeting is called Session of the Contracting Parties.

CONTRACTING PARTIES: When capitalised, the term is used to signify contracting parties acting jointly.

CTD: Committee on Trade and Development. A GATT body which handles issues of particular interest to developing countries.

Council: GATT Council of Representatives which acts in between Sessions of Contracting Parties, meeting about ten times a year, and handles regular GATT business, disputes etc.

Customs Union: Under GATT rules a customs union involves removal of duties and other barriers to almost all of the trade between the countries involved, together with adoption of a unified customs tariff towards non-members.

DC: Developing country.

DMEC: Developed Market Economy Country.

Degressivity: Used in the context of safeguards to suggest that any emergency import controls (safeguards) should be wound down systematically during their operation.

EEC: European Economic Community, a customs union formed under the Treaty of Rome.

EFTA: European Free Trade Association. Members at present are Austria, Finland, Iceland, Norway, Sweden, Switzerland, and Liechtenstein.

Enabling Clause: Decision of the GATT CONTRACTING PARTIES in 1979 for tariff and nontariff preferential treatment in favour of, and among developing countries. In GATT it provides the legal cover for the generalised system of preferences (GSP) schemes of Industrialised countries of tariff preferences in favour of developing countries.

FAO: Food and Agriculture Organisation.

FDI: Foreign direct investment.

FOGS: Functioning of the GATT system - an issue on the agenda of the Uruguay Round.

Free Trade Area: Similar to the customs union, but with each member state maintaining its own individual commercial policy, including tariff towards non-members.

GATT: General Agreement on Tariffs and Trade.

Group of 77 (G77): Group of developing countries in UNCTAD and other UN agencies. In GATT there is only an 'informal group of less developed contracting parties', and includes besides the G77 members of GATT, also Israel and Turkey.

Grey area measures: Term used for bilaterally-agreed and discriminatory trade restrictions (VERs, VRAs, OMAs etc) of very dubious GATT validity.

GNG: Group of Negotiations on Goods - Uruguay Round body which oversees all the negotiations in the area of goods.

GNS: Group of Negotiations on Services - the Uruguay Round body responsible for negotiations on trade in services.

GSP: Generalised System of Preferences, non-reciprocal and non-discriminatory preferences granted by ICs in favour of DCs, established as a result of an agreement in 1968 at UNCTAD.

HS: Harmonised System (of Tariff classifications).

IBRD: International Bank for Reconstruction and Development (World Bank).

IC: Industrial Country (used also as DMEC or OECD countries).

ICAO: International Civil Aviation Organisation.

ILO: International Labour Organisation.
IMF: International Monetary Fund.
IPR: Intellectual Property Right.
ITU: International Telecommunications Union.
LDC: In GATT (and IMF and World Bank), 'less developed country' or 'developing country'. In the UN system it means 'least developed country'.
LLDC: Used in GATT for the UN classification 'least developed country'.
MFA: Multifibre Arrangement. An exception to the GATT first negotiated in 1974 - and extended for the third time in 1986 (till Aug 1991) - under which industrialised countries are able to negotiate and impose quotas on imports of textiles and clothing from developing countries. The MFA had been preceded, from 1961, by similar arrangements restricted to trade in cotton textiles and clothing.
MFN: Most Favoured Nation. The fundamental principle of GATT enshrined in Art. I, and requires non-discrimination with regard to imports. No Contracting Party is to be treated less favourably than any other, and any favourable tariff or other concession granted by one CP to imports from another is to be automatically extended to all other CPs.
Morges group: Informal group of key countries (importers and exporters) involved in the agricultural negotiations in the round (and in the earlier committee on agriculture trade under the 1982 GATT work programme), so named after the place in Switzerland where the group first met. It includes Argentina, Australia, Brazil, Canada, EEC, Finland (for Nordics), India, Japan, New Zealand and US.
MTN: Multilateral Trade Negotiations, usually called trade rounds.
National Treatment: Concept enshrined in Article III, it requires that imported goods, once they have passed customs, be treated no less favourably than domestically produced goods. They are not to be subject to higher

internal taxes or more demanding regulations, standards etc., than domestic goods. Industrial countries are now trying to extend the application of this concept to services, foreign suppliers (firms or individuals) and foreign capital even before they cross the border and come into a country.

NAM: Non-Aligned Movement.

NG: Negotiating Groups, 1 to 14, in the area of trade in goods, and each dealing with individual items for negotiations listed in the Punta del Este Declaration.

Nordics: Informal grouping, consisting (in GATT) of Finland, Iceland, Norway and Sweden. Denmark the other Nordic country is a member of the EEC.

NGO: Non-governmental organisations.

NRPs: Natural Resource-based Products - one of the items on the Uruguay Round agenda and covering trade in non-ferrous metals and minerals, fish and fisheries products and forestry products.

NTB: Non-Tariff Barrier.

NTM: Non-tariff measure, and includes quotas and technical barriers to trade.

OMA: Orderly marketing arrangement.

OECD: Organisation for Economic Cooperation and Development whose members are DMECs.

OPEC: Organisation of the Petroleum Exporting Countries.

PSE: See under AMS.

QR: Quantitative restriction.

Quadrilateral: Term used for the informal group and meetings of the US, EEC, Japan and Canada on trade matters.

RBP: Restricted business practice.

R and D: Research and development.

Request and Offer: Classical form of trade negotiations in which concessions are the subject of direct and, usually, bilateral bargaining. The results of these are later extended to all CPs through the MFN rule.

Safeguards: Emergency protective actions which Article XIX of GATT permits a contracting party to undertake in

specified circumstances to protect a specific domestic
industry from an unexpected buildup of imports.

Sanitary and phyto-sanitary measures: Health regulations relating respectively to animals and plants.

SDR: Special Drawing Rights (in the IMF).

Selectivity: Term used in the context of safeguards to mean
right to apply safeguard actions, not against imports from
all suppliers in a non-discriminatory way as GATT's Art.
I requires, but against individual suppliers in a discriminatory manner i.e. on a selective basis.

S and D: Special and Differential Treatment for developing
countries provided for in Part IV of the General Agreement and by the Enabling Clause; also referred to as
special and more favourable treatment.

SS/RB: Standstill and rollback commitments concerning the
trade policy conduct of participants in the Uruguay
Round.

SUNS: Special United Nations Service (since March 1990
known as South-North Development Monitor), a daily
development bulletin which monitors the GATT negotiating process.

Surveillance body: Uruguay Round body which oversees
the implementation of the standstill and rollback commitments.

TNC: Trade Negotiations Committee - the overall body, established by the Punta del Este Declaration to carry out
the Uruguay Round Negotiations.

TNCs: Transnational Corporations.

TRIMs: Trade-related investment measures - one of the items
on the agenda of the Uruguay Round.

TRIPs: Trade-related Intellectual Property Rights including
trade in counterfeit goods - an issue on the agenda of
the Uruguay Round.

Tariff Peaks: High tariffs (far above the average tariffs of
a country) used to shelter some 'sensitive' industries like
textiles, leather goods, and food products.

Tariff Escalation: When import duties are higher on semi-
processed products than on raw materials, and higher

still on finished products. This escalation serves to keep the market open for raw materials but ensures that domestic industries get the higher added value of processing rather than the countries from which the raw materials originate.

UNCTAD: UN Conference on Trade and Development.

UNCTC: UN Centre on Transnational Corporations.

UNESCO: United Nations Educational, Scientific and Cultural Organisation.

USTR: US Trade Representative.

USITC: US International Trade Commission.

VER/VRA: Voluntary Export Restraint/Voluntary Restraint Arrangement. A bilateral arrangement of dubious GATT validity in which the exporting country undertakes to limit exports of a particular product to a particular market.

WIPO: World Intellectual Property Organisation.

PUBLISHER'S NOTE

A recent event that is little publicised and hardly known to ordinary citizens is likely to influence the shape and structures of the world economy for many decades to come.

That event is the Uruguay Round of trade negotiations under the auspices of the General Agreement on Trade and Tariffs.

What is happening is especially crucial for Third World countries. The industrialised countries are attempting, through the Uruguay Round, to extend and tighten their control of the world economy and the national economies of the Third World.

They are doing it by incorporating new areas (like services, foreign investments and intellectual property) into the GATT framework. If they succeed, then Third World countries will have to "liberalise" or open up their national economies, and allow transnational companies to have sweeping rights not only to export to but set up base in Third World countries, and to be treated like locally-owned companies. This may be the case not only in manufacturing, but also in the service sectors (such as banking, insurance, transport, communications and professional services). Moreover, the Third World's access to industrial technology and to information would be rendered much narrower through new regimes on intellectual property that favour the big companies. GATT itself may be converted into a super trade organisation enforcing the rules and regulations of world trade, mainly in the industrial countries' favour.

As a result, the Third World will be left even further behind whilst the developed countries extend and expand their control over the world economy.

These crucial developments in the Uruguay Round have received scant public attention because the negotiations are conducted behind closed doors, so they remain hidden from the scrutiny of the world's press and citizen groups. Moreover, the discussions are often conducted with the use of technical terms and strange-sounding acronyms (like TRIPS, TRIMS and FOGS), giving the impression that the issues are too complex and beyond the comprehension of ordinary citizens. Yet behind the secrecy and the technicalities of the Uruguay Round negotiations lie critical issues that will affect the lives – and deaths – of ordinary people.

It is our fortune to have a man of Chakravarthi Raghavan's calibre following the Uruguay Round negotiations from its inception in 1986 to its final stages in 1990. With his senior journalist's eye, his wide range of contacts in the diplomatic and UN circles, and most importantly his deep sympathetic understanding of the position of the South in the international economic arena, Raghavan has managed through the years to keep the Third World informed of the many twists and turns of North-South economic battles, including within GATT. More than merely informing, Raghavan has helped to shape the Third World's position by clarifying the issues and their consequences. This book could only have been written by someone like Raghavan, who has made the Uruguay Round talks "transparent" (to use GATT jargon) by unveiling the negotiations and their consequences in incisive analytical terms.

The Third World Network is pleased to publish this book which opens the curtains to explain the history, issues and battles in the Uruguay Round, and its significance and consequences to the Third World. It also provides suggestions as to the positions the Third World countries should take.

We hope this book will be useful for policy-makers (especially in the Third World), economists and social scientists, citizen groups and the ordinary public.

We would like to thank the International Foundation for Development Alternatives, South Commission and Inter-Press Service; Zed Press (which is co-publishing the book); Mr Julius Nyerere, the former President of the Republic of Tanzania and Chairman of the South Commission for his foreword; Martin Khor, Iqbal Asaria and Chee Yoke Heong for editing work; Lim Jee Yuan and Linda Ooi for design and typesetting; and most of all to C Raghavan himself for his scholarship and determination.

S M Mohamed Idris
Coordinator
Third World Network
Penang
April 1990

FOREWORD

At different periods until the Second World War, Spain, Portugal, Holland, Britain, France, Germany were proud of their colonial empires even when they did not give them that name. They saw no reason to hide their domination over others. The domination was total; it was political, and therefore economic, and social. And it was upheld by military power - which had rarely to be deployed while its existence was understood or at least believed in by the colonized. Through this domination, the economic and other interests of the colonial territories and their peoples were subordinated to those of the metropolitan power whenever there seemed to be any possibility of conflict.

Since 1945 there has been a change. National independence has been accepted as a universal right in the statutes of the United Nations. It has been accepted among the peoples of the erstwhile colonial powers as well as among those of the former colonies who had for long been demanding it. Military occupation of another country against the wishes of the people of that country is internationally condemned.

This means that colonialism in the traditional and political sense is now almost a thing of the past. Even the 'gun boat diplomacy' which sometimes supplemented or preceded it, and which was indulged in by other powers also - like

USA - has to a considerable extent been replaced by 'covert action' on the part of the Great Powers. But even 'covert action' by them against governments judged hostile to their economic or strategic interests can be expensive; in democratic states it can also arouse opposition within the country conducting it. And experience has shown that 'covert action' can also lead to international complications if it is not quickly and quietly successful.

Thus, the ruthless pursuit of economic interests by any of these traditional means is either impossible or has very strong disadvantages, however strong a country may be. But powerful nations still seek to spread their domination, and as far as possible their control, over other nations and areas. They still seek to ensure that their domestic interests are served regardless of the interests, or needs, of weaker nations and peoples. The strategy has merely been changed to take account of the rise of nationalism in the Economic South, the world-wide spread of ideas about Human Rights and the rights of Nations to independence, and the existence of the United Nations.

The new strategy is based on the use of economic strength against weakness and dependency; on technological domination face to face with technological backwardness; and on inherited cultural domination combined with control of international information structures.

There are many people in the world - in the field of politics as well as those less active in public affairs - who sincerely believe that the post-1945 period has marked the triumph of genuine internationalism, and of interdependence of equally sovereign nations. They point to the United Nations and its Agencies, the World Bank, the multitude of world functional associations, institutions, and meetings, and to the trade and communications links between all parts of the globe. They believe also that the world's rich are helping the world's poor to overcome their poverty and underdevelopment through Aid and loans and technical assistance. Such people - as well as those to whom the use of strength against weakness is a natural and indeed progressive human trait - would condemn all talk of neo-colonialism or economic colonialism, and the whole purpose of this book.

Unfortunately, such people do not know - or do not understand - the realities of power which underlie the operations of most of these institutions, and which wage constant and too often·successful war with the purposes and ideals for which they were set up. Most ordinary people have heard about Aid. It is from the rich countries in the Economic North to the poor countries of the Economic South. They have never heard of 'Aid' from the South to the North.

What these innocent people do not realise is that through the workings of the present international economic arrangements, wealth flows almost all the time from the poor 'developing' countries of the Third World to the industrialised and rich countries of the developed world. It flows from the primary producers to the industrialised countries, from the ignorant to the knowledgeable. How could they know these things? Virtually nothing in the Northern media gives them such information.

Yet that is the reality. The facts can be extracted from the statistics of all the international organisations; sometimes they are even mentioned in their Annual or Specialised Reports.

Tens of billions of dollars flow every year from the Economic South to the Economic North through movements in the terms of trade which have been adverse to the underdeveloped countries almost continually since the 1950's. The prices of primary commodities like cotton, coffee, cocoa, copper etc. etc. - which are the major export products of the Third World - go down in relation to the prices of machinery, lorries, capital investments of all kinds, and most manufactured goods. To an ever increasing extent, Third World countries sell cheap and buy dear.

Wealth flows also from South to North through financial mechanisms. For example: in the last decade poor nations have found that the Interest Rates on loans they incurred earlier have been increased by their creditors without consultation. They borrow to meet these 'obligations'. And so get further and further into debt even as they transfer huge amounts to their creditors in debt service.

Again, wealth flows through the South's purchase of knowledge - through fees for education and training, through the purchase of books, through subscriptions to vital information agencies, and through payment for the use of patents, or trade marks, or production licences. And so on.

Yet the poor nations of the Third World borrow money, or buy knowledge, or produce primary products for export rather than food for themselves, in order to invest in development - in a less poor future - or to meet their basic human requirements after natural or economic disaster has hit them. It is these purposes which are frustrated when they make a net export of resources to developed countries. This they have been doing for the last six years on account of debt servicing alone, without taking into account the permanent drain constituted by the unfair trading system.

The intellectuals and governments of the Third World have understood the iniquitous effects of the post-1945 world economic order for a very long time. In 1973 they came together and demanded negotiations leading to a new - and more just - International Economic Order. In the wake of the oil crisis of that year, and the work of the OPEC, the matter was put on the World Agenda. Slowly and grudgingly talks about how to organise the negotiations began. The need for them was urged by the Brandt Report in 1980, which made some concrete suggestions about what could be done.

But even as they talked, the industrialised countries organised themselves to resist pressures from the OPEC
and the Third World, and the publication of the Brandt Report
almost coincided with political changes in the major
countries of the North. In 1981 - at the Cancun Conference
- the need for structural change in the international economic
arrangements was firmly denied by the major Northern
representatives. The subject was taken off the World
Agenda; no constructive further discussions have been directed to reform the International Economic Order since that
time.

And now we have the Uruguay Round of trade negotiations.

The Uruguay Round purports to be the eighth in a
series of trade negotiations held under the auspices of
GATT, aimed at encouraging international trade through
reduction of tariff and non-tariff restrictions on imports.
But in fact it is fundamentally different from the previous
seven 'Rounds'. It is a complex undertaking, involving many
different but simultaneous negotiations at different levels,
which taken together could redefine and rewrite the rules
for international trade and those for other new and
important spheres of international economic relations.

In essence, it is an attempt to restructure and refash-
ion the rules of the international trading system to make this
even more favourable than at present to the interests and
concerns of the major trading nations - the industrialised
countries of the Economic North. If the attempt succeeds,
there will indeed be a New International Economic Order.
But it will be even more iniquitous and inimical to the
development aspirations and needs of the poor developing countries than the Order against which they have
been protesting for so many years.

There have been a number of articles and books published on this subject. In particular, the South Commision in
August 1988 published a 'Statement on the Uruguay Round'
which drew attention to its importance to the countries of the
Economic South. It analysed the manner in which the proposals would close off vital development options and opportunities in the future - especially but not only in the increasingly important areas of Science and Technology.
And it pointed out that only co-operation, co-ordination
and solidarity among the countries of the South could succeed in preventing almost irreparable damage to their attempts to develop their countries in freedom and to improve
the lives of their peoples.

This book goes much more deeply into the background,
the history, and the negotiating issues of the Uruguay Round.
It shows how the developed countries did, at earlier periods
of their histories, guard and serve their development interests by protecting their economies against domination by
stronger nations. And it explains how the Uruguay Round -
if the final result is anything like the proposals of the
Industrialised Countries - will prevent the developing countries of the last decade of the 20th century from acting in a
similar manner.

In other words, this book shows how, in area after
area of the Uruguay Round's detailed negotiations, Economic Colonialism is attacking the independent nations of
the Third World and seeking to secure control of strategic
points in their economies. It shows also that this attack
is being pointed by the Transnational Corporations of the
world, in whose interests the Industrialised Countries are
acting, while at the very same time their governments protect
other domestic industries and economic sectors even contrary to the existing GATT rules which they now wish to
extend and twist!

This book will be helpful to negotiators and to
their governments. But it has a much wider interest than

that. In its Epilogue it makes constructive suggestions about how the countries of the South can strengthen themselves in the negotiations. It calls for active interest in the Uruguay Round and in GATT to be taken by the Non-Governmental Organisations and other activists of South and North. And it explains how these expressions of public interest can help to fight this present danger to the future.

This is important. For although the subject of this book is economics and international economic negotiations, it is really about politics, and about national freedom for the countries of the Third World. And the book is written in a manner which can be understood by serious readers who have no economic training. It will therefore be welcomed by genuine internationalists as an alert signal - warning of an attempt to perpetuate and extend the inequities of an international economic structure which is already leading to misery, hunger, ignorance and death in the Third World. And, through its analysis and the suggestions given, it can contribute to the struggle against a serious danger which threatens future world stability and peace.

Julius K Nyerere
February 1990

INTRODUCTION

"The Uruguay Round... is an attempt to tackle issues of strategic importance for the design and management of the global economy, including the linkages between money, trade and finance. In a number of respects the outcome of the Uruguay Round may vitally affect the domestic development and future options of the developing countries."

South Commission [1]

The Uruguay Round of Multilateral Trade Negotiations was launched in September 1986. It had been preceded by more than two years of intense discussions in the GATT, and diplomatic pressures and other manoeuvres (public and private) by the US and other Industrial Nations.

After the initial two years of discussions (at technical level) and the mid-term review (at ministerial level at Montreal in December 1988 and at high-official level in Geneva in April 1989), which provided guidelines and directions for further negotiations, the Uruguay Round has entered its fourth year and is in the final phase of negotiations which are to be concluded at a Ministerial meeting at Brussels (in Belgium) 3-7 December 1990.

The Uruguay Round, both in the plethora of issues for negotiations, as well as in its structures and plans, was imbalanced and weighted against the Third World, when it was launched. It has become even more imbalanced and asymmetric after the mid-term review, and the negotiating process has become an instrument of power play.

But, both before and after the launching of the Uruguay Round, these important developments have received little attention in the Third World - neither in the media nor amongst non-governmental organisations and businessmen.

Even as the negotiations are moving into the final year of its four-year time-span, not all sections and policy-makers within Third World governments seem to be aware of the full implications of the Uruguay Round, whose sweep goes far beyond the normal international trade policy issues of a country. Some of the major Third World countries do not even seem to have a single nodal point or Ministry providing continuity, institutional memory and an overall perspective on the Round, its issues and implications.

This lack of attention is partly due to the fact that peoples and governments in the Third World are daily fighting a battle for survival, and international issues seem so remote. But part of the reason is the dependence of the Third World media on transnational information flows and systems. Some of the transnational news agencies are part of information data networks that would benefit from the liberalisation efforts in 'services', and while they are not deliberately setting out to distort information, the 'demands' of their principal markets in the North and their cultural milieu inevitably result in a one-sided information flow.

As a result, what little has been published are the viewpoints of the dominant North, and its information and disinformation. Even the academic community by and large gets its information mostly from publications emanating from the North and expounding its views - from the IMF/IBRD and GATT or the non-official institutions and think-tanks of the North expounding these philosophies, and their surrogates in the South, often financed by the North.

One recent exception is the publication by the UNCTAD Secretariat of some selected papers, originally commissioned and prepared as part of its technical assistance programme to the Third World countries participating in the Uruguay Round negotiations, and made public at their instance [2].

The present book is an effort to place in the hands of the Third World public, and concerned groups, information on the Uruguay Round and its implications. It is not intended to be an academic or objective exercise, but has been written from a Third World perspective and aimed at filling the gap in other publications. The book is in five parts. The first deals with the political economy of the Uruguay Round and its broad implications in terms of South-North relations. The second deals with the new themes on the agenda of the Round and their interlinkages. The third looks at some of the traditional and old issues of trade and market access, particularly those of importance to the Third World countries. In the light of these, the fourth looks at issues with systemic implications. The fifth deals with the progress in the negotiating processes in the first two years and the outlook in the light of the Mid-term review - the Ministerial meeting at Montreal in December 1988 and the high official level meeting at Geneva in April 1989. It also updates the situation up to January 1990 and presents some views on what positions the Third World countries should take.

In writing this book the author has drawn largely on information gathered by him, as a journalist, in conversations with key participants, and his contemporaneous reporting of these events and processes before and after the launching of the Round. The core of the book is based on two studies done by the author for the South Commission - the first in mid-1988 and the second in May 1989 after the mid-term review. These have been revised and expanded, and are now being published with the permission of the Commission.

Before and after the launch of the negotiations, a number

of key Third World negotiators have discussed the issues in depth and have provided information to the author on material not available on record. It will be invidious to single out any of them, more so as several of them spoke on a background basis. But the author is grateful to all of them. Mohammad Afzal Bajwa, Executive Director of the International Textiles and Clothing Bureau (ITCB), and Jagdish Saigal of the UNCTAD Secretariat went through several of the chapters and offered their helpful suggestions and critical comments, and some source material. The author has benefited greatly by their advice and is grateful to them. All errors and omissions are entirely the responsibility of the author.

Thanks are also due to Dr Manmohan Singh, Secretary-General of the South Commission and his colleagues in the Secretariat, Dr Gamani Corea, former Secretary-General of UNCTAD and member of the Commission, and Mohd Idris and Martin Khor of the Consumers' Association of Penang and Third World Network, for their encouragement. The author is also deeply grateful to the International Foundation for Development Alternatives and its President Marc Nerfin, who conceptualised and published the SUNS [3] for ten years as a source of Alternative Information for the South and but for whose support and friendship all this would not have been possible.

Last, but not least, the author is deeply grateful to Mwalimu Julius Nyerere, former President of Tanzania and Chairman of the South Commission for having agreed to write a foreword.

C Raghavan
February 1990

Notes on Introduction

1. *South Commission, Statement at Third Meeting at Mexico* 5-8 August, 1988.

2. *Uruguay Round: Papers on Selected Issues* (1989), UN Sales No UNCTAD/ITP/10; "Trade in Services: Sectoral Issues", UN Sales No. UNCTAD/ITP/26.

3. *Special United Nations Service,* a daily newsletter devoted to North-South and South-South dialogue. Published by *IFDA* from 1980 till March 1989, it is now being published by the *Third World Network*, in cooperation with the *Inter Press Service News Agency* and the *South Commission*.

PART 1

BACKGROUND

Chapter 1

SOUTH-NORTH RELATIONS AND THE URUGUAY ROUND

The Uruguay Round versus Sustainable Development

On September 20, 1986, at the South American seaside summer holiday resort town of Punta del Este (Uruguay), Ministers of Contracting Parties to the General Agreement on Tariffs and Trade (GATT) launched the Uruguay Round of Multilateral Trade Negotiations (MTNs), the eighth under GATT auspices.

The wisdom of launching the new round and its contents had been the subject of acrimonious debate between the US and other Industrialised Countries on the one side and the Third World countries on the other. It is no exaggeration to say that the Third World countries were virtually dragged into the negotiations, much against their will and better judgement.

The following year, at the United Nations (UN) General Assembly in New York, representatives of these same governments joined others (not members of GATT) in calling for 'sustainable and environmentally sound development'. This was in response to the Brundtland Commission report - 'Our Common Future' - the work of the World Commission on Environment and Development (WCED), chaired by Mrs Gro Harlem Brundtland, Prime Minister of Norway. The Commission had published its report in March 1987 and had forwarded it to the General Assembly and all the UN bodies and specialised agencies [1].

This special independent Commission was set up in 1984, as a result of an UN General Assembly initiative, to formulate a 'global agenda for change'.

While the Brundtland Commission did not challenge the fundamentals of the market economy, it did not endorse the received dogma either. The 'Sustainable Development' advocated by the report, it has to be underlined, does not merely amount to safeguarding the environment from industrial pollution or saving the rain forests to prevent greenhouse effects or reducing or eliminating chlorofluorocarbons to arrest ozone depletion or even birth control to reduce population growth in the Third World. It is all these and very much more - a dimension that is often ignored.

In view of some of the narrow interpretations put on the report, the possibility of new 'conditionalities' being imposed on the Third World countries became very evident. Hence, the General Assembly, while calling upon UN bodies 'to take account' of the report and pursue 'sustainable development', repeatedly qualified all this with the phrase "in accordance with their development plans, priorities and objectives"[2].

After the publication of the report, Mrs. Brundtland carried the campaign of the report and its recommendations to various UN bodies - among others to the UN Conference on Trade and Development (UNCTAD), the International Labour Conference (ILO) and the World Health Organisation (WHO) - and got their endorsement and support for 'sustainable development'.

The executive board of the World Bank, as well as the various regional development banks and agencies, have all come out in support of 'sustainable development' and have said that 'environmental' considerations are being taken into account in their lending policies and programmes (making it however merely another 'conditionality' or an external deco-

ration to their philosophies of market economy development based on deregulation and other dogmas).

The setting up of the Environment Commission and the
embracing of 'environmentalism' by the leading ICs of the
North, was a partial response to the growing concerns over
ecological considerations among the people of the North and
the South. The ecology movements, particularly of the South,
started as responses to local micro problems of water pollution, forest resource depletion and rights of indigenous
peoples. But gradually they began to relate their problems at
micro level to macro-policies of economic development and
the market economy-led linear development models propagated by the international development agencies and international financial institutions like the World Bank [3].

The latter, particularly after the report of the WCED have
also begun to speak of environmental considerations, but
largely these have been external embellishments to the
continued advocacy of resource-intensive (and inherently
wasteful) linear development models and programmes based
on the market. Deregulation and the withering away of government from the economic sectors plays a key role in these
models. To some extent some of the Northern NGOs have
allowed themselves to be co-opted by the Bank and their
own national aid agencies and have agreed to deliver programmes on environment which have been used to mask the
contents of the old development programmes with their
heavy bias in favour of those who already enjoy economic
superiority.

But both the ecology movements of the North and the
South which have related environmental degradation to the
development policies and models of the World Bank and
other development institutions have not yet been able
to relate their problems to the kind of trade policies and activities fostered by the GATT secretariat and its versions of
'free trade', that form the core of the Uruguay Round.

The GATT itself has not so far formally endorsed the concept of 'sustainable development', and it does not figure among the objectives of the new Round either. Mrs. Brundtland has not so far carried her fight into GATT, nor have the Nordic governments who have been trying to get other organisations to adopt the WCED Report.

Perhaps all this is no accident.

For, the two philosophies, that behind the new round (and one which leading Industrial Nations and the officials of GATT advocate) and the philosophy of 'sustainable development' are not easily reconcilable. The basic premise behind the Uruguay Round, and the new GATT that would emerge out of it, is that left to themselves private enterprise and Transnational Corporations (TNCs) function efficiently and for the benefit of all. Thus governments' powers to intervene and regulate need to be curbed.

'Our Common Future' accepts that the State, governments and the international community, have to intervene to ensure 'sustainable development' - eradicate poverty, ensure justice for the poor who are outside the market, regulate market forces, make protection of the environment 'profitable' and penalise, and/or otherwise make 'unprofitable', the degradation of the environment.

A Round to Restrain Competition from Third World

The Uruguay Round is the most complicated and ambitious of any postwar multilateral negotiations, and is unlike the earlier seven rounds of GATT MTNs which had sought to liberalise international trade in goods mainly through tariff cuts and selective lowering of non-tariff barriers.

The new round is really two separate affairs: the GATT MTNs in goods, launched as a decision of the GATT CON-

TRACTING PARTIES and run by the Group of Negotiations
on Goods (GNG), and separate negotiations for a multilateral
framework for 'trade in services', launched by Ministers
meeting on that occasion and run by a separate Group of
Negotiations on Services (GNS). Under the negotiating plan
adopted in February 1987, there is a negotiating group for
each of the 14 areas under 'goods', with the GNG exercising
overall supervision over them. Both the GNG and the GNS
function under the overall jurisdiction of the Trade Negotiations Committee (TNC), established by the Ministers. The
original intention of the US and the ICs was to run all the
negotiations as part of the GATT round, under the TNC as a
GATT body as in previous rounds. But the last minute
compromise at Punta del Este on services, with the negotiations on goods and services being separated and run by two
separate bodies, meant the establishment of the TNC as an
overall political body supervising the entire round (and having
no GATT status). This resulted in some confusion and over-
lapping in the roles of the GNG and TNC. For example, the
surveillance body supervising the standstill and rollback (applicable only to trade in goods) sends its reports both to the
GNG and TNC; and neither really follow it up. The GNG
which is a body created by the decision of the GATT CON-
TRACTING PARTIES at Punta del Este has been blocked from
acting in this matter by the ICs, while the TNC which has no
GATT status has some perfunctory debates and reaches no
conclusions.

With 14 items on the agenda of trade in goods and the
separate 15th on services, the Uruguay Round is to be
completed in four years, by 1990. The Tokyo Round, with far
fewer items on its agenda, took seven years and left behind
much unfinished business (mostly those of concern to the
Third World).

Launched at US initiative, with the support of most of
the major ICs, the Uruguay Round negotiations are really
about global production and production capacities, and other
wider issues. The European Community's chief spokesman in

GATT, Amb. Tran Van-Thinh, for example, told newsmen from EEC countries (in February 1987) that the new round is not about technical GATT issues like tariff and non-tariff measures, but about wider economic issues and trade policy, and thus the main negotiations would be a trilateral affair involving the US, EEC and Japan [4]. The new round is essentially for reorganising the international economy and international economic relations into the 21st century. It has also to be seen in the wider geopolitical context of the efforts of the United States to maintain its position as a global superpower. The US finds its power under challenge not only militarily, but also in terms of its post-1945 status as the dominant Centre in the Capitalist world [5].

"Like all major powers in history occupying the number one position, the US is now facing two great tests: whether in the military/strategy realm it can preserve a reasonable balance between the nation's perceived defense requirements and the means it possesses to maintain these commitments; and whether.... it can preserve the technological and economic bases of its power from relative erosion in the face of the ever-shifting patterns of global production...The final question about the relationship of the 'means and ends' in defense of American global interests relates to the economic challenges bearing upon that country..the first of these is the country's relative industrial decline, as measured against world production, not only in older manufactures such as textiles, iron and steel, shipbuilding, and basic chemicals, but also - although it is far less easy to judge the final outcome of this level of industrial-technological combat - in global shares of robotics, aerospace, automobiles, machine tools, and computers... the second, and in many ways less expected, sector of decline is agriculture... the scenario (in the 1970s of global imbalance between feeding requirements and global output)... stimulated two powerful responses... a massive investment in American farming from the 1970s onward... and the enormous western-funded investigation into scientific means of increasing Third World crop outputs, which has been so succesful as to turn growing numbers of such countries as food exporters...these two trends have coincided with the transformation of the EEC into a major producer of agricultural surpluses, because of its price support system... along with these difficulties affecting American manufacturing and agriculture are unprecedented turbulences in the nation's finances... which has transformed it from the world's largest creditor to the world's largest debtor-nation in the space of a few years" [6].

The response of the US and other ICs to this 'industry-technology' combat has been to protect their markets and industries and prevent emergence of competition elsewhere, particularly from the Third World.

As the UN Conference on Trade and Development points out: "In recent years in the face of market losses suffered by national enterprises, trade imbalances and structural adjustment problems, governments of most developed market economy countries have become relatively less preoccupied with ensuring free competition and its corollary, free trade, as with the competitiveness of their enterprises. The growing perception that technological advance is a key element in trade performance and economic growth has led governments of these countries to adopt a broad range of measures intended to stimulate such advances. It has also led them to take measures to protect or bolster their national industries from competition arising from technological advances or catching-up by industries of other countries" [7].

There is "the persistence of trade measures in the developed market economy countries aimed at protecting their industries, but equally adaptable to the promotion or protection of domestic technology.... Other governmental measures... have aimed at promoting the technological edge of domestic enterprises by restructuring the legal framework governing competition among them, and by enlargement or strengthening of the patent or copyright privilege.... However, since national regimes... are territorially limited, bilateral and multilateral initiatives have been undertaken aimed at ensuring world-wide protection of technological assets through har-

monisation in all important respects of the standards of protection prevailing in all countries... For the first time, a linkage between adequate and effective intellectual property
protection in other countries, and market access for their goods
has been established. The threat of trade retaliation has suf-
ficed to induce a number of developing countries to change
their intellectual property regime. In a few cases, failure to
make the changes suggested has led to actual retaliation" [8].

But as Dieter Ernst, Senior Advisor of the OECD Development Centre puts it, "as ever more countries are pursuing
national economic security with a vengeance, global economic security has been increasingly threatened... current
policies of export-led growth, based on 'neo-mercantilist' trade
and industrial policies, are leading us into a dangerous
impasse.... I use the term 'neo-mercantilism', in order to indicate that global competition has become increasingly politi-
cised. Heavy state involvement is geared to an improvement,
not only of the balance of payments, but to a strengthening
of the so-called 'strategic' industries, ie. industries producing
generic technologies, such as advanced electronics. In short,
we are talking about an increasing convergence between
industrial and trade policies which is driven by an over-riding
concern with the rapid and worldwide commercialisation of
temporary technology leadership positions.

"Two main aspects are involved. First, a far-reaching
promotion and protection of industries which generate or
heavily rely on generic technologies... second, and at the
same time aggressive policies to open up foreign markets, in
particular some potential future growth markets in Asian and
Latin American Newly Industrialising Economies, by means
of a rude 'beggar-my-neighbour export promotion' and the
insistence on 'reciprocal market access'. But neo-mercantilism is not restricted any longer to national policies. Bilateral
and even multilateral arrangements to restrict access to key
technologies seem to have recently increased quite substantially in importance... the European communities sectoral
research consortia... the still quite pervasive restrictions to the

international dissemination of so-called 'dual-use' technologies, as codified in the current COCOM lists, is basically an instrument of such neo-mercantilism. Finally, the US-Japanese trade agreement on semiconductors... has probably been the most far-reaching attempt so far to create a bilateral, cartel-like 'managed trade' agreement" [9].

All the moves of the US and other ICs, leading to the launch of the Uruguay Round, with its new themes and their proposals and efforts on these are related to this pursuit of national economic security, at the cost of global economic security, through these neo-mercantilist policies.

Flag, Trade, and Gunboat Diplomacy

From the viewpoint of the Third World the Uruguay Round is an exercise with very far-reaching implications - "under the new trade regime (that would emerge) the autonomy of developing countries in pursuing their development policies will be seriously compromised unless of course they decide to withdraw completely from the international economic system which, in view of the social and economic structures of these countries, does not seem to be a feasible option"[10]. It will curb the right of governments to intervene in the economy for the benefit of their people while expanding the 'space' for TNCs.

The thrust of the US effort vis-a-vis the Third World in the Uruguay Round, and more so on the new themes where it is backed by the Europeans and Japan, can also be better understood in the context of the continuous efforts of the European powers in the inter-war years, and of the US since 1945, to create and maintain an international regime to protect foreign capital and secure compliance [11].

In the 17th and 18th centuries trading, investment and property rights of foreigners had evolved from European practices and treaties, and were accepted by the US after its independence - a legal expression of reciprocal obligations undertaken to safeguard the mutual economic interests of their nationals. But these norms were imposed hegemonically on the Third World without any pretensions of reciprocity and enforced through naked power and colonialism - with Britain and other Europeans flaunting racial superiority and asserting inapplicability of 'rights' evolved in Europe to the colonised peoples.

"Vasco de Gama and his associates, even before they reached the coast of India, began to enforce the claim of his sovereign to be the 'Lord of Navigation'...The Portuguese armada ran across some unarmed vessels returning from Mecca. Vasco de Gama captured them and in the words of Lendas, 'after making the ships empty of goods, prohibited anyone from taking out of it any Moor and then ordered them to set fire to it'. The explanation for capturing the vessel is to be found in Portuguese historian Barros' remark: 'It is true that there does exist a common right to all to navigate the seas and in Europe we recognise the rights which others hold against us; but the right does not extend beyond Europe and therefore the Portuguese as Lords of the Sea are justified in confiscating the goods of all those who navigate the sea without their permission.'

"Strange and comprehensive claim, yet basically, one which every European nation, in its turn, held firmly almost to the end of Western supremacy in Asia. It is true that no other nation put it forward so crudely or tried to enforce it so barbariously as the Portuguese in the first quarter of the sixteenth century, but the principle that the doctrines of international law did not apply outside Europe, that what would be barbarism in London or Paris is civilised conduct in Peking (e.g. the burning of the Summer Palace) and that European nations had no moral obligations in dealing with Asian peoples (as for example when the British insisted on the opium trade against the laws of China, though opium smoking was

prohibited by law in England itself) was part of the
accepted creed of Europe's relations with Asia. As late
as 1870 the President of the Hong Kong Chamber of
Commerce declared: 'China can in no sense be considered a country entitled to all the same rights and privileges as civilised nations which are bound by international law.' Till the end of European domination the fact
that rights existed for Asians against Europeans was
conceded only with considerable mental reservation. In
countries under direct British occupation, like India,
Burma and Ceylon, there were equal rights established
by law. But that the law was not enforced very rigo-
rously against Europeans was a known and recognised
phenomenon. In China, under extra-territorial jurisdiction,
Europeans were protected against the operation of Chinese laws. In fact, except in Japan, this doctrine of different rights persisted to the very end and was a prime
cause of Europe's ultimate failure in Asia" [12].

In Latin America and the Caribbean these rights were
enforced by the UK and other Europeans, through private
sanctions of the foreign money lenders and a suitable mix of
gun-boat diplomacy (as when British, Italian and German
naval vessels bombarded and blockaded Venezuelan ports in
1902 for satisfaction of claims including defaults on bonds,
and in 1904 when Germany blockaded Santo Domingo). In
the early 20th century the US, while seeking to keep the
Continental Powers out of the region, took on this role of
enforcing 'international property rights' by use of force,
through the Roosevelt Corollary to the Monroe doctrine (in
Theodore Roosevelt's message to Congress in December 1904)
[13].

From the early part of the 19th century, when Britain
was the dominant centre and capital exporting country, and
right till the first world war there was no challenge to these
principles, but only some limited challenge from Latin
American States to its unilateral enforcement. But after the
first world war and the efforts under the League of Nations

to obtain legitimacy for the earlier regimes, there has been a steady erosion of these international norms or their enforcement. After World War II, when the US put together the Bretton Woods institutions for the monetary and financial system and sought to create the parallel Trading system through the International Trade Organisation and the Havana Charter, there were efforts to include provisions about international property and investment rights. But these did not succeed, and in any event the US itself killed the Havana Charter.

Thereafter, there has been a steady erosion of the 19th century international regime (property rights of foreigners were inviolable except in conditions of war, and could be 'expropriated' only under strictly defined public purpose and after compensation, and disputes to be subject to international arbitration). Through successive resolutions and declarations in the General Assembly, starting with the 1952 resolution on Permanent Sovereignty over Natural Resources and culminating in the 1974 Charter of Economic Rights and Duties of States [14], the supra-national rights of foreigners have had to give way to assertion of national sovereignty and domestic law.

Over the last two or three decades, the nature of interference with property rights of foreign investors have changed - from simple expropriation to a variety of regulatory measures on investment, business, imports and exports. These have made the old norms irrelevant. The gunboat diplomacy of the 19th and early 20th centuries was replaced for a time by covert operations (e.g. against the Mossadeg government in Iran and the coup against Allende in Chile). But even these have become increasingly difficult. The US and other capital-exporting ICs are hence trying to create new definitions of property and impermissible interference with its enjoyment, and create a new international regime (which the Third World countries will subscribe to). This will be a regime with credible enforcement measures through trade retaliation, rather than overt or covert use of force that is no longer feasible or acceptable.

Freedom of Transnational Capital

The current US effort, backed by other capital exporting states which are bases for TNC operations in the world, have to be seen in this context. It is an US-led effort for rewriting the rules of international economic relations, embracing many new areas never before dealt with in GATT. Through the Uruguay Round, the US is attempting to incorporate into the GATT framework areas of economic activity and relations that are not strictly 'trade' issues - intellectual property rights, services and investment rights - and whose legitimacy for inclusion in GATT has been sought by prefixing the words 'trade', 'trade in' or 'trade-related' before them.

"The introduction of these new areas within the ambit of trade negotiations under the auspices of GATT could best be described as the concerted efforts on the part of the developed countries to reshape the existing international trading system that would promote maximum freedom of TNCs to operate world-wide" [15].

It is an effort to put in place a new international regime for rights of foreigners - with norms relating to investment, right of establishment and business, patents, trade marks and other such rights, coupled with enforcement of all these through trade-retaliation.

Third World economies undoubtedly do need Foreign Direct Investments (FDI), for capital, technology, know-how etc. But they must retain the capacity to decide their own priorities and regulate the inflow of capital. Hence, for example, the various performance requirements that Third World governments stipulate in permitting FDI and disciplining its operations in the country. Third World countries should have the capacity to determine these matters autonomously, without any international framework or agreement that would in any way undermine this capacity.

If the US-led effort succeeds, Third World countries may find themselves obliged to reduce or eliminate conditions regulating investments and operation of foreign companies on their territories - in mining, manufacturing, and services such as banking, insurance, transport, wholesale and retail trade and professional services like audit, advertising and legal practices and assure TNCs complete freedom of operation. Under penalty of retaliatory measures against their exports, they would also be obliged to introduce laws protecting and enhancing patents and other industrial property rights of TNCs. As a result, their consumers could find themselves paying higher prices for essential drugs, for example [16]. Even the traditional rights of their farmers to store seed (from their harvest) for the next season or breed cattle could be in jeopardy [17].

The powers and position of the TNCs would be enhanced, the sovereign space of countries would be reduced and the process of transnationalisation of the world economy (and of the Third World) would be carried forward to an extent where it would not be easily reversible. It will divide the world between the 'knowledge-rich' and 'knowledge-poor', with the latter permanently blocked from acquiring the knowledge and capacity to be rich. The global economy and international relations would have been restructured for a Transnational World Order, rather than the NIEO (New International Economic Order) [18]. In economic and social terms, Third World countries and their peoples could be said to be on the point of being rolled back to the colonial era.

These far-reaching effects may not come about. Much could still depend on how the Third World countries act in the remaining period of the negotiations, individually and collectively. But time is running out on them.

The concerns over the moves of the ICs in the Uruguay

Round in the Third World, concerns simmering just below
the surface even in countries where seemingly there is no
overt opposition, is partly the reflection of the rise of economic nationalism in the Third World. But underlying these
is the reaction of the peoples of these countries, and particularly of Asia and Africa, to their historical colonial experiences of the last two centuries. European traders came to
trade, preceded and followed by naval and other expedi-
tions of their governments asserting a divine right to trade
(including the British assertion of the right to sell and promote consumption of opium in China), and brought most of
Asia under colonial rule, with Japan joining the Europeans in
these matters [19]. Those underrating the influence of these
events in shaping the response of Third World peoples may
be in for some surprises in the long run.

Notes on Chapter 1:

1. For a critique of the report see Taghi Farwar in *Special United
Nations Service (SUNS)* 1800, 1802.

2. See 'Development: Oslo Statement of UN Heads Questioned',
SUNS 1982, for objections in ECOSOC to statement of UN executive
heads at OSLO that they would prepare their biennium budgets on
basis of the WCED report, and discussions and conclusions at
UNCTAD Trade and Development Board on 'sustainable development', *SUNS* 2121 and 2125.

3. Jayanta Bandyopadhyay and Vandana Shiva, 'Political Economy of
Ecology Movements', *International Foundation for Development
Alternative (IFDA) Dossier* 71, pp 37-60.

4. 'Trade: Uruguay Round Negotiations mainly triangular - EEC',
SUNS 1659 pp 3-4.

5. See Paul Kennedy, *The Rise and Fall of the Great Powers'* (1987),
Random House, New York.

6. *Ibid* pp 514-528.

7. *'Impact of technological change on patterns of international trade'*, UNCTAD TD/B/1246.

8. *Ibid* pp 16-17.

9. Dieter Ernst, *'Technology, Global Economic Security and Late-comer Industrialization - An Agenda for the 1990s'*, paper for UNCTAD/UNDP Round table on technology and trade policy, 22-24 April 1989, mimeo available from UNCTAD Secretariat, pp 17-24.

10. Jagdish C. Saigal (1986), 'Why Fear Free Trade in Services?', *Economic and Political Weekly*, Bombay (India) Vol. XXI No.13, pp 551-552.

11. For an understanding of these issues, see Charles Lipson, *'Standing Guard'* (1985), University of California Press.

12. K.M.Panikkar, *'Asia and Western Dominance'*, George Allen & Unwin (1953), pp 42-43.

13. *Encyclopaedia Brittanica* (1971), Vol 19, pp 608-609, 660.

14. UN General Assembly Resolution 3281 (XXIX), 12 December 1974, A/9631 pp 50-55; Karl Sauvant *'Collected Documents of The Group of 77'* (hereafter cited as Collected Documents), Oceana Publications, Vol V, pp 567-572.

15. Jagdish C. Saigal, *op.cit.*

16. The abuse of process and product monopolies in the area of drugs was brought out in UK in an inquiry by the Monopolies Commission. Until the early 1970s, Italy provided no protection for drug patents, with the result that drug prices in Italy were lower than in the UK. The inquiry found that the British National Health Service was being charged for 'substances' used in two commonly used tranquilisers, Librium and Valium, about 40 times the prices at which alternate products could be bought in Italy. On the recommendation of the Monopolies Commission, the UK government ordered Roche Products, a British subsidiary of Hoffman La-Roche AG of Basel, to cut its selling prices by 60 to 75 percent and refund $27.5 million to the National Health Service for overcharging. (cited

in Surendra J. Patel, 'Indian Patent's Act: Implications of Controversy', *Mainstream*, February 18 1989, pp 12-13).

17. Pat Roy Mooney, 'Biotechnology and the North-South Conflict', in *Biotechnology Revolution and the Third World,* Research and Information System for the Non-aligned and other Developing Countries (RIS), New Delhi, 1988 pp 268-269.

18. For a fuller discussion, see Chakravarthi Raghavan, 'A Rollback for the Third World', *IFDA Dossier* 52, Nyon, Switzerland, pp 57-67.

19. For a better appreciation of the reactions in much of the Third World and particularly the countries of Asia to foreign investments and efforts of foreign powers to assert rights on behalf of their nationals, see Panikkar *op.cit.*

Chapter 2

BACKGROUND TO GATT AND THE URUGUAY ROUND

Any appreciation of the situation of the South in the Uruguay Round requires an understanding of the GATT, and the events of the 1960s and 1970s.

The General Agreement came into being in 1948 as a temporary arrangement, until the Havana Charter and the International Trade Organisation (ITO) envisaged under it came into being. But the US Congress refused to ratify the Charter - since it would have meant ceding to the ITO some part of US sovereignty and agreeing to forego some rights of the Congress and the US government in the area of trade policy. As a result, the General Agreement has remained for 40 years as a provisional treaty - a contract among governments acceding to it, and not a definitive treaty with its own institutional arrangements. The provisions of the General Agreement are basically akin to those of the Havana Charter for exchange of tariff and trade concessions. Additionally, there are ancillary trade policy provisions to ensure that the concessions granted to imported products are not negated by other actions of governments.

One of the myths surrounding the GATT is that its seven trade rounds brought about the liberalisation of trade and the expansion of the world economy since 1945. It will perhaps be more correct to say that the post-war expansion of the world economy, the so-called Golden Age of the industrial world, has been the result of the operation of a number of macro-economic processes including application of Keynesian economics and state intervention to promote expansion. The expansion of trade was an *effect*, rather than the *cause*, of world economic expansion. In fact the GATT process was instrumental in satisfying the demand for space from the Transnational Corporations and their 'trade' - within TNCs amongst the principals and subsidiaries, and among TNCs [1]. All the tariff cuts in past rounds echoed this purpose, and dealt essentially with issues of 'market access'.

It is perhaps true that Europe and Japan benefitted by the GATT MTNs and their exports expanded. However, the post-war reconstruction and expansion of production in Europe was essentially the result of the massive US Marshall Plan aid. This was backed by favourable trade policies and relatively unencumbered flows of technology. The US encouraged and enabled the formation of the European Payments Union to finance intra-European Trade and the adoption of trade policies for such intra-trade that discriminated against the US. Thus, in the European context the expansion of trade and economic activity was more the result of the Payments arrangements and the intra-European trade arrangements rather than the GATT MTNs.

The GATT modality of negotiating and extending concessions, tariff and non-tariff, meant that the ICs in successive negotiations reduced their mutual tariff and non-tariff barriers, but not those in respect of exports of Third World countries. Thus Third World countries did not benefit, by and large, from the tariff reductions or other trade liberalisation measures of these MTNs. They did derive some indirect benefits because of the trickle-down effects of global economic expansion and the exchange of trade concessions among the major ICs in industrial products where the Third World countries were minor suppliers.

But side by side with these tendencies for trade liberalisation, set in motion by these complex set of factors, there were also contrary trends. Japan was allowed to join the General Agreement only after it had agreed to bilateral restraints on exports of textiles to the US. When the cotton-producing Third World countries (some like Egypt, India and Pakistan were GATT cps from outset) began exporting cotton textiles, the protectionist counterforces to trade liberalisation and free trade based on comparative advantage, began asserting themselves. These resulted first in the 'temporary' Short-term and then the Long-term arrangement in cotton textiles. These have since been institutionalised in the Multi-Fibre Agreement (MFA) and its successive protocols of extension.

All such discriminatory and 'managed trade' arrangements represent the price paid by the Third World countries for the launch and conclusion of successive GATT MTNs for trade liberalisation. The concessions exchanged among ICs would normally have had to be extended to Third World countries under Article 1 of the General Agreement for most-favoured-nation treatment.

Initially, and even for quite some years afterwards, there were few Third World countries in the GATT. Of the 23 original signatories, eleven were 'less developed contracting parties'. Two of them (Lebanon and Syria) dropped out and the third, China (Taiwan), withdrew in 1951. In the initial or first phase of political decolonization, the newly independent countries all joined the United Nations, and most of them the IMF and the World Bank. But very few rushed into GATT. As colonies, the General Agreement had been applied in their territories by the metropolitan powers; after independence many of them continued to apply GATT in practice but joined only very slowly. As of November 1988, there are 96 CPs of whom 67 are 'less developed' (66 from the Group 77 countries, who now number 127, and the territory of Hong Kong) [2].

After the initial flush of independence, and hopes that with independence economic prosperity would be automatic, disillusionment soon set in. By the late 50s, the countries of the South became dissatisfied with the Bretton Woods institutions, and their prescriptions. The GATT theories and the actualities of the trade negotiations, with the Third World having no voice and deriving no substantive benefits, were additional factors in their disillusionment. The efforts of these countries to get development issues addressed in an integrated way via ECOSOC got nowhere either. This led to the founding of UNCTAD as an organ of the UN General Assembly, where wider issues of international economic relations could be addressed through 'Trade and Development'.

In GATT, the Heberler Committee's report and recommendations led, at the 1963 GATT Ministerial meeting (when the decision to launch the Kennedy Round was taken), to the adoption of conclusions and recommendations on a Programme of Action [3] for measures for expansion of trade of Third World countries. These, among others, called for standstill on new barriers to export trade of these countries, removal of quantitative restrictions inconsistent with GATT, duty-free entry for Tropical Products, elimination of tariffs on primary products and reduction and elimination of barriers on semiprocessed and processed exports of the Third World, and progressive reduction of internal charges on products wholly or mainly produced by Third World countries. But these have remained largely unimplemented, though figuring on the agenda of successive GATT rounds.

In 1964, the General Agreement sought to accommodate the Third World by incorporating special provisions relating to 'Trade and Development' in Part IV. Essentially a best endeavour framework involving no commitments, these provisions came into force the next year. But they have remained pious exhortations, and have not been translated into commitments or obligations like the other parts of the General Agreement.

The Rise and Fall of the New International Economic Order

Until the mid-1970s, the South's major effort - through appeals, declaratory statements, and political pressure through resolutions in the UN General Assembly or UNCTAD and elsewhere - was to seek benefits through minor reforms of the international economic systems and their rules. In most cases, this amounted to pleas for special treatment and exceptions favouring the Third World. Some progress was achieved such as in Generalised System of Preferences (GSP), Overseas Development Aid (ODA) targets, and multilateral concessional financing etc. But there were no fundamental challenges to the system [4].

By the early 1970s, the Third World's 'reformist approach' gave way to the restructuring phase. The countries of the South had begun to realise that however hard they strove, and whatever the 'special treatment' given to them in principle, they could not develop without changing the asymmetry in international economic relations and systems. The breakdown of the Bretton Woods institutions, and the 1973/74 OPEC action (and the vista it seemed to open of raw material producers joining hands to regain control over their terms of trade), provided the overall setting for the Sixth and Seventh Special Sessions of the UN General Assembly, and the adoption of the NIEO Declaration and Programme of Action, and the Charter of Rights and Duties of States [5].

The NIEO decisions and programmes led to the Paris negotiations at the CIEC [6] (Conference on International Economic Cooperation), which involved a limited number of countries of the North and the South. Parallel to the CIEC negotiations, UNCTAD took up several of the NIEO platforms and (at Nairobi, 1976) fashioned a number of mandates for negotiating changes in structures and rules - in commodities, trade, shipping, money and finance and debt (already a Third World problem), Economic Cooperation among Developing

Countries (ECDC) etc. Various UN agencies also got into the act, with a series of special UN conferences convened by the UN and/or the specialised agency - employment at ILO, Primary Health Care and essential drugs at WHO, food security at FAO, revision of the Paris conventions at WIPO etc. Many of the UN agencies brought up their own long-pending issues for negotiations at this time as part of the NIEO, and helped to confuse and diffuse the debates. On the other hand the IMF/IBRD and GATT ignored NIEO altogether - even the words not figuring in their literature.

The CIEC ended without results [7]. Beyond declarations and programmes, largely ignored by governments, the sectoral conferences too led nowhere - except perhaps in spawning institutional rivalries and helping the North's "forum game". The NIEO issues went back to the UN General Assembly and led to the establishment of the Committee of the Whole (COW), whose attempts to pursue the NIEO Programme and North-South dialogue for restructuring also ended in failure. There were fundamental differences about the nature of the world economy, and its functioning, and the type of reforms needed - all of which involved issues of power and power relations. The discussions could not bridge these differences.

Meanwhile, oil prices went up sharply in 1979, the so-called 'second oil price shock'. This time, it unified the leading ICs against the South and resulted in monetarism, high interest rates and policy-induced recession. Then came the Non-Aligned Movement (NAM)/G77 initiative for Global Negotiations. This was accepted in principle and placed on the agenda of the 1980 UN General Assembly Special Session on Development. But the Assembly was unable to launch Global Negotiations, in the face of the US opposition over IMF and GATT jurisdiction. By then monetarism had gained the upper hand in the US Federal Reserve, brought Reagan and his new agenda to the White House, enabling the US to reverse itself openly, not only on this but on other earlier commitments for international cooperation.

The global negotiations issue dragged on, figuring on the UN General Assembly agenda even in 1986, after the launching of the Uruguay Round negotiations at Punta del Este. But for all practical purposes (and at least in retrospect) the UN effort for NIEO and restructuring through Global Negotiations came to an end after Reagan said "NO" at the meeting of 22 heads of governments in Cancun, Mexico in November 1981 [8]. This is how Julius Nyerere, Chairman of the South Commission and former President of Tanzania, a participant at Cancun, describes what happened there:

"When we met at Arusha, at the ministerial meeting (of the Group of 77) in 1979, there was optimism and hope about the thrust for NIEO etc... even at Cancun (1981), there was still some hope. But the hopes were dashed there because Reagan said 'no' and that was it. It was all very revealing.

"The other members from the North at Cancun, at least some elements of them, agreed with much of what we had been talking about. I had hoped at that meeting that we would try and persuade Reagan. The meeting itself had been postponed to suit his convenience. We from the South thought that even if we cannot persuade Reagan, the rest of them who agreed with us would go ahead.

"What was very revealing, and very depressing, was that after Reagan said 'no', the other leaders from the North said that was the end" [9].

The Group of 77 did not fully grasp Cancun and its outcome [10] and (or despite it) persisted in its efforts to launch Global Negotiations by appeals to reason, and offering procedural and other compromises. But these efforts got nowhere, though the issue has remained on the UN agenda.

However, from the point of view of the US and other

leading Industrial Countries, checkmating the South over the
NIEO and maintaining the status quo were not enough. They
had to bring about changes in the international systems and
rules. The postwar systems created in 1945, and particularly
the monetary and financial systems, centered around the
Bretton Woods institutions and based on fixed exchange
parities and dollar-gold parity, had collapsed in 1973 and the
subsequent reforms and changes did not amount to a system.
The floating exchange rate system, which it was thought
would cure most problems merely created a new set of
problems, and adversely affected the trading system.

Decline of US Economic Dominance

The postwar economic system was postulated on
US power and lead in technology and productivity, the US
vision of the world based on self-confidence, and a certain
homogeneity of industrial and economic culture and similar
levels of development. However, after the collapse of the
Bretton Woods system, and the subsequent political and
economic upheavals of the 1970s, it is perhaps true to say
that the US power had been relatively reduced, in military
terms through the Soviet emergence as a nuclear and space
power and in Economic terms by the new centres in Europe
and Japan. Nevertheless, US power - political, military and
economic - is by no means as diminished and ineffective
as that of Britain, the centre power of the 19th and early
20th centuries, in the inter-war period and specially during
and after the Great Depression of the 1930s [11]. In fact it
may be true to say that US power is at its height in that the
ideological appeal of a different approach than the ugly face
of 'capitalist path' which the Soviet and Chinese achieve-
ments represented, has been tarnished, particularly in the
face of the post-Mao developments in China, the major
economic problems in Eastern Europe and *perestroika* and
glasnost campaigns in the Soviet Union under Gorbachev.

When the Reagan administration came into the White

House, there was an effort to reassert power, but on the basis of waving the flag and resort to some sabre-rattling. In the economic arena, there was an effort at blind pursuit of national interest in relations with other powers, in the Industrial and Third World - with confrontation and threats often replacing the post-war efforts at cooperation and consensus [12]. To make up for the lack of vision and a well-thought out programme for reforms for a new system, there was an attempt to propagate globally the ideology of the domestic radical right (that was not always practised at home), and talk of pushing back the East and the South too. Instead of the NIEO agenda (some of which could be faulted as mere sloganeering) for North-South negotiations and restructuring, the US sought to formulate its own agenda in the political and economic fields.

The ideology preached by Reagan, and on his election by the World Bank and the IMF as if the domestic elections of its 15 percent shareholder was a mandate by the entire membership, was on the misguided view that the US had reached its position by laissez-faire and others have only to follow the same policies to reach the same goals. As Keohane pointed out:

"Growth took place in the antibellum United States as a result of a conjunction of favourable internal and external conditions. The United States prospered without developing a coherent economic growth strategy, either of disassociation or managed association. Yet its economic successes were accompanied by the political failure of secession and civil war. Despite this mixed record, and the difficulties of generalising from the American experience (or from myths about it) to contemporary less-developed countries, Americans characteristically view their own history as demonstrating the virtues of laissez-faire and economic openness. In this respect, American ideology reinforces the interest of the twentieth century United States in maintaining a liberal world economy. It is therefore difficult to persuade

United States policymakers of the virtues of state-run
strategies of 'self-reliance' in the Third World. To a
country that was born free and born lucky, the protective actions of the less free and the unlucky do not
strike a responsive chord."[13]

Some of the issues for this agenda had been under discussion within the US establishment for quite a while, and
certainly from the 1970s. Ranging from the move in the mid-
60s for the nuclear non-proliferation treaty (which at its
core was aimed at preventing the rise of new military powers
that would threaten the two super-powers and the North;
and with China, which had blasted its way into the nuclear-
weapons field, reluctantly admitted as a member), the gradual shaping up of the so-called 'terrorism' agenda, the 'drugs'
issue (where the South is being asked to control supplies) to
the idea of a GATT for investment [14].

Some of the US moves and demands, though accentu-
ated by the US system of government and the jockeying for
power between the Executive and Legislative branches,
could be rationalised, and perhaps justified, from the purely
narrow national interests of the US. But reforming a failed
system or putting in place a new one, needs something
more than a focus on national self-interest, particularly in an
inter-dependent global economy. Unfortunately, this sense
of vision, and self-confidence to use that vision to create a
new world that would accommodate the interests of the
emerging Third World and the rising competition there, has
been lacking in the US which still plays a lead role in the
world economy and its management.

The US moves, from 1981, have to be seen against this
background. In the economic arena, after the 'adjustment'
forced on the Third World via the IMF and World Bank, the
US sought to restructure the international economy and
economic relations on the basis of its own agenda. There is
as yet no consensus among the major ICs on the changes to
be brought about in the monetary and financial system. But

there has gradually developed among them a consensus on the changes to be brought about in the trading system, to subserve their ends rather than the NIEO perspectives which they had opposed and blocked. For the US, liberalisation of trade in 'goods' had become largely irrelevant. In terms of economic exchanges in the area of 'goods', opening up export markets in Europe and Japan for agriculture, long excluded from GATT rules or treated as an exception, had become important. For the TNCs, investment and trade in 'goods' and 'services' had become substitutable, and the US needed new rules and disciplines to deal with some of these issues, which could no longer be dealt with purely in intra-OECD terms but needed to involve the major economies of the South.

While the agenda involved also US relations with Europe and Japan, the near equivalance of economic power of the three, and mutual conflicts among them, also resulted in a situation of commonality vis-a-vis the new rising competition from the Third World, and the need to reshape the world from the worldview of the North.

Why the North Chose GATT to Reshape World Economy

In order to implement radical changes in the framework of world trade and economy, the Northern countries had to find a 'vehicle'. They decided that the vehicle would be GATT. The choice of GATT for launching a new round of 'trade' negotiations, but with new themes and agenda have to be seen in this perspective. The choice was not by accident:

Firstly, trade (with communication) is the biggest interface of nations with others. The Third World nations, struggling to sell abroad and earn foreign exchange to import necessities and investment goods and intermediate inputs, are most vulnerable on this front. One can, by not seeking their resources, at least for a while, defy the IMF and the World Bank, and escape their influence and conditionalities

(for opening up the domestic economy to foreign investments and exchanges). But it is difficult for any country to
close its frontiers   and shut itself off from trade with the
outside world. Very large continental economies, with considerable domestic reorganisation and repression (political,
economic and social), could perhaps do this for a time, but
not the vast majority of the Third World nations. Even now,
the IMF and World Bank, particularly the latter, though
contributing   only to about five percent of Third World investment for development, exercise an enormous influence
on the economic   policies of these   countries   including in
the area of Trade policy. However, while the World Bank
is able to hold out a carrot, it is unable to wield the stick,
which   the   trading   system and its   retaliation   provisions
provide. One of the efforts in the Uruguay Round (negotiating group on the Functioning of the GATT System, FOGS) is
to enable the three to combine forces in influencing trade
and economic policy in the countries of the South.

Secondly,   among the fora dealing with   such issues,
the Third World countries are at the weakest inside GATT,
in terms of collective organisation and bargaining. They do
not negotiate or bargain collectively inside GATT. This is
despite the fact that, objectively, all the Third World countries have   more fundamental common interests than their
differences on individual trading issues. They have much
more at stake, and disunity only means that each is picked
separately and   coerced in negotiations based on power.
They have accepted the dogma that GATT is a 'contract'
among individual 'contracting parties' with varying interests,
and that there   are no North-South differences but only
differing trading interests [15]. At one stage, in the preparations for the 1982 GATT Ministerial   meeting, the US itself
had spoken of North-South trade negotiations in relation
to the new round, but later dropped the use of such
terminology. Third World countries   had   opposed any
such North-South negotiations in the GATT [16].

Unlike in UNCTAD, UN or other parts of the UN system, inside GATT there is only a tenuous informal group of 'less developed contracting parties' (the GATT term for Third World countries) that meets from time to time to exchange information, and occasionally present a joint paper or statement. The informal group includes Israel and Turkey (an OECD member). Until their accession to the European Community, Greece and Spain in Europe also formed part of the group.

Helped by the 'non-transparent' (hidden and lack of openness) processes of GATT, the representatives of some of the Third World countries take positions inside GATT that are contrary to what their Heads of States/Governments in NAM or Trade Ministers in the preparatory four-yearly meetings before UNCTAD sessions or Foreign Ministers at New York, have collectively decided. This is no reflection on the diplomats who, by and large, carry out instructions they receive. It is a result of the internal contradictions inside these countries and their governments and leadership.

But the major trading nations, despite their mutual differences and trade quarrels, have always been aware of their general common interest against the South and have been concerting together. The US, EEC, Japan and Canada meet regularly on trade issues, at so-called quadrilateral meetings and overall economic co-ordination is done at the meetings of G5, G7, G10, and at annual Ministerial sessions at the OECD.

ICs do not also break ranks among themselves, even to side with the Southern members of their particular coalitions and interest groups, as the behaviour of Australia, Canada and New Zealand (in the Cairns group) at the Montreal midterm review meeting of the Uruguay Round showed [17].

Thirdly, unlike in other fora where the South can muster at least the verbal and rhetorical support of the Socialists, in GATT, the Socialists' support cannot be counted on. In the current state of East-West relations, there are even doubts as to whether the East could any longer be counted on to support the South [18].

For their own reasons, including their primary aim of reducing or eliminating the built-in discrimination against them on the ground of the role of their state enterprises and trading entities, the East European socialist countries inside GATT (Hungary, Poland, Czechoslovakia) take a low profile, and sometimes take positions closer to that of the West. China is trying to 'resume' its status as a GATT contracting party and is negotiating the terms of its 'resumption', and thus taking a relatively low profile. Bulgaria has applied to join, but the terms of reference of the working party to examine its request are yet to be settled at the time of writing.

The Soviet Union is not in GATT. From 1983-84 it had been making unofficial soundings about joining GATT. In March 1986, when preparations for the round were under way, the Soviet Union expressed an interest in the GATT and as a preliminary step Soviet diplomats and officials undertook a number of soundings on becoming an 'observer'. But the US and the EEC strenuously opposed. Since the GATT Council acts only by consensus, and they were not ready to force an open confrontation the Soviet Union publicly made known its wishes, but made no formal application [19].

The Soviet Union had also expressed an interest in participating in the proposed new round of negotiations, citing the wide range of international economic relations sought to be addressed. But unlike in the Tokyo Round, where participation was open to all countries, participation in the Uruguay Round was restricted to GATT Contracting Parties, and some other categories of countries, using a careful terminology aimed at blocking Soviet participation [20].

Fourthly, while all inter-governmental negotiations are in private, the GATT processes are the least transparent. With very rare exceptions for ceremonial purposes, all GATT meetings are behind closed doors, without the obtrusive presence of the media or non-governmental organisations of consumers and other public interest groups. Major TNCs and their organisations quite often are around such meetings as advisors to their delegations. GATT documentations are all 'restricted', except when there are specific decisions to be made public, often long after the event.

The subjects dealt with are technical, but are also made obfuscatory in the terms and acronyms used, though occasionally the chosen acronyms are more suggestive [21]. The media reportage of GATT activities, and of the Uruguay Round, is mostly based on what the GATT spokesmen reveal to the Press (copious on viewpoints of the industrial world but very sparse on that of Third World countries), or what any interested delegation chooses to reveal often in unattributable background briefings. Coupled with the US domination of information channels, this makes manipulation of the media and management of news easier in GATT. The public, and even some militant NGO groups espousing public causes, are seldom aware of what is taking place except long after the events and decisions.

There is no group or representational system of negotiations in GATT, as in UNCTAD and other UN agencies, but only the informal 'green room consultations'. This makes it easier to forge and strike deals which may be against the public interest before the public is fully aware of what is happening.

The 'green room consultations' is the code name for GATT's (consultative) decision-making process, and is so named after the wall-paper decor of the GATT Director-General's conference room in Geneva where these consultations take place. The understandings reached in these consultations are presented formally to others, often with only a few hours notice, and rammed through.

Participation in these consultations is by 'invitation', and those invited are selected by a non-transparent process. There

is a predominance of Industrial Nations - the US, the EEC
(with its 12 member states sitting behind), Austria, Australia,
New Zealand, Canada, Japan, Switzerland, a representative
of the Nordics (Finland, Iceland, Norway and Sweden), Turkey
(OECD member classified as a 'developing country' inside
GATT), and Hungary from Eastern Europe. Third World
invitees vary (with some invited because their diplomats if
excluded could be a nuisance at the formal meetings) and
include Argentina, Brazil, Chile, Colombia, Egypt, India,
Jamaica, Korea, Nigeria, Malaysia and/or Singapore (for
Asean), Tanzania, Yugoslavia and the territory of Hong Kong.
Since 1986, Uruguay and Pakistan have been brought in.

The very atmosphere and makeup is intended to over-
awe anyone opposing the viewpoints of the major industrialised nations. There is a fetish about participation at level of
ambassadors. Third World countries, who can't always field
ambassadors (who in Geneva are often delegates to several
UN agencies) are often represented by their junior officials,
who are expected only to take notes and are 'discouraged'
from active participation. The lack of transparency often
enables some countries to adopt positions in the 'green room'
quite different from their public positions.

In theory, all contracting parties are equal; and GATT's
consensus decision-making process is the most democratic
with the big and the small having the same equal voice. But
in practice when the small have tried to assert themselves,
they have been ignored or sought to be overawed by arguments that the countries with the largest share of the world
trade have more at stake in the trading system and its rules,
and hence their views should prevail. This was openly stated
during the preparatory stages of the Uruguay Round when
repeatedly the US spoke of the 'trade weight' of the US, EEC,
Japan and the OECD countries that supported the Round and
its new themes as against the low 'trade-weight' of the few
who opposed it and whose voice should hence be ignored.
This concept is practised even more widely in GATT's actual
decision-making. In the full meetings of its bodies the adop-

tion of decisions is only a formality. Real decisions are taken in the green room consultations and other informal channels of negotiations, chaired by the GATT Director-General or his representative.

The position of the GATT secretariat is also anamalous. Legally, the 'secretariat' and the Director-General (DG) are officials of the Interim Committee for the International Trade Organisation (envisaged under the Havana Charter), but this is now maintained as a fiction. The DG is appointed by the GATT Council, with the Interim Committee meeting formally to adopt it. The General Agreement even now, has no provision about the GATT secretariat or its executives and officials. The GATT is not an international organisation like the UN or its agencies. It is a Contract among signatory governments, and the Director-General and his subordinate officials are only 'contracted parties', basically only to service the Contract and carry out what the Contracting Parties direct them to do from time to time. Yet, the present Director-General and other senior officials have been bending over backwards to espouse or pursue a particular policy line which is mostly the line favoured by the US and/or the EEC. According to some of the old time GATT officials, this is in sharp contrast to the situation under the previous DG Olivier Long. According to some of these officials, towards the end of the Tokyo Round, the US and EEC informally presented Long with a text agreed between them for a so-called counterfeit code and asked him to hold 'consultations' and secure adherence by others. Long refused, ruling it to be 'out of court'.

Notes on Chapter 2:

1. See Vijay Kelkar *'On the Reforms of the International Trading System',* UNCTAD mimeo, 1986, paras 28-30.

2. Israel and Turkey are considered less developed contracting parties

in GATT. But they are not included on this count, even though they designate themselves as such and participate in the meetings of this 'informal group of developing countries in the GATT'.

3. *GATT - Basic Instruments and Selected Documents* (hereafter cited as BISD), Twelfth supplement, pp 36-47.

4. *Trade and Development Report*, 1981 (UNCTAD), pp 24-25.

5. Karl Sauvant, *'Collected Documents'*, Vol V. Declaration on establishment of NIEO pp 557-559; Programme of Action on NIEO pp 559-566; Charter of Rights and Duties of States pp 567-572.

6. Twenty seven countries (19 from the South and 8 from the North) participated in the CIEC, which owed its origin to an initiative of French President Giscard d'Estang. The participants were: Algeria, Argentina, Australia, Brazil, Cameroon, Canada, EEC, Egypt, India, Indonesia, Iran, Iraq, Jamaica, Japan, Mexico, Nigeria, Pakistan, Peru, Saudi Arabia, Spain, Sweden, Switzerland, US, Venezuela, Yugoslavia, Zaire and Zambia. The Third World countries had established their own ad hoc secretariat to service them at the meeting. For details of the documents and final communique see Collected Documents, *op.cit.*, Vol VI, pp 401-572.

7. Perhaps the only outcome of the CIEC was the impetus it gave to on-going negotiations in UNCTAD on Common Fund and on ODA debt of the 'poorer countries'.

8. Heads of States/Governments of 22 countries met on October 22-23 at Cancun, the Mexico, in an effort to get the North-South dialogue and Global Negotiations going. The meeting of the limited numbers of countries at summit level had been suggested by the Brandt Commission. The invitations to the meeting were issued jointly by the Austrian Chancellor and the Mexican President. The countries of the south who attended were Algeria, Bangaldesh, Brazil, China, Guyana, Cote d'Ivoire, India, Mexico, Nigeria, Philippines, Saudi Arabia, Tanzania, Venezuela, and Yugoslavia. Those from the North were: Austria, Canada, France, West Germany, Japan, Sweden, the UK and the USA. The Soviet Union which had been invited did not participate.

9. Chakravarthi Raghavan, interview with Nyerere, (1987) *SUNS* 1669.

10. But they were not alone. A number of prominent personalities attempted to put the best interpretation on the outcome in the effort to keep the North-South dialogue going. See comments of Gamani Corea (who was at Cancun as one of the advisors of the UN Secretary-General) in *SUNS* 402, Willy Brandt *SUNS* 408, and Shridath Ramphal *SUNS* 420.

11. See Kennedy, *op.cit*

12. Some of the motivations and the underlying forces have been briefly touched upon in Chapter 1.

13. Robert O.Keohane in *"The Antimonies of Inter-dependence'*, ed. by John Gerard Ruggie, (1983) Colombia University Press, p 90.

14. Paul Goldberg and Charles Kindleberger in "Towards a GATT for investment: A proposal for supervision of the International Corporation." *Law and Policy in International Business 2* (Summer 1970) 295-325, cited by Lipson, op.cit, p 298 (fn 27 in chapter Five).

15. In the beginning, when it broached the subject, the US had talked of a new North-South trade round, of the Industrialised Countries exchanging trade concessions with the Newly Industrialising Countries, and in return for their own concessions to the NICs forcing them to open up their markets to other Third World countries. But very soon this North-South dimension dropped out of the US terminology.

16. *SUNS* 631 p 4.

17. Chakravarthi Raghavan, 'Montreal GATT Talks', *Deccan Herald,* Bangalore, India Dec 30, 1988.

18. 'Group of 77: Sees dangers of East-West consensus against South', *SUNS* 2113 p 3.

19. Press conference of Mikhail Pankin, head of the Department of International Economic Organisations of the Soviet Foreign Trade Ministry, *SUNS* 1481.

20. See Part I section F, of the Punta del Este Declaration in Annex I.

21. The acronym for 'Trade-related Intellectual Property Rights' is TRIPs. All the proposals of Industrial countries in this group are aimed at tripping the Third World efforts at industrialisation and development and preventing them from emerging as competitors. The acronym for the 'Functioning of the GATT System', a mandate for negotiations for improving surveillance of trade policies affecting the trading system and improving the overall effectiveness and decision-making of GATT, is FOGS. The working of this negotiating group is under such a fog that even the word 'surveillance' has dropped out of its terminology.

Chapter 3

THE EFFORT TO ROLLBACK

The US Push for a New GATT Round

The efforts and initiatives for the new round have to be seen against the background of the present state of the world economy and the situation of the US which, after being the Centre for well over four decades, now feels its power and hegemony threatened and challenged from diverse sources. As the dominant power, economically and militarily, the US had brought about a postwar world order to accommodate and further its interests.

Since then, and particularly over the last two decades, there has been an increasing interdependence of economies and issues (as a result of which actions in one area or state affect others, and actions or inactions of others affect one's own capacity to act, even of the most powerful). The transnationalisation of the world economy has been going on at an accelerated pace. But the TNCs are now coming up against the reality of the nation state and the postwar order, and find it constraining [1]. The US which still is the dominant home of the TNCs and the leading country in outward foreign direct investment (FDI) is hence directing its effort to limit national space of others, through demands for 'liberalisation' and 'deregulation'.

But this is confined to selected areas and sectors, and there is little talk of it in the high technology areas, which are subject to high degrees of regulation and state support and intervention. Often in these areas mercantilist concerns for goods, services, patents and other industrial property protection to ensure monopoly rentier incomes, are masked under pleas of 'security' and safeguarded and protected. From an agreement for free trade based on comparative advantage, GATT is slowly becoming a neo-mercantilist instrument of the Centres.

In 1981, in Congresional confirmation hearings, key cabinet aides of Reagan, like US Trade Representative William Brock, laid out their ideas and intentions about a new GATT round, but few outside the US paid any attention.

By early 1982, the US began pushing for a new round, at official and non-official gatherings. In January 1982, at the Davos symposium of the European Management Forum, Brock laid out US ideas at some length. He called for a Ministerial meeting to launch a new round to deal with problems of investment and all attendant problems of liberalising the free movement of capital, liberalising the trade in services (which should include issues of capital investment and free movement of capital, banking, insurance, shipping, consultancy, data systems etc), the challenges of trade in technology, the question of safeguards and problems of structural adjustment, perfecting the arrangements for trade in agriculture, improving the rules and methods to deal with non-market economies ('so that they compete fairly in the world markets, fairly and without exporting their price and cost distortions'), non-tariff barriers and other trade matters "not even contemplated when GATT was set up", methods to bring the Third World into the world trading system (both to provide them market access in products where they have competitive advantage and encourage them to assume full share of responsibility for managing the world trading system) [2].

The GATT secretariat was sceptical and cautious [3]. There was also resistance, inside and outside GATT, from the EEC and other industrial nations, apart from Third World countries. But at US insistence, a GATT Ministerial meeting was convened, with a preparatory committee drawing up the agenda and draft recommendations for Ministers. The GATT Contracting Parties convened at ministerial level in November 1982, and the US formally proposed a new round of GATT negotiations and for putting on the agenda new issues not governed by GATT rules or not dealt with at all so far in GATT - agriculture, services, high-technology, investment measures, and trade in counterfeit goods (which as presented was in terms of the alleged manufacture of spurious spare parts for automobiles or brand-name watches etc, and their being fraudulently passed off as genuine originals, by a few Far Eastern economies, and the need to tackle this) [4].

At the ministerial meeting, there was resistance to the US, not only from the Third World but also from the EEC and the smaller industrial nations, though for different reasons. The resistance from some of the EEC member-States was because they were not ready to give up agricultural protection or allow any impediments in their efforts to catch up with the US and Japan in High Technology (HT).

Japan, a target of US and EEC pressures to open up its market, was ambivalent. But within a year it joined hands with the US [5]. The Japanese Prime Minister, in a joint statement with the US President in 1983, called for a new GATT round. Perhaps Japan saw in this a way of escaping bilateral pressures over its own trading practices. But there was also the compelling force of Japanese capital. Japan has now become the most dynamic country for outward investment in the world. In its efforts to break down some of the barriers in the US, and with an eye to the emerging prospect of a single EEC market by 1992, Japan has been promoting aggressively outward FDI and production operations in the US and the European Community.

Ultimately a compromise was reached at the 1982 Ministerial meeting by putting everything on a GATT Work Programme. With a number of Latin American nations under pressure over the debt crisis that had just erupted, the Third World countries compromised on 'Services', but with about a score of them entering specific reservations about their GATT rights. The services issue was included on the work programme in a separate track: 'for interested countries to undertake national studies and exchange information on such studies *inter alia* through international organisations such as GATT', leaving further actions, if any, to be decided at the 1984 Session (later postponed to 1985) of the Contracting Parties [6].

During the preparations for the 1982 meeting, the GATT Director-General had spoken of the importance of tackling 'grey area' measures to restore the credibility of GATT [7]. In the declaration adopted, all the references to measures 'to circumvent GATT rules' were deleted, and the commitment to abide by GATT obligations was changed into making 'determined efforts to ensure that trade policies and mea-sures are consistent with GATT principles and rules'. GATT was thus degraded from a 'contract' with 'rights and obligations' to a 'best endeavour' agreement [8].

The US appeared to give up the investment issues. The Third World thought it had achieved a major victory and relaxed, only to find, in a matter of two years, the US coming back with full vigour on all the same issues and more (so-called workers' rights were added by then).

Trade in counterfeit goods (about which the EEC was also concerned) had been put on the 1982 work programme. But in the working party that went into it the scope was slowly expanded - thanks mainly to the negligence of the disorganised Third World countries, most of whom thought that it did not affect them but only the supporters and allies of the US (Hong Kong, South Korea, Singapore and Taiwan) - with the US and others relating it to the issue of intellectual property rights (IPRs).

Immediately after the 1982 Ministerial meeting, the Third

World countries thought that the work programme was a self-executing process. But the US and others did not see it that way, and the entire work programme was made a kind of preparation for the new round envisaged by the US. By 1985, the US was again calling for a new round and including in it all the new issues [9]. It sought to justify the new issues being brought into GATT by just prefixing the words 'trade' or 'trade-related' before services, IPRs and investment.

The Role of the TNCs

In the 18th and 19th centuries, access to markets and natural resources, and capital accumulation to the centres, were secured through colonialism; countries professing anti-colonialism like the US may not have had colonies (though there was colonial rule over Philippines) but resorted to force as in the interventions in Central America and the naval expedition to open Japan to foreign commerce.

The postwar order of the UN Charter eschewed all these. In the economic sphere too (learning from the disastrous experiences of the inter-war years and the Great Depression), unilateral trade and other economic retaliations were replaced by principles of international cooperation in trade - with rules for permitted and not-permitted state actions, consultations and dispute settlement procedures and mechanisms. Retaliation was to be by withdrawal of concessions granted and only as a last resort after collective authorisation by the international community.

Now all this is being reversed. S.301 of the 1984 US Trade and Tariff Act, and the 'super S.301' of the 1988 Omnibus Trade and Competitiveness Act, are nothing more than an assertion of unilateral retaliation rights to secure one's demands [10]. Only instead of use of guns to open up markets [11], there is now talk of using 'crowbars' to pry open markets [12]. Both in the new themes and in the systemic issues on the agenda of the Round, these types of actions are now sought to be legitimised and internationalised.

The driving force behind all this is the TNCs. Through the trade liberalisation efforts of the 1950s and 1960s, they had expanded. The trade liberalisation and tariff reductions of earlier Rounds were undertaken in their interest, and it was they who benefited; contrariwise the lack of liberalisation and growth of protectionism in the textiles and clothing sector is due to the fact that TNCs are not a major force in production in this sector [13].

The TNCs (which have now become giant conglomerates linking industry, trade, capital and finance, technology and other services) find themselves constrained by the existing order and its relations and are demanding *lebensraum*. They are demanding new rules and international regimes guaranteeing them the freedom to expand, maximise their profits and enhance their global capital accumulation process. The push on new issues is thus part of a grand design. Even the push for 'free trade' in agriculture is related, at least partly, to the fact that the major actors now (in the US) in international trade in agriculture are a few TNCs.

It is not as if there is a monolithic view inside the US or other ICs on the new round and the 'free trade' flag under which it is all being pushed. In the US (and other ICs) the manufacturing sector, particularly that in the older and established branches which are not part of the new 'high technology', has been feeling the rising competition from the Third World. Not only do they not want any free trade or further liberalisation of market access, but they want curbs and cutbacks on existing access. The industrial capital engaged in traditional sectors and facing competition from the newcomers in the Third World wants to draw up protectionist walls around the country; but finance capital wants to expand and break down walls in other countries. This conflict is reflected in the approach to new themes and traditional ones. The contradiction is sought to be resolved through rules for 'free trade' in the new areas and changes to enable 'managed trade' in the traditional sectors [14].

GATT was designed for, and its rules and principles deal with, issues of market access for products. The new process being set in motion seeks something much deeper. It is not only intended to seek markets, but to change production patterns and the capacity to produce. By granting foreign capital internationally assured privileges in investment, intellectual property, and services, its monopoly of knowledge and technology is sought to be perpetuated. All this will affect the structures of production and constrain the capacity of others to produce and compete. The net outcome is much more sinister for the weaker countries. In economic terms, it will take the Third World back to its colonial days and stifle development.

The Breaking Up of Third World Unity

The US effort and policy was well-orchestrated, and from the beginning it was consciously aimed at breaking up any solidarity of the Third World countries. Neo-classical economists in international financial institutions and conservative outfits like the Heritage Foundation let loose a barrage about these countries being 'free riders'. Disillusionment with several Southern governments, their dictatorial regimes and the high life-styles of their elites, and development fatigue among Northern NGOs, also contributed to the general atmosphere of decrying governments and their interventions in the market. These northern groups became the reverse side of the Reagan coin (of leaving it to the market): by talking against planning and three decades of international development efforts and strategies, and calling for 'grass-roots action' and leaving things to the people - which in reality in Third World conditions amounts to laissez-faire of the robber baron variety.

From 1979, soon after the end of the Tokyo Round, the Third World nations and the smaller industrialised countries, like Australia, had begun to feel that world trade was being distorted by the policies of the three major trading blocks (US, EEC, and Japan), and the system was being brought into disrepute. This was why there was a broad measure of solidarity between the Third World nations and the smaller industrial nations at the time of the 1982 GATT Ministerial meeting. But this solidarity soon receded as a result of discussions and pressures within the OECD.

In the beginning the Third World countries inside GATT joined hands to resist the US on the new round, and the initial US efforts to break up the Third World unity did not succeed. But gradually it began making headway. The US and the international institutions under its influence, propagated the thesis that Third World countries were at different levels of development and had nothing in common. They began efforts to create new groupings of North and South, led by the North - for example, the countries primarily dependent on agriculture for external trade. This last tactic finally resulted in the formation of the Cairns group, and alienating many of its Third World members (but not its Industrial-country members who never gave up their basic OECD alliance) from other Third World countries who saw little of benefit to them in the new round.

By the end of 1985 and early 1986, Third World unity faded away, under bilateral pressures applied by the US: political in terms of support to beleaguered regimes against their domestic opponents or externally against neighbours; financial in terms of debt negotiations; and economic, in the area of trade, by using its vast panoply of powers to reward or punish - capacity to maintain or deny GSP benefits, threat of harassing actions like anti-dumping and countervailing proceedings, quotas under the Multi-Fibre Agreement (MFA) etc. The EEC and Japan too joined these efforts in influencing and weaning away the Francophone bloc and the countries in the Far East.

But the EEC quickly recognised the firm positions of

countries like Brazil and India and the need at some point to reach some compromise acceptable to them.

As a result of the US pressures, a number of countries (that ultimately became the 'Group of 20' under the leadership of Colombia and Uruguay) either abandoned their opposition and/or provided some support to the US on the new round or remained silent. These included ASEAN countries, South Korea, Pakistan, Sri Lanka, Bangladesh, Colombia, Chile, Uruguay, and some Francophone members like Zaire, and Senegal.

But a smaller group [15], led by Brazil and India, remained together and resisted the US. The 'Group of Ten' as they were known, managed to manoeuvre within the limited space available to them, and exploited the US-EEC differences to forge a tactical alliance with the EEC. This ultimately led to the compromise agreements at Punta del Este on the services issue, almost identical in language to what had been earlier agreed to between the EEC and India and Brazil [16].

In this fight, and the efforts of the 'ten' to block 'services', the other traditional GATT issues got relegated to the background. The group of about 20 Third World countries, the nine EFTA countries and Australia, Canada and New Zealand, (with participation but not commitment of US, EEC and Japan), and led by Colombia and Switzerland, forged compromises on both the traditional and other issues, and produced a compromise text which became known in GATT circles as the *cafe au lait* paper, after the Geneva concoction of black coffee and milk, because of the Colombian (coffee) and Swiss (milk) leadership for it!

Promised Concessions That Never Came

The expectation of those who sided with the US or remained quiet, while others were opposing, was that if they made some concessions in the new areas they would get concessions in the traditional areas like textiles, tropical products etc. Many of these countries felt there could be a genuine trade off between the old and the new issues. But there was no such trade off and, in terms of the negotiating mandate, the Third World lost on the old issues too.

In the wording of the standstill and rollback commitments, GATT obligations and 'derogations' from GATT (like the MFA) were placed on an equal footing. Pakistan and some others had hoped that in return for their agreeing to include services in the new round, the US and others would agree to negotiate an end to the MFA. At Punta del Este even the reference to the MFA was eschewed, though privately it was made to appear that it was in deference to the pending Textile Bills in the Congress. Instead the mandate spoke of 'integrating' the trade in this sector into GATT. Now the US is even saying that it wants the MFA, the present 'global system governing this trade' to be incorporated into the GATT! [17].

Efforts to ensure conclusion of a comprehensive safeguards agreement as a condition for other negotiations or priority for the long-pending Tropical Products issue also failed, both figuring merely as two items on the long agenda in goods, and merely opening the possibility of some early action. Some, like South Korea and Singapore, subsequently lost their GSP benefits - to safeguard which they had sided with the US.

At Montreal (in December 1988), at the mid-term review meeting, where a so-called 'X'mas package' in tropical products was evolved, Colombia got nothing. On coffee, its main export crop, there was no move to reduce the consumption taxes on coffee in Europe. On cut-flowers, another major Colombian export item, the tariff reduction was of two percentage points (from an EEC-MFN external rate of 17-20 percent, intended to protect EEC producers) [18].

Notes on Chapter 3:

1. See Lipson, *op.cit.* chapter one pp 1-33, chapter four pp 85-139, chapter five pp 140-194, chapter six pp 200-226, and chapter eight 258-275.

2. *SUNS* No.462 pp 5-7.

3. *Ibid.*

4. For reportage on 1982 meeting see *SUNS* 655, 656, 657, 658, 659, 661, 662. For text of the 1982 Ministerial Declaration and GATT Work Programme for the 1980s, see *GATT Activities in 1982,* GATT Secretariat, Sales No. GATT/1983-2, pp 8-26.

5. 'Third World cool to US move for new trade negotiations', and 'Japan, a stalking-horse for the USA?' *SUNS* 889.

6. *Ibid.*

7. Dunkel's speech in Hamburg, *SUNS* 659.

8. *SUNS* 659 and 660.

9. See reports on Special Session of CPs (Scp 30-Oct 2, 1985) and annual session (Nov 25-28, 1985), *SUNS* 1332, 1333, 1372, 1374.

10. See in Chapter 5 below.

11. Panikkar *op.cit.* on European and US opening up of Asia for trade. see pp 201-202 for an account of Commodore Mathew Calbraith Perry's expedition and US-Japan trade treaty followed by similar treaties with other European powers.

12. Testimony of Mrs. Carla Hills, US Trade Representative in the Bush Administration, before Senate in confirmation hearings. 'Senate backs hardliner as Trade Representative', *Financial Times,* Jan. 30, 1989.

13. Kelkar *op.cit.* paras 27-29.

14. 'Limit Free Trade with Japan, US is Advised', *International Herald*

Tribune Feb 25, 1989; 'US May Reverse Free Trade for Japan', *International Herald Tribune,* Mar 3, 1989. The managed trade approach in economic relations with Japan has been advocated in the US by the high-level private sector business advisory group, headed by chairman of American Express Company, James D Robinson III, who is spear-heading the drive for free trade in services.

15. Argentina, Brazil, Cuba, Egypt, India, Nicaragua, Nigeria, Peru, Tanzania, and Yugoslavia. On the eve of Punta del Este, Argentina detached itself from the group, while Kenya and Zimbabwe joined them.

16. Interview with S.P.Shukla in *SUNS* 2100.

17. Carla Hills' testimony before Congress, *USIA Bulletin,* 2 March 1989, pp 8-9. Also, de Clercq's statement in the European Parliament, *European Report* No.1484, 18 January 1989.

18. Subsequent simulations done in UNCTAD show that the additional trade that could be created would be about US$333 million annually, or two percent of the 1986 imports, and of this only US$90 million will come from the Third World countries. The balance of benefit will accrue to the ICs themselves. See tables 3 and 4 in Chapter 11 under Tropical Products.

PART II

NEW THEMES FOR GATT

Chapter 4

THE NEW THEMES AND THEIR INTERLINKAGES

15 Items on Agenda

The 15 items on the agenda of the Uruguay Round are quite a mix of new and traditional issues. There are the normal issues of market access for products. In the same category, but not entirely, is 'Agriculture' – an area where existing GATT rules and disciplines have not been applied or have been treated as an exception, and where application of existing rules or creation of new disciplines are now envisaged. In the same category perhaps is Textiles and Clothing – an area of trade, governed for nearly three decades by a regime of its own, as a derogation from GATT rules and principles, and which enables imposition of discriminatory restrictions against the Third World. In a second category, are a group of what might be called 'systemic' issues about the General Agreement and its provisions, related to products and their market access. In the third category are the 'new themes' - Trade in Services, Trade-related Intellectual Property Rights (TRIPs) and Trade-related Investment Measures (TRIMs).

Strictly, TRIPs and TRIMs are solely in relation to 'goods' and are a part of the GATT MTNs launched as a decision of the GATT CONTRACTING PARTIES. The inclusion of 'Services' is a decision of Ministers, acting as representatives of their countries and not as Contracting Parties. The Punta del Este Declaration placed it in a 'separate track', delinked from the GATT agenda, and thus separate from TRIPs and TRIMs.

But they have interconnected effects [1].

Unilaterial Actions Show US Intentions

From the outset, both in its bilateral and multilateral relations, the US saw the three issues as one. Title III of the US Trade and Tariff Act of 1984, particularly the coercive powers vested in the Administration under its S.301, and which have been reinforced and vastly expanded under the Omnibus Trade and Competitiveness Act of 1988 and its 'super S.301', leave little room for doubt about US intentions.

Under S.301, domestic producers and other interests could petition the USTR about 'unfair' trading practices of foreign countries. The provisions for authority to the President to enforce US trade rights through negotiations was first enacted in 1962, revised in 1974, and again in 1984, and has now been vastly expanded under the 1988 law.

Before the latest amendments, private parties had to petition the USTR and seek investigations. After inquiry by the US International Trade Commission (ITC) and recommendations and findings to the President (who has discretionary authority to pursue the matter or not), the USTR could aggressively negotiate with the foreign country concerned to comply with US demands and failing a satisfactory conclusion impose unilateral tariff and non-tariff barriers to imports from the country concerned.

The USTR also had powers to self-initiate some cases under S. 301, particularly with respect to intellectual property protection. Cases were initiated in 1985 against Brazil over its informatics policy (involving copyright issues for computer software, but also non-IPR issues like investments, import restrictions and production subsidies etc) and against South Korea over its alleged failure to provide adequate protection for US intellectual property.

The Brazilian policy, relating to copyright protection for software was determined to be 'unreasonable' by
the President, and there were on-again and off-again bilateral negotiations, with the threat of retaliation (and possible
targets) announced in November 1987. It should be noted
that the Brazilian policy on the informatics front had been
already a subject of domestic pressure from the consumer
industries, and it would probably be true to say that the
US pressure was used by Brasilia (and some of the con-
suming industries) to bring about changes. Brazil changed its
informatics   law, particularly copyright protection for software, in 1988 (though not to the full satisfaction of the US).
The USTR backed away from the threat of retaliation, but announced the decision to continue to monitor.

In the case of South Korea, a bilateral agreement was
concluded in July 1986, under which that government committed itself to making several changes in its laws and their
enforcement. The investigation was thereupon terminated in
November 1986, but the USTR is continuing its monitoring of
the Korean actions.

In July 1987, acting on a complaint filed by the US Pharmaceutical Manufacturers Association over Brazil's patent
regime for pharmaceuticals, the USTR began investigations,
and a determination was made by the US President in July
1988 that the Brazilian regime was 'unreasonable'. In October, 100 percent tariffs were imposed on about 40 million
dollars worth of annual imports from Brazil. Following Brazil's
complaint in GATT, the dispute was referred to a panel for
adjudication in February 1989, but that too only after the US
found itself completely isolated in resisting reference of the
dispute to a panel [2]. But the USTR told Congress that even
if the GATT panel holds S.301 to be contrary to GATT, the
'retaliation' against Brazil will continue, and so would US use
of S.301 to gain its ends [3]. After some further foot dragging
on the US part, only in June 1989, the panel's terms of reference were settled in the GATT Council, but on the understanding that only the US measures, and not the legality of

S.301 vis-a-vis GATT was to be ruled upon. As a price for this, the US had also to agree that the panel would not also rule on the Brazilian patent law [4].

During 1975-84, Third World countries were targets of S.301 investigations in 14 out of 47 cases instituted. After the 1984 amendments, they have been targets in 11 of 20 investigations. The latest amendments could result in a sharp upsurge of US actions against Third World countries.

Super 301 and Special 301 Give US Stronger Powers

Under the amendments to S. 301 by the latest law (s. 1301 of the Omnibus Trade and Competitiveness Act), the USTR himself could initiate actions. The USTR is also mandated to initiate actions on receipt of petitions, and the President's discretionary authority is very much circumscribed. Practices of foreign countries deemed 'unjustifiable' and which 'burdens or restricts' US Commerce are made subject to mandatory actions.

The changes introduced by the 1988 US Trade and Competitiveness Act, in S. 301 as well as other provisions, which are known as the 'Super 301' and 'Special 301' provisions have brought about a new situation enabling the US to engage in coercive negotiations with trading partners to secure a broad range of objectives in the trade and economic fields [5]. The terms 'Super 301' and 'Special 301' are not actually used in the law, but have been adopted as common names identifying these new mechanisms. They are essentially sections 1302 and 1303 of the Trade and Competitiveness Act which respectively, and retroactively, create new sections 310 and 182 of the Trade Act of 1974, vesting in the administration coercive powers of negotiations during 1989 and 1990 to secure stated objectives from various trade partners.

Even before the amendments, the USTR had to send to Congress every year a National Trade estimate listing the

'Foreign Trade barriers' to US Commerce. Under the latest amendments in the 1988 law, the term 'commerce' has been expanded to include services (including transfer of information) associated with international trade whether or not related to specific goods, and foreign direct investment by US persons with implications for trade in goods and services.

Under 'Super 301', in 1989 and in 1990, within 30 days of sending the annual National Trade Estimate Report on Foreign Trade Barriers, the USTR has to identify the US trade liberalisation priorities including priority practices (major trade barriers and trade distorting practices) whose elimination would have the most significant potential to increase US exports, and the priority foreign countries. Within 21 days of this, investigations are to be started under S.302 and simultaneously the governments identified as the target of investigations would be asked to hold bilateral consultations [6].

The investigations (whether on complaints or self-initiated) are to determine whether the policies and barriers complained of are 'unreasonable', 'unjustifiable' or 'discriminatory' (all the terms are definied in the Act) and whether they burden or restrict US Commerce. If the determination is affirmative, and the bilateral consultations do not result in acceptable concessions, the USTR may threaten retaliation, which is usually done by announcing a large number of import products from the country as the likely targets for tariff or quantitative restrictions. This is part of the effort at coercive extraction of concessions, and is intended to bring pressure on the government of the country concerned from its exporters of these products. If everything fails, the USTR may impose the 'retaliation'. Under the US law, such 'retaliation' is mandatory if the actions are deemed to be 'unjustifiable' (with some exceptions), and at USTR's discretion if the actions are considered 'unreasonable' or 'discriminatory'.

As already noted, when the USTR identifies under 'Super 301', the priority countries and their practices, the USTR has to initiate the investigations and seek consultations within 21 days. If the countries concerned do not agree within a period of 12-18 months either to (a) eliminate or provide compensation for the practice within three years, or (b) reduce the practice within three years, the USTR may 'retaliate' against the country. While the 'Super 301' instrument has its own procedures, the final effect would be the same, excepting perhaps the discretion to 'retaliate' or not. The retaliatory provisions are the *means* rather than the *objective*. The goal is to use the threat of retaliation to gain concessions without actually using the retaliation. The whole effort is to shift the burden of adjustment entirely to the trading partner.

The term 'unreasonable' has been defined in the US law to include any policy or practice which, *while not necessarily in violation of or inconsistent with international legal rights of the US* (emphasis added), is otherwise unfair and inequitable. It will include all policies and practices that deny (a) 'fair and equitable' opportunities for the establishment of an enterprise, (b) adequate and effective protection of intellectual property rights, (c) market opportunities for US goods (including where governments are seen by the US as tolerating anti-competitive activities of private firms). The term also includes countries said to be engaging in export targeting, or deny workers rights - deny rights of association, right to organise and bargain collectively, permit forced or compulsory labour, fail to provide minimum age for employment of children, and standards for minimum wages, hours of work, occupational safety and health of workers. The term 'export targetting' has been defined as meaning "any government plan or scheme consisting of a combination of co-ordinated actions (whether carried out severally or jointly) that are bestowed on a specific enterprise, industry or group thereof, the effect of which is to assist the enterprise, industry or group to become more competitive in the export of a class or kind of mechandise". The definition is so wide that it can be used to take any action the US wants against any country that is likely to emerge as a competitor.

Under the 'Special 301', there is a special procedure

created for identification by the USTR of countries considered to be providing inadequate intellectual property protection, and for self-initiation of proceedings against them. The USTR has to annually (by May 30, 1989 and April 30 of subsequent years) identify countries that are considered by the USTR to be denying adequate and effective intellectual property protection, and deny market access to US producers that rely upon intellectual property protection. The USTR has also to identify the priority countries (based on the annual trade barriers report, petitions received from firms and industry groups and consultations with other officials within the US government). A foreign country is to be deemed to be denying protection of IPRs, if it denies "adequate and effective means... for persons who are not citizens or nationals... to secure, exercise, and enforce rights relating to patents, process patents, registered trademarks, copyrights and mask works". A country is to be considered to be denying fair and equitable market access if it denies "access to a market for a product protected by a copyright, patent or process patent" through laws or regulations that violate international law or international agreements or constitute discriminatory non-tariff trade barriers.

Within 30 days of identifying the priority countries, the USTR is to initiate actions (investigation under S. 301 etc), but has discretion not to do so if such actions would be 'detrimental to US economic interests'. Cases where actions have been initiated will require resolution within two years, depending on progress of the talks and steps taken. Thus the cases will be 'adjudicated' by the USTR (combining the roles of prosecutor, jury and judge) concurrently within the final two years of the Uruguay Round.

The US is thus negotiating with its trading partners, while holding a gun at their heads - the threat of unilateral trade restrictive measures (already a reality as in respect of Brazil), if they do not yield [7].

US negotiators publicly and privately often adopt

the posture that they are reasonable people, but that they have to deal with a Congress which is more protectionist. But this is an effort to translate into trade negotiations the 'good cop, bad cop' tactics in police investigations, and can impress only the unwary. This kind of negotiations, under threat of worse Congressional actions, have been a consistent tactic of the US under the Reagan administration. At the 1982 GATT Ministerial meeting, then USTR, William Brock, held out similar threats [8].

US Objectives in New Themes

In its latest Trade Law, Congress has clearly spelt out the negotiating objectives in services, intellectual property, high technology goods, and investments. It has also provided for unilateral determination of 'unfair trade practice' by any country that does not yield to US demands in these areas, whether bilaterally or in multilateral negotiations, and for imposing tariff and other trade restrictions.

In the area of services, the principal negotiating objectives are spelt out as reduction or elimination of barriers to or other distortions of international trade in services, including barriers that deny national treatment and restrictions on establishment and operation in such markets, and develop internationally agreed rules, including dispute settlement procedures, which are consistent with US commercial policies and will reduce or eliminate such barriers or distortions and ensure fair and equitable opportunities for foreign markets. Legitimate US domestic objectives (and laws and regulations relating to them) including protection of legitimate health or safety, essential security, environmental, consumer or employment opportunity interests, are to be taken into account by the negotiators in pursuing negotiating objectives.

In the area of intellectual property, the negotiating objectives are (a) to seek enactment and effective enforcement by foreign countries of laws which recognise and

adequately protect intellectual property including copyrights, patents, trademarks, semi-conductor chip layout
designs, and trade secrets, and provide protection against
unfair competition; (b) establish GATT obligations (i) to
implement adequate substantive standards based on standards in existing international agreements that provide adequate protection or standards in national laws if international agreement standards are inadequate, (ii) establish
effective procedures to enforce, both internally and at the
border, the standards, and (iii) to implement effective dispute
settlement procedures that improve existing GATT procedures, and (c) to supplement and strengthen standards in
existing IPR conventions administered by other international
organisations, including their expansion to cover new and
emerging technologies and elimination of discriminatory or
unreasonable exceptions or preconditions to protection.

In the area of foreign direct investment (FDI), the objectives are (i) to reduce or eliminate artificial or trade-distort-
ing barriers to FDI, to expand the principle of national treatment, and to reduce unreasonable barriers to establishment,
and (ii) to develop internationally agreed rules, including
dispute settlement procedures which will help ensure free
flow of FDI and reduce or eliminate the trade distorting
effects of certain trade-related investment measures.

In the area of High Technology [9], the negotiating
objective is to obtain the elimination or reduction of foreign
barriers to, and acts, policies, or practices of foreign governments which limit equitable access by US persons to foreign-
developed technology, including barriers, acts, policies, or
practices which have the effect of (i) restricting participation
of US persons in government-supported R and D projects, (ii)
denying equitable access by US persons to government-held
patents, (iii) requiring approval or agreement of government
entities, or imposing other forms of government intervention
as a condition for grant of licenses to US persons by foreign
persons (except for approval for national security purposes
to control critical military technology), and (iv) otherwise

denying equitable access by US persons to foreign-developed technology or contributing to the inequitable flow of technology between the US and its trading partners.

For the ICs, All the Issues are Interlinked

A detailed perusal of the US position papers and statements before [10] and at the 1982 GATT Ministerial meeting and during the 1982 Work Programme, particularly in the exchange of information on 'Services', in the subsequent discussions in the GATT Council and the group of senior officials, and in the preparatory committee for the new round, shows that for the US all three areas overlap. It has framed issues under each heading in such a way that they are substitutable, with rules under one being able to achieve the objectives sought in the other.

The TNC conglomerates are involved in inter-linked operations through their control of access to finance, technology and services, and the oligopolistic market structures. The right of 'establishment' and 'national treatment' under the services framework would achieve the same purpose as similar proposals under investment rights; and any TNC starting operations inside a country, whether as a producer of services or of goods, under the proposed new rules for either would be entirely free to expand its activities into any other area. They would create a new international regime of norms for property rights of foreigners, which would be superior to those of nationals. The US has never hidden this hegemonistic demand. In 1965, when codifying its foreign relations law, the US State Department declared: "Some states maintain that an alien is not entitled to a higher standard of justice than a national...this Section [of US law] follows the prevailing rule that such national treatment is not always sufficient..." [11].

Rules under TRIMs, for freedom for investors and national treatment for them, would enable TNCs to produce or import as they wished 'goods' or 'services', and obtain the same privileges as 'right of establishment' under Services. GATT norms for intellectual property protection would enable TNCs, the major source of technology flows, to decide autonomously what technology (whether in goods or services) could be used inside a country or prevented from use, what goods could or could not be exported, and where and under what conditions and terms, and secure for the TNCs monopoly rents through their global control of finance, technology and services.

At Punta del Este, and afterwards, when a number of countries of the Third World spoke of the 'delinking' of goods and services negotiations, the US made clear in no uncertain terms that it saw the two as interlinked and that there could be no progress in goods without parallel progress in services, and within the goods without equal progress on the new themes of TRIPs and TRIMs.

Even apart from US intentions and objectives, the three new themes are really inter-connected and constitute a single rubric relating to production, comparative advantage and compétitiveness of countries - a result of the fundamental structural changes in global production and trade that have already taken place, and are in progress, due to qualitative changes and advances in information and communications technology and its applications.

Double Standards in the Theory and Practice of "Free Trade"

In present day international political and economic relations, there are double standards with glaring inconsistencies between policies preached and practised [12]. While neoclassical economics and liberalism are thrust on the Third World countries, government intervention is growing in the major industrialised countries. Such intervention and support is particularly noticeable in research and development in new technologies [13]. There are also growing university-industry and industry-industry links in R and D and their commercial utilisation [14]. This has reached a point where science and knowledge, once considered a common heritage of mankind, are no longer so and are increasingly kept secret. Direct government actions abroad in support of private enterprises have become quite common - ranging from heads of governments and states actively promoting the interests of particular enterprises in contracts and sales abroad to retaliatory actions against foreign countries in support of domestic corporations.

Simultaneously, doctrines of deregulation and liberalisation have been used to reduce the capacity of national and international institutions and instruments to intervene and safeguard public interest. Liberalism and 'free trade' are preached to increase access to foreign markets. But there is a high level of protectionism and state intervention, particularly in the areas of new technologies, and new products and industries. In these matters the stengthening of the role of the state is found in countries professing far right and highly conservative ideologies.

Theories of free trade, whether the classical theory of Ricardo or its modern versions in neo-classical economics, are based on the premise that production and trade take place between independent entities in different countries, and that free trade among countries, based on comparative advantage (with immobility of land and factors of production), is for the benefit of all. Free trade theories have always been advanced by the centre countries to advance their own interests [15]. Even in Ricardo's example of free trade in Portuguese wine and British cloth being to mutual advantage, the capital, land (where Portuguese vines were grown), and trade and shipping services, were all in British hands [16].

GATT economists and their apologists, when confronted with the negative consequences of 'liberalisation' simply ignore the distributional effects and argue on the basis of trade theory that in the long run everyone gains because of comparative advantage. But 'comparative advantage' is a

much misused term. "Comparative advantage... has acquired
a powerful ideological role and has been used to rationalise
almost any type of international division of labour. Poli-
ticians, journalists and other professionals use the term with
universal and accepted ease, without ever questioning what
it actually means. Theories of free trade based on comparative advantage have never evaluated the nature of speciali-
sation - 'who developed, who controlled and who used the
productive knowhow'." [17]

Moreover, under conditions of the new technological
and structural changes, comparative advantage is no longer
static and based on natural resource endowments, but can
be created - through innovation, adaptation and improvements in existing technology and products - to ensure international competitiveness. This has made technology a crucial
element. It comes with investment flows, and enables rapid
expansion of so-called 'trade in services', both of the service
and the information and communication flows that enable
transborder flow of services.

Trade is not an end in itself, even under theories of 'free
trade'. It must result in net gains for society, and enable Third
World countries to develop and bring about equity within
and among countries, without which there will never
be peace. This involves issues of gains and their distribution.

"Distributional conflicts and contradictory perspectives
aggravate relations among nations as well as within them.
None of the insights provided in the general case for
international trade sheds any light on the way in which
the gains from trade (or, for that matter from advanced
technology) are distributed among nations. It is comfort
indeed, but cold comfort, for developing nations to
suspect that although trade strengthens their economy,
it strengthens the economies of developed nations far
more. They are confronted constantly with the exaspe-
rating anomaly that international trade may well make
the rich richer relative to the poor, thus increase inter-

national income inequality... ... gains from international trade are distributed among nations roughly in proportion to their market power. To the strong go most, to the weak only what their residual veto , 'we will not trade' can extract.

"Distribution based on market power is worse than arbitrary from the perspective of developing countries; it is inimical. It condemns them to a vicious circle of relative poverty, from which they can emerge only by chance. Their relative poverty requires national spending on the necessities of the day, on penalty of collapse. Little is left over for the accumulation of capital and technology at a faster rate than developed-countries, which would enable them to close the international gap in living standards and end their relative poverty" [18].

Keeping the Third World Technology Poor

In effect there are now two classes of countries, the knowledge-rich in the North and the knowledge-poor in the South, with the position of the latter continuously declining in the world economy and international division of labour to the point where they find themselves relegated for ever to be mere hewers of wood and drawers of water.

The Third World countries are not reconciled to this and, individually and collectively, they are attempting to persuade and pressure those holding technology (mainly TNCs) to transfer it to them, and are also trying to develop their own indigenous capacities.

The TNCs are a major source of technologies, and they control it through patents, investments, cross-licensing and the services. Increasingly, governments in the Industrial Nations, in an effort to maintain the international competitiveness of their economies and exports are underwriting considerable amount of research and development in new technologies. "... the scale, nature and distribution of government support to high technology industries is a determinant factor of the growth and competitiveness of the private or other enterprises involved" [19].

Given the vast outlays in R and D and investments, as well as the short-life cycle of some of these products, the leading Industrial Nations are trying to prevent emergence of competition by controlling (on claims of security and other specious reasons) the flows of technology to others. The Uruguay Round is being sought to be used to create export monopolies for the products of Industrial Nations, and block or slow down the rise of competitive rivals, particularly in the newly industrialising Third World countries. At the same time the technologies of senescent industries of the North are sought to be exported to the South under conditions of assured rentier income, while keeping domestic markets of the North closed to products of such industries in the South.

The entire TRIPs negotiations are intended to internationalise what so far has been in the domestic domain, namely, establishment of the norms and criteria for industrial (intellectual) property protection, broaden the scope of protection, extend the lifetime of protection (and thus monopoly rights of the TNC holding the patent), reduce or eliminate the capacity of the Nation-State to regulate or attack such monopolies, block technical development and rise of competition in the periphery, and enhance the enforcement of rights of TNCs, nationally and internationally.

The TRIMs negotiations are related to the fact that the TNCs, who wish to extend their activities in the Third World and set up operations which are vertically integrated into their global production and distribution systems, are the major source of the new technologies. Third World countries have been using their regulatory powers of restrictions on inputs and investment to encourage TNCs to supply the competitive technologies and set up production with forward and backward linkages to the domestic economy. Through the new

TRIMs rules, these powers of the Third World governments are sought to be restrained, and TNCs allowed a free hand to maximise their profits and global capital accumulation for the benefit of their home countries.

Intellectual (industrial) property protection, involving grant of monopoly privileges statutorily, have always been and still are tempered in the ICs by use of competition laws to attack any abuses [20]. But internationalising the norms and ensuring their protection - without the countervailing international instruments to ensure competition in international trade (and with powers of enforcement) and without home-states assuming obligations to supervise and control export cartels operating from their territories - and restricting host states from regulating activities of TNCs through TRIMs, would in effect mean that Third World countries would be left without any defences.

Advances in information and communication technologies have made it possible to deliver services across the border more easily. By ensuring 'free trade' in services, access to new markets is secured and the countries to which the services are exported are made more dependent on the foreign suppliers (for a wide range of upstream and downstream producer services vital for production and trade, and social well-being) who can control, if not block, the emergence of new competition.

Thus, while traditional GATT trade liberalisation measures are intended to break down barriers to imports, and make the imported goods competitive with domestic production, the new themes are really about ability of countries to develop comparative advantage and compete, and would be a zero sum game. Internationalisation of industrial property system would result in blocking diffusion of knowledge and block Third World access to new technologies or development of technological capacities. International rules on investment would reduce Third World bargaining power vis-a-vis the TNCs. Rules for 'national treatment' obligations towards foreign capital, and free flow of data and data services through a services agreement, would eliminate the capacity of any country to 'protect' its domestic market and enable establishment and growth of industries. International rules on services would block or inhibit Third World countries developing indigenous service industries or keeping control over key service sectors. Trade retaliation would enable enforcement of all these on recalcitrant Third World countries refusing to fall in line.

Cumulatively, Third World governments would not only be unable to act positively in the economic fields to advance the well being of their peoples, but would be obliged to protect the interests of the TNCs and foreign enterprises and foreign nationals against their own peoples. The only role left for governments would be maintaining law and order, and keeping labour under control. Governments of independent countries in the Third World would thus be left doing what the metropolitan powers did during colonial days.

Notes on Chapter 4:

1. Murray Gibbs and Mina Mashayekhi, 'Elements of a Multilateral framework of principles and rules for trade in services', *Uruguay Round: Papers on Selected Issues* (1989), UN Sales No. UNCTAD/ITP/10 pp 83-88.

2. *SUNS* 2035.

3. *Daily Bulletin of the US Mission* Geneva of 2 March 1989.

4. *SUNS* 2184.

5. In May 1989, the USTR has initiated actions under 'Super 301' and 'Special 301'. see Chapter 12 infra.

6. Brazil, India and Japan have been identified as 'unfair traders' and priority countries for negotiations under 'Super 301', by an announcement of the USTR on May 25.

7. The US has in May 1989 invoked these provisions, naming Japan, Brazil and India under Super 301, and identifying 25 countries under Special 301. See Chapter 12.

8. *SUNS* 655.

9. The contrast between US objectives in intellectual property rights and in High Technology is striking.

10. See Brock at Davos, *SUNS* 462.

11. American Law Institute, Restatement of the Law, Second: Foreign Relations Law of the United States (1965), cited by Lipson *op.cit.* p 8.

12. Constantine Vaitsos, "Radical Technological Changes And The New 'Order' in *The World Economy*, pre-publication article made available at UNDP/UNCTAD Roundtable on Services at Salzburg, Vienna July 1988.

13. *'Protectionism and Structural Adjustment'* (TD/B/1196), UNCTAD (1988) pp 16-18.

14. *Biotechnology Revolution and the Third World,* Ed. Nagesh Kumar, Research and Information System for Nonaligned and Other Developing Countries (RIS), India p 6, pp 154-155.

15. Eli F.Heckscher, *Mercantilism,* (London: George Allen and Unwin Ltd.) Vol.2, p.13.

16. Stuart Holland, speech at UNCTAD 20th anniversary symposium, UNCTAD TAD/INF/PUB/85/1, p.48.

17. Vaitsos *op.cit*

18. *'The New International Economic Order: A US Response',* Ed. by David B.H.Denoon (1977), a UNA-USA Book, McMillan, London, p 44.

19. Vaitsos *op.cit*

20. Robert Merkin and Karen Williams, *'Competition Law: Antitrust Policy in the United Kingdom and the EEC'* (1984), Sweet and Maxwell, London pp 294-359.

Chapter 5

SERVICES

How Services Were Brought Into GATT

As already noted, when the issue of 'services' [1] was first raised by the US, it was on the basis that this is a growing area of economic activity and trade, and that it should be brought under GATT rules and disciplines to expand world trade and make GATT more relevant to the changes in the world economy. Somewhat deliberately and always shrouded by the rhetoric of the benefits of liberalisation, the US never spelt out clearly what was sought but left things vague enough to bring everything under it.

Gradually, other Industrial Nations began to support and fall in line with the US views. As already noted in Chapter 3, the European Community was less strident and, just before Punta del Este, conducted negotiations with Brazil and India to evolve what the Geneva diplomats of the three used to characterise as the 'common platform'. This compromise was ultimately substantially incorporated into the Punta del Este mandate on Services [2].

According to the mandate:

"Negotiations in this area shall aim to establish a multi-lateral framework of principles and rules for trade in services, including elaboration of possible disciplines for individual sectors, with a view to expansion of such trade under conditions of transparency and progressive liberalisation and as a means of promoting economic growth of all trading partners and *development of developing countries.* Such framework *shall respect* the policy objectives of national laws and regulations applying to services and *shall take* into account the work of relevant international organisations" (emphasis added) [3].

While the Third World countries concerned agreed to end their opposition and negotiate a multilateral framework, the negotiations are in a separate track, delinked from the goods negotiations and with the decision on how to implement it and where left to be determined at the end when the shape of the framework would be better known. The end objective is to be the 'economic growth of all trading partners' and the 'development of developing countries'. Development which had never figured in the GATT, and came in as a subsidiary and an exception meriting special treatment, is to be a central objective in the services framework. The expansion of trade in services is an immediate goal to achieve economic growth and development; and the expansion of trade in services is to be brought about under conditions of transparency and progressive liberalisation. Liberalisation is thus relegated to the status of a 'means' rather than an end in itself.

Thus any framework of rules that would not contribute to expansion of trade, and would not result in both the end objectives (of economic growth and development) have been ruled out. Also, as between various methods for expansion of trade, the preferred means is 'progressive liberalisation', and under conditions of 'transparency'.

The Negotiating Plan agreed to in January 1987 identified, for discussions and negotiations, five elements, listed under five indents, with the stipulation that neither their formulation nor order prejudged their relative importance or order for negotiating purposes. The five were:

• Definitional and statistical issues

• Broad concepts on which principles and rules for trade in services, including possible disciplines for individual sectors might be based

• Coverage of the multilateral framework for trade in service

• Existing international disciplines and arrangements

• Measures and practices [4] contributing to or limiting the expansion of trade in services, including specifically any barriers perceived by individual participants, to which the conditions of transparency and progressive liberalisation might be applicable.

Unlike in the MTNs in 'goods', where there is provision for early accords and their implementation by agreement but subject to a final assessment on the 'overall balance', the implementation of results in the services area is to be decided only at the end of the Uruguay Round negotiations. In its final, concluding part, the declaration says: "When the results of the Multilateral Trade Negotiations in all areas have been established, Ministers meeting also on the occasion of a Special Session of Contracting Parties shall decide regarding the international implementation of the respective results".

North and South Disagree on Priorities

The discussions [5] in the GNS have shown considerable North-South differences on the weight to be given to the various elements, the extent to which each of them have to be satisfactorily addressed, whether solutions or agreement on each is essential for progress on the others, and particularly in drawing up rules and principles. However, unlike before Punta del Este, there is now an acknowledgement, on the part of everyone, of the linkages. But there is also an effort to argue that some of the elements (such as statistical problems) are not amenable to early solutions, and while there should be agreed measures to solve them, progress on other elements should not be held up.

In their papers and views so far, the industrial nations led by the US have concentrated on the second and fifth indents, and have tried to focus debates on them. Even among the issues in the fifth indent, attention has been sought to be focussed only on so-called 'perceived barriers' to trade, ignoring the rest.

While the main guiding principle is to be 'promoting economic growth of all trading partners and development of Third World countries', there has been no effort to address these questions. Nor has there been any effort to tackle 'definitions' (what 'services' are and what is meant by 'trade in services' which is to be negotiated) or 'coverage' (what sectors would be included in the proposed framework and what would not). Terms like 'trade' and 'transactions', which have different connotations and implications, are being used by ICs synonymously, as part of a deliberate effort to confuse the unwary and extend GATT and international jurisdiction beyond 'trade'.

Statistical issues too have not been tackled, except perfunctorily, on the ground that improvement of statistics is a long-term project, and negotiations cannot wait for it. Third World countries are being asked to agree to international obligations without even knowing what it would cost them, even in terms of balance-of-payments. The statisticians who were consulted (from the UN, UNCTAD, EEC etc), while explaining the deficiencies of UN and IMF data and difficulties of getting better data for statistical purposes and analyses, said they could suggest solutions only if they were told what 'services' are to be covered and what would be the definition of 'trade' in services.

Despite all this, the problems about definitions, statistics etc have been sought to be put aside. There has been a deliberate effort to use the nebulous situation, where the large majority of Third World countries have no clear idea of what they would be committing themselves to, to forge a framework that would have no clear definition and bring under 'services' only those sectors of advantage to the ICs while excluding those where the Third World may have an advantage. Also, with 'trade' itself not being defined, the agreement could be made to cover not merely instances where the 'service' crosses the border for delivery, but right of 'establishment' for the providers of service to locate themselves in the foreign country and produce the service.

To get around the problems created by the definition and coverage issue, a suggestion has been put forward by some that the general framework should have only broad concepts such as 'transparency', non-discrimination, national treatment, right of establishment and/or commercial presence, standstill on new regulations restrictive of trade, and mechanisms for international scrutiny of existing and new or proposed national regulations. Liberalisation would be left to future rounds of negotiations. Also, separate and more detailed sectoral agreements are envisaged, and provision for each signatory to have right of 'limited exclusion' from the general framework (which could be used by the industrial nations to exclude labour or labour-intensive services). The latter are also sought to be excluded, by providing for exclusion of matters governed by consular regulations.

The US Position

The US has spelt out its ideas and proposals on some of these concepts, and how to reach them [6].

Under 'transparency' it wants an international structure to enable examination of national measures on services, both those promulgated by governments for reasons unrelated to trade   and others so related. Such an examination would enable multilateral scrutiny of intended and unintended effects of such measures on access to markets and treatment of foreign service suppliers in a particular market. Governments would be obliged to publish all their rules and regulations, provide interested parties an opportunity to comment on proposed rules (an obligation to foreigners in the legislative or quasi-legislative   powers of a state not existent in any other area of economic or other activity of a government), and review of such measures, considered by others to be inconsistent, under   normal consultation and dispute settlement   procedures as in the General Agreement.

Signatories to the agreement would be obliged to extend its   benefits unconditionally to all other signatories, subject to provisions for some exceptions (like those in the General Agreement).

Foreign services providers would be entitled to a treatment   no less favourable than that granted to domestic providers of such services. Except in cases of proven legitimate regulatory needs and regulations that have a clear nexus, all other restrictions on establishment or investment would in effect be invalidated, and foreign service providers would be able to sell their services freely across the borders.

In pushing for a general multilateral framework of broad principles to be quickly concluded, even ahead of sectoral agreements, the US and Japan are also having an eye on internal market integration within the Community beginning 1992. The EEC has tried to reassure its trading partners that it will not become 'inward-looking' from 1992, and would continue to be as open to the outside as before. But it has also said that while it would fully abide by its GATT obligations in matters covered by it (trade in goods), in areas where there are no multilateral disciplines it would demand reci-procity.

This implies, for example, that if a bank, based in Japan

or the US, is to get the privilege of operating throughout the EEC, when it gets authorisation and establishes itself in one of the EEC countries, banks based in the EEC states should have equal and similar rights in Japan or the US as the case may be. The US is in no position to assure this, since this is a matter involving the power of the states, and even federally authorised US banks cannot operate in all the states. The problems in the insurance sector will be even greater.

The US, and its banks, have expressed great concern. Following some protests, the EEC has slightly backed off, but has not abandoned its ideas. In view of such concerns, the US negotiators privately say that while before and at Punta del Este their main targets for liberalisation and market access were the major Third World economies like India or Brazil, they are now even more concerned over the 1992 prospects in Europe and want a multilateral framework of general principles concluded quickly. If this does not happen or is likely to be delayed, they may want to conclude a bilateral or plurilateral agreement within the OECD context. Japan also is similarly concerned.

The EEC Position

The EEC [7] has also favoured a multilateral framework of principles and rules involving: progressive liberalisation of market access and respect for policy objectives, international competition, transparency, and 'development compatibility' [8]. The EEC has sought what it calls 'commercial presence', but this is just the thin end of the wedge, and over the long term might achieve the same purpose as the 'right of establishment' sought by the US. Unlike the US, the EEC is of the view that not all 'perceived barriers to trade' could be the subject of negotiations for liberalisation, since regulations could be the outcome of national policy objectives and thus have to be respected in terms of the mandate. While talking of 'development compatibility', the EEC is of the view that 'expansion of trade' is the absolute criterion, and that 'development' (and rules and principles for that) must be tested against the absolute criterion of expansion of trade.

The EEC negotiators, having ruled out labour movements, have also been frank enough to say that for the foreseeable future they do not see any 'comparative advantage' for Third World countries in any sector of service trade, and that mutuality of benefits could best be assured by providing in the agreement obligations on service providers to transfer technology, ensure access to networks and their information etc. However, they also rule out the home countries of the TNCs assuming any duties to ensure that their TNCs abide by these obligations, nor any other enforcement measures (beyond normal GATT trade retaliation by withdrawal of concessions) for enforcement of such obligations - a 'right' that the weaker Third World trading partners can never exercise [9].

Sign Now, Define Its Meaning Later

The Industrial Countries have been generally taking the position that a prior definition of 'trade in services' might not be necessary, and that either a definition would develop over time or one could be evolved in the light of the multilateral framework and the sectors to which it would apply. In support of this, the argument has been advanced that when the General Agreement was signed, there was no attempt to define 'trade in goods'. This is a somewhat specious argument, since the General Agreement was preceded by almost a century of bilateral trade agreements, and a few centuries of commercial usage, where these terms had acquired some accepted meanings.

If Third World countries accept the view that an agreement on 'trade in services' could be concluded without a definition of 'trade' or 'services', because of lack of clearly established parameters of negotiations, they would find themselves unable to prevent modification of the mandate in subsequent rounds of negotiations, and would be compelled to deal with 'investment' and 'right of establishment' and other issues, not related to 'trade' but to production. They would also open themselves to coercive pressures from their powerful trading partners, based on the latter's own view of the definition [10].

On the statistics issue too, the Industrial Countries have been taking the position that developing adequate statistics would be a long-term project, and a multilateral framework should not be held up for this. But this means Third World countries would be entering into commitments without even knowing what would be its impact on their overall economies and balance of payments, and without any clear idea as to the sectors where liberalisation would benefit them and where it would be adverse to them. Without this they cannot negotiate intelligently and achieve a balanced compromise.

Liberalisation also poses its own problems, and unless these are clearly dealt with in the proposed framework, a general provision for liberalisation would pose serious dangers for the Third World.

In the scheme of GATT, whose model is sought to be injected, everything that is not prohibited is permitted, but could be the subject of negotiations to reduce protection. Customs tariffs are legitimate, but could be negotiated down and 'bound'. However, quantitative restrictions would be illegitimate - unless specifically excepted when they are not subject to negotiations. The 'national treatment' to the imported product after it crosses the border, an obligation under Article III, is thus a corollary to ensure that countries do not cheat on their negotiated concessions and bound tariffs and that after importation they do not impose discriminatory obligations vis-a-vis the domestic product that would impede access to markets for the imported product.

Services are not capable of frontier customs or other price measures to protect the domestic industry, and access to   markets involves cross-border movement of persons, capital, goods and information. Hence regulations to deal with trade in services have to deal with all these movements. The right of establishment, coupled with national treatment, in effect thus would rule out completely any domestic measures to protect any domestic service industry. Even more, these two concepts are presented as basic obligations, and not in terms of frontier measures, and would amount to encroachment on national 'economic space' and sovereignty.

Apart from the 'definition' and 'statistics' problems, the issues relating to 'coverage' and the 'existing international disciplines and arrangements' have been sought to be brushed aside by the Industrial Nations. The principal effort is to create a framework in such general terms that it could be viewed in international law as over-riding any specific sectoral international agreements - such as the agreements under ITU in telecommunications, agreements about civil aviation in ICAO, liner code and other shipping agreements negotiated in UNC-TAD, and other international accords about which even details have not been gathered.

Existing agreements in fact are sought to be dismissed by US and its supporters as mere 'technical agreements', setting standards etc, and as not covering 'trade' aspects that fall within GATT jurisdiction or that of the new trade in services framework.

Apart from the US and EEC, other Industrial Nations (Japan, Australia, Canada, Switzerland and the Nordic countries) too have formulated proposals and positions. There are some nuances and differences in their approaches, in the context of their mutual relationships and rivalries [11].

The Position of Some Third World Countries

Some of the Third World countries have made general statements on the mandate and the economic and legal issues, and have also made comments on the papers and proposals of the various Industrial Nations, and some of them have been elaborated and circulated within the GNS as documents [12].

All of them have been fairly unanimous in underscoring the importance of the 'development' concept and the need to provide for it as an integral part of the agreement. All of them have sharply distinguished between 'trade' that crosses the borders and thus the subject of negotiations, and domestic trade, investment, establishment etc which are outside the scope of the mandate. Some have envisaged the possibility of negotiations to enable temporary presence in the market for delivery of the services, and special measures (through 'relative reciprocity or 'preferential access') to enable Third World countries to export services, develop capacities to set up service industries, and secure access to technology, networks etc. They also insist that behaviour of private parties in the markets are also a legitimate area to be covered by any agreement.

Brazil has termed as 'naive' and 'theoretical' assumptions that unilateral liberalisation would intrinsically benefit the Third World. India has said that the mandate did not enable any 'open-ended scrutiny' of national regulations in services or subjecting them to any multilateral determination about their appropriateness or legitimacy; also, existing international agreements in various sectors should be examined to see whether these sectors need to be covered or incorporated in the multilateral framework. India has also insisted on 'development' being the criterion to be obeyed. Mexico has said 'development' should be a central objective to be achieved through the agreement, and not merely provided for through 'exceptions' and 'waivers' (as in GATT). Argentina has put forward detailed suggestions about the various elements of a possible agreement; while insisting that national policy objectives cannot be questioned, it also envisages practical procedures for parties to gradually adjust their national regulations.

Notes to Chapter 5:

1. The developments in the negotiating process set out in this chapter have to be read in conjunction with relevant portions in Chapter 11.

2. Since much of the compromises and understandings (including the organic delinkage of goods and services negotiations) were in informal negotiations, these were brought on record at the very first meeting of the Group of Negotiations on Services in Feb 1987 by two of the key Third World negotiators - Paulo Nogueira Batista of Brazil and Shrirang P Shukla of India. Neither the US nor the EEC, the other parties to the compromise negotiations at Punta del Este, challenged them. See *SUNS* 1664.

3. Annex I.

4. From the beginning Third World countries said the mandate and the plan covered not only 'measures and practices' of governments but of private parties too, meaning TNCs and their Restrictive Business Practices.

5. For discussions and proposals see *SUNS* 1695, 1748, 1784, 1817,1818, 1846, 1860, 1871, 1908, 1940, 1947, 1984, 1985, and 2038; also see 'Uruguay Round', *op.cit.* pp 90-105.

6. For details see *SUNS* 1817 and 1940: also *News of the Uruguay Round,* NUR 012, published by the GATT information service.

7. For details of EEC proposals in the GNS see *SUNS* 1846 and *NUR* 016.

8. *SUNS* 1846, and also *NUR* 013.

9. 'Economists challenge some service theories', report on roundtable at Salzburg, *SUNS* 1978 pp 3-8. see in particular remarks of EEC negotiator John Richardson at pp 6-7.

10. See infra Chapter 12 about the Montreal mid-term review agreement on further work on definition in the negotiations in the GNS for a multilateral framework. Though the agreement would appear to rule out factor movements except in relation to 'discreteness of

transactions', and 'limited duration', during the post-Montreal discussions in the GNS on the sectoral testing of concepts, both the notes on individual sectors prepared by the secretariat, and views advanced by the US and other ICs, have blandly ignored these limitations. The ICs have been pressing for definitions that would secure 'right of establishment' for their service industries.

11. For details of some of these see various issues of *SUNS*: Australia 1786 and 1984, Canada 1786 and 1940, Japan 1786 and 1985, Nordics 1908, Switzerland 1988.

12. For details see *SUNS* Nos. 1664, 1786, 1908, 1909, 1984.

Chapter 6

PROTECTION OF INTELLECTUAL PROPERTY

Changing Concepts and Laws Regarding Patents

Of all the issues that have been brought on the agenda of GATT in the Uruguay Round, the subject of 'Trade-related Intellectual Property Rights including Trade in Counterfeit Goods' is one area where the most determined and combined effort of the Industrialised Countries is deployed against the Third World [1]. Through the negotiations in TRIPs, the industrialised countries are seeking to establish new international rules to protect the monopoly rentier incomes of their TNCs, deny Third World countries access to knowledge, block their capacity for innovation and technical change and prevent any rise of competitive capacity in the Third World.

The efforts of the US and other industrialised countries, directed against the Third World countries, and aimed at constricting their process of industrialisation and autonomous development and blocking competition to themselves, is not without parallel. Capacity of countries and governments for 'folly' is apparently endless [2]. In the 18th century, Britain sought to enforce the mercantilist system on its North American colonies. It sought to ensure that the colonies would serve as "the source of raw materials and the market for British manufacture, and never to usurp the manufacturing function...Transportation both ways in British bottoms and reexport of colonial produce by way of Britain to foreign markets were aspects of the system, which was regulated by some thirty Navigation Acts and by the Board of Trade, the most organised and professional arm of the British Government" [3]. The American colonies hit at the powerful British interests, and encouraged domestic manufacture through home-spun flax textiles, and hit the entire British Trade. To rescue the East India Company and its finances, and monopoly trade interests in North America in tea, the Tea duty was imposed, which triggerred the Boston Tea Party and set in motion forces that brought Independence and gave birth to the United States. Nearly 150 years later, Gandhi in India hit at the British through his home-spun Khadi movement. The efforts of the US and other ICs, through the instrumentality of the Uruguay Round and the instruments to be fashioned through the new themes, will perhaps in the long-term be a repetition of the same 'folly' with the same consequences.

The proposals of the industrialised countries in the negotiations are a 'complete reversal' of their past commitments to assist in promoting the development of the Third World. "The clock is not simply being put back. It is to be remade to move only backward" [4].

Patents, trademarks and other intellectual (industrial) property rights are not natural human rights. Ancient Greece (7th century BC) granted to cooks a monopoly for one year to exploit new recipes. But a few centuries later, Emperor Zeno in Rome (480 AD) rejected the concept of monopoly. The City State of Venice, the first to establish a patent law in 1474, granted the 'rights' on condition that the patent is worked; otherwise the patent rights were 'forfeited' [5].

When European countries began creating patent rights, at the dawn of the industrial revolution, there were conflicts whether the 'monopoly' to exploit the invention granted to the inventor is a natural right or an exception to the natural right of citizens to the invention. The 1791 French patent law said that the 'monopoly' of an inventor was 'a natural right'. Not so said Austria in 1794. While accepting patents, it rejected the concept of natural right and called patents an 'exception' to the 'natural right of citizens to have access to inventions' [6].

There is no definition of 'patent' in the 1883 Paris Convention. In the UN Secretary-General's report on 'The Role of Patents in the Transfer of Technology to Developing Countries' [7] a patent was defined as "a statutory privilege granted by the government to inventors, and to other persons deriving their rights from the inventor, for a fixed period of years, to exclude other persons from manufacturing, using or selling a patented product or from utilising a patented method or process. At the expiration of the time for which the privilege is granted, the patented invention is available to the general public or, as it is sometimes put, falls into the 'public domain'."

Later, for purposes of the 1975 joint study by the UN, UNCTAD and WIPO [8], the International Bureau of the WIPO provided a description of the patent as 'a legally enforceable right granted by virtue of a law to a person to exclude, for a limited time, others from certain acts in relation to a described invention; the privilege is granted by a government authority as a matter of right to the person who is entitled to apply for it and who fulfils the prescribed conditions'.

Patents and other intellectual or industrial property are thus statutory rights - benefits created by law by the State. Even to call them 'rights' is a misnomer. They are really 'privileges' granted by the State by statute - a form of government intervention in the market place, a government subsidy not unlike tax credits, export incentives etc [9]. They were created to reward inventive work of individuals and enable spread of knowledge useful to society, make inventions more widely available for productive use by granting, for a limited duration, the patent-holder monopoly rights of exploitation and excluding others from using them without the authorisation of the patent-holder.

Gradually there has been the development of the concept of Science and Technology as a common heritage of mankind but this is now being challenged. In the postwar decades, patents etc have been garnered by the TNCs who have created a monopoly right for themselves. Patent laws were originally established to reward invention and promote industrialisation as well as prevent import monopolies within the country concerned. However, through efforts to universalise patent laws that give owners the right to exploit the patent at international level (and not only at national level), the industrialised countries are in fact trying to reward export monopolies in the industrial centres which would slow down industrialisation and spread of technology in the Third World.

A major argument advanced for intellectual property protection and for uniform international norms is that this rewards innovation and inventiveness, and without it there would be no technological advance or flows.

But a study in the UK in 1973 on the economic effect of the patents system on manufacturing industry reached some broad conclusions at variance with this argument [10]. The study came to three broad conclusions:

"First, the patent system per se appears not to promote innovation significantly, and in only a few industries, notably drugs and chemicals, were patents widely used. The study also confirms that most inventions would be made with or without a patent system, and that the elimination of free-riding by competitors seeking to use rival research costlessly is of greater theoretical than practical importance [11]... Secondly, monopolistic conduct by patentees in relation to prices and output is not wide-spread, although in some industries prices did exceed competitive levels. The absence of abuse was at least partly attributed to legal controls, particularly Crown use of drug patents. Thirdly, the publication of patent specifications, demanded by the Patents Act as a condition of grant, has led to a beneficial circulation of information and as a result licences have been applied for

and granted to those best suited to exploit inventions"
[12].

The major thrust for internationalising standards and
norms for Patents have come from the US pharmaceutical
industry and the European fashion and designer clothes
industries. But their efforts to hit at the Third World may
ultimately have negative effects on the overall economic
sectors of the North, both Industry and Services. As Tuchman
points out, the British attempts to safeguard its mercantile
interests through the tea duty and other measures ultimately lost Britain its colonies. In the current age, the efforts
to ensure rentier incomes for drug and other TNCs, would
perhaps be the trigger to set off economic decolonization
movements in the South over the medium to long-term.

Ensuring worldwide rights for processes and products for drugs, it is argued, is essential to encourage new
research and discovery of new drugs. But Patents no longer
seem to serve their original purpose of innovation of things
useful to society and spread of knowledge. In the area of
pharmaceuticals, patents and excessive secrecy associated
with them appear to be reducing innovation and scientific research, and have not helped produce new drugs needed
for the ailments afflicting humanity, particularly the poor.

According to an article in *The Economist* magazine:
"Two-thirds of the 50 top selling drugs are retreads of old
therapies. Drug research used to be simple... Now, biotechnology has made cleverness essential again... Unfortunately
academic culture and drug-industry culture seem to react as
tastelessly as port poured into gin... Those scientists who
come to the drug industry to get rich and recognised are
soon disappointed. Researchers in the industry rarely get a
share of the profits from the products they discover" [13].

In Europe, where grant of patents privileges by the State
began, at the onset of the industrial revolution (in the 17th
and 18th centuries), it was used as an instrument for promot-

ing technological and industrial progress in the country granting the patent, and benefited the inventor or the person importing the invention into the national territory for industrial exploitation. The purpose of patents and patent regulations "has been and still is determined basically by the technological and industrial interests of the country enacting the patent legislation" [14].

The Paris Union Conventions, which balanced the right of the inventor with the wider public interest, took note of the differing economic and other circumstances in each country and gave considerable leeway to its member states, not only in fixing the duration of a patent in any particular area but even whether something should be allowed to be patented or the knowledge remain in the public domain.

In England, where patents were originally introduced, the 'period' was fixed at 14 years, the time needed to train two journey-men apprentices in succession. The presumption was that when two journeymen had learnt the technique and set themselves up independently, the technique or innovation was already public, and there can be no more such rights. By this logic of course, given the lesser time now needed to train people, and the shorter lifespan of the product, the life of a patent should be shorter. But they are sought to be extended to protect the modern corporations, particularly the TNCs and their investments and monopoly profits. The Paris Conventions were continuously amended to tilt the balance away from patent rights combined with requirement of local exploitation to protect public interest, to patent rights and monopoly import privileges to benefit the corporations.

According to Dr Alberto Bercovtitz:

"For a long time, the patent laws required that the patented invention be actually exploited within the national territory. Patents were devised as incentives for development of industries in the patent-giving country... The privilege had no value unless it was exploited...With increase in international trade it was (soon) possible to profit from a patent... by importing from abroad the products protected from patents. The response... to this phenomenon was to counter by making use of the patent as an export monopoly a ground for forfeiture of the patent... Originally designed as a means of fostering the technological and industrial progress of the State granting the patent... there has been a continuous trend towards internationalising the functions so as to enable owners to exploit them not at the national but at the international level... The notable weakening of the obligation to exploit the patent in the country granting it facilitates the exploitation of the patented invention through exports. This leads in turn to patents being utilised for securing exclusive rights on export markets" [15].

Bringing 'Intellectual Property' into GATT

The terms 'intellectual property' and 'industrial property' are being used co-terminously in recent years. Intellectual property strictly means copyright for literary and artistic works and related rights, and are governed by the Berne Convention (of 1886, and revised in 1928 and 1948) and the much later (1952) UNESCO-sponsored Geneva Convention of Universal Copyright. 'Industrial property' on the other hand covers patents, utility models, inventors' certificates, trade marks and similar rights. In recent years, copyright has been extended in some countries to computer programmes, integrated circuits and informatics.

Some of the complaints and issues now being agitated about lack of adequate protection or enforcement etc, were never even raised in the WIPO, which administers the Paris Conventions on Industrial Property and the Berne Convention on Copyright. According to the WIPO Director-General, Dr. Arpad Bogsch (a US national), at no stage within the WIPO had the US and others put forward any proposals for changes in the Paris Conventions or other ancillary instruments, either about securing greater protection for intellectual property rights or to deal with counterfeit goods in international trade. "Very little effort has been made within WIPO to improve protection, with the exception perhaps of the proposed treaty on integrated circuits," says the WIPO Director-General [16].

In bringing the issue on the Uruguay Round agenda and by using the term 'intellectual property right', the US and other ICs have managed to inject some value-loaded words, like 'piracy' and 'counterfeiting', to describe those who are not prepared to accept their demands. With the help of the media, they have made these terms current coin, confusing the public and legitimising their own demands, and painting those opposing them as indulging in some immoral acts or near criminal conduct or behaviour.

In the Uruguay Round the ICs are using the term 'intellectual property' in an all-embracing manner, to include all types of industrial property rights. The US, Japan, EEC, Switzerland, and the Nordics have all put forward their proposals in this area, all of them on the basis that 'indequate, excessive and discriminatory protection' of IPRs impedes and distorts trade and should be dealt with in GATT. But the US papers merely talk of 'inadequate' protection. With some varying approaches, all of the ICs want norms and standards to be established under GATT auspices. Switzerland has suggested specific amendments to GATT for this purpose, while the others call for a GATT agreement [17].

Switzerland has sought establishment within GATT of a set of general normative principles to be enforced by GATT procedures. The US and Japan want a GATT agreement with annexes specifying the norms for protection of IPRs and to which national IPR laws should conform. The EEC is not seeking any 'harmonisation' of national laws, but agreement on a set of principles for substantive standards that everyone should respect. Both at the preparatory stage, as well as in the initial consideration of the issue, the EEC was rather reticent. But in 1988, it put forward proposals that were as far-reaching as those of the US or Japan.

The US has also said that the rights to be protected should include 'trade secrets', while the EEC wants protection to include 'coverage of neighbouring rights', geographical indications including appellations of origin and protection against acts contrary to 'honest commercial practice', which would amount to the US demand for protection of trade secrets. The US has said 'trade secrets' should be defined broadly to include 'undisclosed valuable business, commercial, technical or other proprietory data as well as technical information'.

The attempts to get 'trade secrets' given statutory IPR protection is a contradiction of the basic theory behind IPRs, namely statutory protection of such rights to enable full disclosure and spread of knowledge more widely. In the case of a patent, the applicant has to make a full disclosure with all technical details, and all this is carefully scrutinised before the patent is granted (and the information published by the authority granting the patent) before the holder gets exclusive rights of exploitation for a limited time after which it passes into the public domain. But under the proposals about 'trade secret', an enterprise concerned would be keeping its 'information' secret, but others using the information in their activities would be presumed to have 'pirated' them and would be penalised.

Why Patent Moves May Harm Third World

In international trade, 'patents' and 'trade marks' far from expanding trade are really trade barriers in as much as the owners are given some monopoly import privileges. Historically, there have been intense fights between the so-called free traders and those pressing for patent monopolies. Several of the currently industrialised countries, when they were in the stage of industrialisation resisted patent laws. The Dutch in 1869 repealed their existing law enacted in 1809, and did not introduce patent laws until 1912. In Switzerland, attempts to introduce patent laws were successively turned down in referendums, and a law was enacted only in the last decade of the 19th century. Till very recently a number of OECD countries (the Federal Republic of Germany till 1967, Switzerland till 1978, Japan till 1976 and Nordics till 1968) did not provide patent protection for chemicals; and pharmaceuticals were denied such protection in FRG and France till 1967, and Italy till 1979. In Spain chemicals and pharmaceuticals will become patentable only in 1992 [18].

Many of the countries that became independent after the war inherited patent laws introduced by the colonial metropolitan powers. India's patent law was introduced in 1859, just two years after it came under British Crown rule. Similar was the case in a number of other colonies in Asia and Africa, where patent laws were introduced to protect the metropolitan interests and ensure import monopolies. It was only much after independence that some of these countries revised their patent laws to provide the balance between the rights of patentees and public interest and to promote industrialisation and secure transfer of technology.

The imbalance between the North and South is seen in the fact that over 80 percent of the patents in Third World countries are owned by foreigners, mainly TNCs of the US, UK, FRG, France and Switzerland, and over 95 percent are not used at all in production in these countries.

In bringing the issue into GATT - an agreement intended to expand world trade - and insisting on creating new norms in areas where none exist or enhancing norms in areas already subject to the Paris Union Conventions administered by the WIPO, the US and other ICs are demanding that the new round not reduce trade barriers but enhance them. While the US and some of its supporters want to reduce or eliminate subsidies to farmers, through the IPRs they want consumers around the world to subsidise their TNCs, "subsidise American companies to the manner they have grown accustomed at home" [19]. Under S.301 of the US Trade and Tariff Act, the US unilaterally determines failure of other countries to provide the same level of protection to the US enterprises as they enjoy at home as an 'unfair trade practice' that would invite unilateral US trade actions; and the US now wants, through the Uruguay Round, GATT provisions to legitimise such unilateral actions.

Historically, biological processes and products have not been eligible for intellectual (industrial) property protection. The US and other ICs, through the WIPO and GATT, are now trying to make manipulated genes and altered species, and their characteristics, patentable. The vast biological diversity of the Third World - whether discovered or altered and adjusted - would become the intellectual (industrial) property of private interests. The extension of some of these rights, for example by seed companies and animal 'breeders', would result in farmers being denied their traditional right to save seed. They would be forced to pay a royalty everytime a 'seed' with a 'patented characteristic' is used or grown or a cow or farm animal with a patented gene or characteristic gets an offspring. Even incorporation of a characteristic of one crop into another would be subject to this royalty [20].

Third World consumers would be forced to pay higher prices for their drugs. Till recently, Italy did not allow patenting of drugs and their processes, while such protection was available in the UK. As a result, Roche Products, a British subsidiary of Hoffman La-Roche AG of Basel (Switzerland) was selling the British National Health Service two patented products used in the formulation of Librium and Valium (both widely used tranquilisers), at over 40 times their prices in Italy. The British Monopolies Commission found that Roche Products was paying its parent company $925 per kilo for a substance that could be bought in Italy (where these products were not under patent protection) for $22.50 per kilo and $2,305 per kilo for another substance that could be bought in Italy for $50 per kilo [21]. If this could happen in an industrialised country, it is easy to visualise what would happen to consumers in Third World countries.

US Double Standards

The US negotiating objectives on intellectual property protection in the Uruguay Round, as spelt out by Congress in the Omnibus Trade and Competitiveness Act of 1988, exhibits some double standards. As already noted, while spelling out the objectives for a new GATT-based international regime in this area, the law has reinforced existing provisions to enable unilateral actions. Under the latter (S.1303), there is a special procedure for the USTR to identify priority countries that are indulging in unfair practices (by denying protection and/or access to their markets for US enterprises relying on intellectual property protection), for bilateral negotiations to resolve the problem, and failing that to take trade 'retaliation'. While the USTR is not obliged to take actions against countries identified, there is a presumption that special attention will be devoted to such a country. Another provision in sec. 1101 (b) (10) directs negotiators to obtain enforcement of GATT rules against 'statutes, practices or policies of any foreign government which, as a practical matter, unreasonably requires that... intellectual property be licensed to the foreign country or any firm of the foreign country.'

But the same section, 1101 (b) (15) provides:

"(A) The principal negotiating objective of the United States regarding access to high technology is to obtain the elimination or reduction of foreign barriers to, and acts, policies, or practices of foreign governments which limit equitable access by United States Persons to foreign-developed technology, including barriers, acts, policies or practices which have the effect of -

(i) restricting the participation of US persons in gov-

ernment-supported research and development projects,
 (ii) denying equitable access by US persons to government-held patents,
(iii) requiring the approval or agreement of government
entities, or imposing other forms of government interventions, as a condition for the granting of licenses to
US persons by foreign persons (except for approval or
agreement which may be necessary for national security
purposes to control the export of critical military technology), and
(iv) otherwise denying equitable access by US persons
to foreign-developed technology or contributing to the
*inequitable flow of technology between the United States
and its trading partners."* (emphasis added)

This is purportedly a Congressional response to concerns of US industry over restrictions of Japan and other
advanced ICs to participation of US persons in research
projects and access to their results. But it is difficult to see
how it is different from the concerns and arguments of other
countries that very strict intellectual property protection and
enforcement is an unreasonable barrier to transfer of technology. The only US logic appears to be "What I have I keep;
what you have we shall force you to share".

Uruguay Round Mandate on IPRs

The Uruguay Round mandate stipulates, in three separate paras or indents:

"In order to reduce the distortions and impediments to
international trade and taking into account the need to
promote effective and adequate protection of intellectual property rights, and to ensure that measures and
procedures to enforce intellectual property rights do not
themselves become barriers to legitimate trade, the
negotiations shall aim to clarify GATT provisions and
elaborate as appropriate new rules and disciplines.

"Negotiations shall aim to develop a multilateral framework of principles, rules and disciplines dealing with international trade in counterfeit goods, taking into account work already undertaken in the GATT.

"The negotiations shall be without prejudice to other complementary initiatives that may be taken in the World Intellectual Property Organisation and elsewhere to deal with these matters."

This was a carefully crafted and negotiated mandate.

In the first para or first indent, the preamble has balanced the issue of adequate protection of IPRs with the need to ensure that enforcement of such rights does not become a legitimate barrier to international trade. In the light of this, negotiations were restricted to 'clarification' of existing GATT provisions and for elaboration of new rules and disciplines *"as appropriate"* (emphasis added).

The rationale for the mandate on 'clarification' and 'further elaboration... as appropriate' flows from the fact that laws and regulations for protection of IPRs could become disguised protectionist measures. Hence various GATT provisions, even when recognising the enforcement as an exception - in Article XX (d) for example - balance it with the demand for non-discrimination and no disguised protection. The provisions in Article IX relating to marks of origin call for these marks of origin, appellations etc not to be used to unncessarily hamper international trade or discriminate among contracting parties. Thus the whole scheme and objective of the provisions relating to IPRs in GATT has been to ensure that their enforcement does not hamper or retard international trade. All this is now being reversed.

Under the second indent, kept separate from the first, the negotiators have been asked to develop a multilateral framework to deal with international trade in counterfeit goods.

The mandate under the third indent has qualified both the first and the second, by making clear that the GATT negotiations *"shall be without prejudice"* (emphasis added) to any complimentary initiatives in WIPO and elsewhere on these matters.

The negotiating plan adopted in January 1987 maintained this balance, and provided for separate consideration of each of the three indents.

But from the outset the ICs have sought to blur these distinctions and have been insisting that the negotiations should deal with all aspects of IPRs in GATT on the ground they are all trade-related. On the other hand it has been the consistent position of the Third World countries that the negotiating mandate for TRIPs is limited to a clarification of the relevant GATT provisions and to promote cooperation among the CPs to deal with these issues, but without imping-ing on the competence of international organisations with competence in this area, such as WIPO, UNCTAD and UNESCO. This has resulted in the group being embroiled from the outset in disputes about its mandate.

The ICs are attempting to use the mandate to create international substantial norms in the GATT - new norms where none now exist and enhance existing norms - and force all countries to adopt such norms, and ensure its implementation and enforcement through GATT procedures of consultation, dispute settlement and retaliation etc.

Even an ordinary reading of the Punta del Este mandate does not suggest that it was the intention to use the nego-tiations to create a new international framework governing these matters. This is even more clear when the negotiat-ing history is considered.

The intense negotiations on this issue at Punta del Este (involving the US, EEC, Brazil and India) resulted in the compromise mandate. The GATT Contracting Parties had before them two drafts of a Ministerial declaration for launching the round. The first was the paper by the group of ten Third World countries [22] and the second a Colombian-Swiss paper [23].

The first had nothing on any of the new themes. The second was de facto used as the basis for negotiations at Punta del Este, but was significantly altered in important respects in the mandate that was ultimately adopted. In both, the portions relating to trade in counterfeit goods and on respect for jurisdiction of existing international organisations and their work in these areas are same and have not been reproduced. But on the issue of IPRs, the two versions are given below, with the differences in italics.

Swiss-Colombian draft	**Punta del Este mandate**
- In order to reduce distortions and impediments to international trade *arising from the lack of* adequate and effective protection of intellectual property rights, negotiations shall aim:	In order to reduce the distortions and impediments to international trade, and
- *to promote a more effective and generalised application of existing international standards in intellectual property matters;*	*taking into account the need to promote effective and adequate protection of intellectual property rights, and*
- to ensure that measures and procedures to enforce intellectual property rights do not themselves become barriers to legitimate trade; and	to ensure that measures and procedures to enforce intellectual property rights do not themselves become barriers to legitimate trade,

- to clarify and elaborate rules and disciplines *with respect to these matters.*	the negotiations shall aim to clarify *GATT provisions* and elaborate *as appropriate new* rules and disciplines.

The 'judgement' in the Swiss-Colombian text that 'lack of adequate and effective protection' of IPRs is the cause of trade distortions and is an 'impediment' to international trade was eliminated in the mandate. In the Swiss-Colombian draft, the mandate to the negotiators was spelt out as the promotion of 'a more effective and generalised application of existing international standards' and ensuring that measures and procedures to enforce IPRs do not themselves become barriers to legitimate trade. In the Punta del Este mandate, these are merely factors to be 'taken into account', and have the same status as the need to ensure that enforcement of IPRs do not themselves become barriers to legitimate trade. And, while the Swiss-Colombian draft had called for clarification and elaboration of rules and disciplines to achieve the two 'aims' of the mandate, the Punta del Este declaration has qualified it by asking for clarification of GATT provisions, and elaboration of new rules and disciplines only 'as appropriate'. Also, while the US and others are now seeking new norms where there are no international norms and for enhancement of existing norms, the wording in the Swiss-Colombian draft (which was dropped from the Punta del Este mandate) only spoke of more effective and generalised application of 'existing international standards'.

The North Pushes Its Version of TRIPs

In the course of the first two years of negotiations, the ICs have sought to brush aside all this negotiating history and the wording of the compromise.

The US and Japan, as their proposals show, want to go the whole hog and want GATT rules for (a) substantive enhancement of IPRs where there are already international norms and standards, and creating norms where none now exist; (b) better enforcement (i) at the time of importation, a traditional function of customs, and (ii) at the stage of exportation and production by the country concerned; and (c) dispute settlement as a form of enforcement on the countries and governments.

The proposals of the US and some others under the first indent, have called for establishment of 'adequate' international norms to protect IPRs, and providing for such norms in respect of patents, trademarks, copyright, layout rights for semiconductor integrated circuits, trade secrets, designs etc. The new norms proposed would be more than those under the WIPO Paris Union conventions. Several call for the enforcement of the new norms (and some say established international norms) through GATT Dispute Settlement Procedures. This would enable the major trading nations to 'retaliate' against Third World countries allegedly not providing or observing such norms. A variant proposal envisages the creation of a code, as in the Tokyo Round, whose signatories will agree to oberve the new norms and in return will get bencfits, perhaps in the form of assurances against harassment at customs for purported violations.

Under the second indent, some Third World countries have indicated their willingness to proceed to negotiations, on basis of work already done, in developing some draft agreement or code to deal with trade in counterfeit goods. But a number of ICs have expressly linked this work to work under the first indent.

An issue under the third indent has been the relationship of any accords reached in GATT to existing agreements - under WIPO and UNESCO. While some of the industrial countries have suggested that the GATT accords would override the commitments under the other agreements, a number of Third World countries have insisted that changes or amendments to those accords have to be sought according to the procedures set in them, and GATT can't be used either to amend them or create new agreements in these areas.

In the light of their own stand on the jurisdictional issues, the leading Third World nations have not put forward or formulated any proposals of their own. It is not merely a question of choice of forum or GATT vs WIPO.

Until the Uruguay Round, GATT never concerned itself with these IPRs [24], and the few GATT provisions were put in to ensure that patent and trade marks protections do not become disguised barriers to trade. The substantive issues were dealt with in WIPO, which administered the Paris Union Conventions on industrial property and the Berne Conventions on copyright. Signed in 1883, for a long time the Paris Union remained a 'rich men's club'. Of the original signatories, four were from Latin America - of whom three (Ecuador, El Salvador and Guatemala) soon dropped out, leaving for a long time Brazil as the sole Third World member. The convention was subsequently revised six times (1900, 1911, 1925, 1934, 1958 and 1967), with each revision tilting the original balance between public interest and monopoly interest of the patentee in favour of the latter. Nevertheless, the convention maintained the compromise between private interests of the patent holders and the public interest, as well as the differing situations in different countries, by recognising the basic autonomy and freedom of member-states to legislate according to their own perceptions of national and public interest. Member states were left free to legislate on the criteria for patentability, whether a patent should or should not be examined to determine whether a patent should at all be granted, whether the criteria have been met, to whom the patent is to be granted (first inventor or first applicant), for products, for proceses or for both, and in which fields and for what terms [25].

In the wake of the collapse of colonialism, and emergence to Independence of many of the colonies in Asia and Africa, several countries, (more so in Africa than in Asia) joined the Paris Conventions (to which they were in a sense parties when they were colonies). But soon they began to see the inequity in the Paris Convention and began their efforts to change it - through the Non-aligned Movement and the Group of 77. The issue was originally raised by Brazil in 1961 in the UN General Assembly, and the Assembly called for a study by the UN Secretary-General and for an international conference. The report [26] came out in 1965, but no conference was called. The issue was again taken up in the formulation of the International Development Strategy for the Second Develoment Decade, and the strategy called for a review and revision of the international conventions on patents. Then in 1973, at UNCTAD-III in Santiago, UNCTAD, WIPO and the UN were asked to update the 1965 study with a view to a revision of the international conventions. The study [27] was published in 1975. That same year the UN Special Session adopted by consensus a resolution which called for the revision of international conventions in this area.

After further expert group and inter-governmental studies in UNCTAD, a consensus resolution in 1975 set the broad guidelines for the revision. This was endorsed by the UN General Assembly and the task of revision of the Paris Union Conventions was entrusted to the WIPO, and this resulted ultimately in the convening of a UN Diplomatic Conference, which has been unable to make any progress because of the stands of the US and other major ICs [28]. Simultaneously with all these efforts, work also began in UNCTAD on a code of conduct for Transfer of Technology, which after considerable headway and agreement on most of its provisions, remains stalled, among other things, on the issue of 'restrictive practices' of TNCs. The decade-old efforts to reform and change the Paris Union conventions to secure development objectives have been blocked by the US, Japan etc, who are now pushing the issue in GATT, and by emphasising 'trade' want to tilt the balance in favour of the holders of IPRs to the detriment of public interest.

TRIPs will Roll Back Third World's Interests

By bringing up the issues now in the Uruguay Round, the ICs are going back on all their past commitments and trying to reverse the process of history. Their proposals in the TRIPs group have no reference to promotion of the techno- logical development of the Third World to which they committed themselves nearly two decades ago. The propos- als ignore the role of IPRs in technological innovation, access to and transfer of technology, and the entire issue of public good. They abrogate the century old balance in this area between rewarding creativity and safeguarding public inte- rest, a balance that has to be struck in each country, taking into account its circumstances.

As already noted, historically countries in the process of industrialisation have always limited the scope of protection granted to foreign technologies, often excluding whole areas of activity from protection. This is on the sound view that when a country has a weak technological capacity and base, and its enterprises cannot take significant advantage of the incentives of the IPR regime, benefits from such protection would outweigh the disadvantages of being unable to ac- quire and adapt foreign technology or import new products and processes from other and cheaper sources.

Being a statutorily granted right, the most important con- sideration in granting IPR protection is public interest - counter-balancing the rights of IPR owners by their obliga- tions to the country granting them such rights, such as through local working, and compulsory licensing in the absence of local working. It may be in the interests of the dominant industrialised nations now to shift the balance more to pri- vate rights of their corporations than public interest; but this cannot negate the right of the Third World to maintain this balance and ensure public good and public welfare.

Any international regime, with norms and standards ap- plicable uniformly in all countries, would really mean that the Third World countries would be powerless to act against abusive use of the rights granted. Such abusive practices characterise the licensing agreements by which the patent-holding foreign enterprise authorises its working in the territory of any particular country. Industrialised nations counter such abusive practices through their anti-trust and competition laws and policies, which they are able to enforce on the enterprises which are located on their territories or are dependent on the market. Third World nations are disadvantaged in this. International efforts in UNCTAD to deal with this through the International Code of Conduct on Transfer of Technology, as already noted, have been blocked by the dominant Industrial Nations on this very issue of restrictive practices and the role of TNCs.

Acceptance by Third World countries of these demands in the Uruguay Round would amount to abandonment of their two decades' old effort over a technology transfer code in UNCTAD and the reform of the industrial property system through amendments of the Paris Conventions. It would extend the GATT system to areas where there is no international consensus on the appropriate means for protection of new technologies, including biotechnology where moral and ethical questions, apart from public policy questions, are involved. All these need to be considered in more universal fora with wider mandates than the GATT with its less universal adherents and narrower focus on trade.

In all states, when property rights are created or are natural civil rights, if there is a violation, the only responsibility for the state is to provide a judicial or quasi-judicial process for determination of rights among parties and for remedies. The Paris Union Conventions accept this, and on this basis "obliges each of its 98 member States to grant to nationals and residents of the other member states, under the 'national treatment' principle, the same legal remedies for infringement of patent rights as those it grants to its own nationals, possibly subject to the provisions of the national law relating to judicial and administrative procedures and to jurisdiction" [29].

A panel ruling in GATT, in a dispute between the EEC and US, has brought out that the US not only does not provide 'the same' legal remedies to foreign nationals, but discriminates against them [30]. Now through their proposals for enforcement, and for issues involving private rights of individuals and enterprises to be a matter of dispute among states, the US and other ICs are claiming in this area for foreign enterprises a greater right than is available to domestic holders of such rights.

Two years of discussions in the group have not been able to bridge the gap between the ICs and the Third World countries on what to negotiate. In their formulations for the Montreal meeting, the Third World countries said:

- Substantive matters relating to IPRs have to be dealt with in WIPO, UNCTAD and UNESCO,
- The negotiating group should deal strictly with 'trade-related' aspects as different from substantive norms or establishing such norms,
- GATT provisions should be clarified so that measures and procedures to enforce IPRs do not become barriers to legitimate trade, and
- A multilateral framework to deal with trade in counterfeit goods should be concluded expeditiously.

The US has called for negotiations to complete an agreement providing for adequate substantive norms and standards, drawing such standards from international conventions 'where adequate' and from national laws where international conventions are inadequate, and with provisions for 'national treatment' and 'transparency' drawn from GATT principles. It has also called for provisions for border and internal enforcement measures, a dispute settlement mechanism taking account of existing GATT procedures and adapting them. One of the US proposals would prohibit compulsory licensing or any State intervention to fix royalty and licence fees.

Two other proposals on the table, one from the Chairman of the Negotiating Group and the other from Switzerland are less forthright than the US but seek to achieve the same purpose. The Chairman's text calls for work in the negotiating-group on commitments to provide effective and appropriate enforcement of IPRs and specification of 'reference points' on availability, scope and use of IPRs. The Swiss call for elaboration within GATT of norms and standards for IPRs, and multilateral procedures for settlement of disputes. Both papers also call for dispute settlement procedures in GATT [31].

In the various proposals and concepts advanced by the ICs, rights are being claimed abroad that are not even available in the countries themselves. Intellectual property protection laws have always to be assessed along with the competition laws that also apply to these areas.

In the UK, for example, "the law confers monopoly rights on proprietors of the property but there is no uniform treatment, and the nature and extent of monopoly vary between the different types of rights, as do measures taken to regulate their exercise... First, each statute creating an intellectual property right imposes its own internal form of regulation, ranging from compulsory licensing in the patent system as a defence against underproduction, to compulsory arbitration over the terms of certain copyright licences. Secondly, the ordinary competition laws... remain applicable... The definition of 'anti-competitive practice' in the Competition Act is wide enough to allow any practice related to intellectual property to be investigated.." [32]

While the Rome treaty creating the European Community guaranteed the continued existence of national systems of intellectual property protection, the European Court of Justice has interpreted the applicability of EC's anti-competition laws and jurisdiction in such a way as to distinguish between existence of national intellectual property protection laws and the exercise of those rights which fall under community jurisdiction. This differentiation between 'rights' and their 'exercise' has been used to attack practices of firms having parallel rights in a number of EC states and using them to operate a discriminatory price policy along national boundaries [33]. As a result of some of these decisions, compulsory licences may be available in the UK simply by infringement and payment of a royalty [34].

Under UK law itself licensing provisions by a patentee could be modified on a finding by the Monopoly Commission, after an anti-competitive policy investigation. These modifications could relate to any conditions in a licence relating to the licensor's use of the invention, a licence condition limiting the patentee's right to grant further licences, and any refusal by the patentee to grant licences on reasonable terms [35]. Once three years have elapsed after grant of patent, compulsory licences can be obtained on five grounds:

- The patented invention is capable of being worked in the UK, but is not being worked or worked fully,
- The demand for a patented product is not being met on reasonable terms, or is being met to a substantial extent by importation,
- The patented invention is prevented or hindered from being commercially worked in the UK by importation,
- Where by a patentee's refusal to grant one or more licences on reasonable terms (a) an export market is not being supplied, (b) the working of any other invention patented in the UK is prevented or hindered, or (c) commercial activity in the UK is unfairly prejudiced,
- Where use of non-patented material is unfairly prejudiced by reasons of conditions imposed by the patentee on the grant of licences or subsqent use of goods manufactured under the patented process [36].

Notes on Chapter 6:

1. Developments in the negotiating process set out in this chapter have to be read with the relevant portions in Chapter 12 on the mid-term review accord reached in April '89.

2. See Barbara Tuchman, 'The British Lose America' in *'The March of Folly'* (1984) Chapter 4.

3. Tuchman pp 159-160.

4. Surendra J.Patel, 'Indian Patents Act: Implications of Controversy', *Mainstream*, New Delhi (India), 18-2-1989, p 17.

5. 'The Laws of Life', *Development Dialogue*, 1988: 1-2, Uppsala (Sweden), p 251.

6. *Development Dialogue*, p 251.

7. UN publication, sales no 65.II.B.1.

8. UN publication sales no E.75.II.D.6 para 6.

9. Pat Roy Mooney, 'Biotechnology and the North-South Conflict' in *Biotechnology Revolution and the Third World (1988)*, RIS, India. Also, see preface to *'Working Paper on Patent Law Review'*, 1976, prepared for the Department of Consumer and Corporate Affairs, Canada, p 5, cited by Pat Mooney.

10. Taylor and Silbertson, *The Economic Impact of Patents* (1973).

11. That patents are not essential to innovation (in the area of bio-technology) is brought out in 'From Cabbages to Kings', *Development Dialogue*, 1988:1-2, pp 246-247.

12. Robert Merkin and Karen Williams, *Competition Law: Antitrust policy in the United Kingdom and the EEC* (1984), Sweet and Maxwell, London, p 317.

13. 'Drugs need new boffins', *Economist*, London, July 16.

14. Dr. Alberto Bercovtitz, *'Historical Trends in Protection of Tech-*

nology in Developed Countries and Their Relationship to Protection in Developing Countries', a forthcoming UNCTAD study, UNCTAD/TT/Misc.75.

15. *Ibid.*

16. *SUNS* 1677 p4.

17. For various proposals and discussions and comments on them see *SUNS* 1683, 1732, 1812, 1900, 1944, 1979, 1988, 2007, 2032.

18. Surendra Patel, op.cit, p 11; also *'Technology-related policies and Legislation in a changing Economic and Technological Environment'*, UNCTAD TD/B/C.6/146, p 28 fn 27.

19. Pat Mooney *op.cit.* p 264.

20. *Ibid* p 268.

21. Surendra J Patel, *op.cit.* p 13. for details of the case see Hoffman-la Roche v Secretary of State for Trade and Industry (1974), cited by Merkin and Williams.

22. GATT document of the Preparatory Committee, PREP.COM(86)W/41/Rev.1, cited as W/41.

23 PREP.COM(86)/W/47/Rev.2, cited as W/47.

24. The US and EEC had sought to introduce in the Tokyo Round agreements, at the final stages, a code on 'trade in counterfeit goods', and gave their draft to then GATT Director-General, Olivier Long, asking him to hold consultations and table it. According to those in the secretariat and some of the participants in that round, Long ruled it 'out of court'.

25 G.H.P.Bodenhausen, *'Guide to the Application of the Paris Convention for the protection of Industrial Property'*, pp 15-16, cited by S.J.Patel.

26. *'The Role of Patents in the Transfer of Technology to Developing Countries'*, UN publication, sales no 65.II.B.1.

27. UN publication sales no E.75.II.D.6

28. 'GATT vs WIPO', *SUNS* 1657.

29. Note prepared by the International Bureau of WIPO for the Negotiating Group on TRIPS, MTN.GNG/NG11/W/24/Rev1, p 12.

30. United States - Section 337 of the Tariff Act of 1988, Report of the Panel, *GATT Document,* L/6439, p 58.

31. As pointed out in chapter 12 infra, the opposition of the Third World countries collapsed at the April TNC, and they have agreed to encompass the substantive issues in the negotiations, though there still seems to be some doubts as to what is the substance they have agreed to. The collapse is attributable to the US pressures, under threat of initiating S 301 actions against them. In the event, they did not escape these actions either. On May 25, the US did initiate actions against Brazil and India under 'Super 301', and against 25 countries under 'Special 301'.

32. Merkin and Williams, *op.cit.* p 295.

33. *Ibid* p 298.

34. *Ibid* p 320.

35. *Ibid* p 320.

36. *Ibid* pp 322-324.

Chapter 7

INVESTMENTS: TRIMMING THE NATION-STATE

In its mandate on investment questions [1] under the title *Trade-related* investment measures' (emphasis added), the Punta del Este Declaration provides that:

> "Following an examination of the operation of GATT Articles related to the trade restrictive and distorting effects of investment measures, negotiations should elaborate, as appropriate, further provisions that may be necessary to avoid such adverse effects on trade".

Any investment resulting in production is bound to have an effect on trade and is thus 'trade-related'. But it is clear from the actual wording of the mandate (rather than its title) that not every investment measure which is trade-related can be considered in the Uruguay Round but only those having a 'restrictive' or 'distorting' effect on trade. The language used was the result of some last minute negotiations, involving particularly the US and some of the Latin American Nations with several of the latter, after the adoption of part I of the Declaration by the Contracting Parties, making their own interpretatory statements that general 'investment' issues were beyond the scope of the negotiations.

The US objectives and efforts in the negotiations have to be seen against the background of the evolution of the international regime on property rights of foreigners in the 18th

and 19th centuries and the erosion of these rights in this
century - in the inter-war periods and in the post-war era in
the aftermath of decolonization which began with the Indian
independence in 1947 and swept through much of Asia and
most of Africa in the 1960s.

The standards for treatment of foreigners and their
property evolved in Europe in the 17th and 18th centuries
(treaties of Westphalia 1648 and Paris 1745). Arising out of
their extensive and ongoing economic ties with each other,
all the European powers had reciprocal interests in protecting the trade and property interests of their nationals in other
countries. These norms included the concept that the property of foreigners cannot be expropriated except for recognised public purpose and on payment of compensation according to international standards and subject to international
arbitration. After its own independence, the US accepted these
norms, and from the early part of this century tried to enforce
them on the Caribbean and Central American States.

Until World War I these norms were largely unchal-
lenged. At the 1909 The Hague Peace Conference, the Latin
American States challenged only the right of unilateral enforcement. But the situation changed after World War I. At
the series of economic conferences convened by the League
of Nations, these norms about property and other rights of
foreigners came under increasing challenge, and failed to be
incorporated into the new international treaties.

After the second world war, when it took the lead in
fashioning a new post-war system of political and economic
relationships and institutions governing Trade, Money and
Finance (Havana Charter and the Bretton Woods agreements)
the US revived the efforts to incorporate into them international norms and standards relating to the property rights of
foreigners. But the US did not succeed [2].

The US, like the Europeans, through the interwar period
had continued to assert the validity of the 19th century inter-

national standards, and tried to do so forcefully, for example against Mexico after its revolution in the 1930s. Even earlier, the interventions in the Dominican Republic (under Theodore Roosevelt) and the so-called Roosevelt Corollary to the Monroe doctrine, sought to establish the European-US 'international property norms' and enforce their observance by the Latin American Nations. When codifying its foreign relations law in 1965, the official comment said: "Some states maintain that an alien is not entitled to a higher standard of justice than a national... This Section (of the Law) follows the prevailing rule that such national treatment is not always sufficient, and that there is an international standard of justice that a state must observe... even if the standard is inconsistent with its own law" [3]. But this was only an US assertion, like those of colonial powers in the 19th century, and cannot be reconciled with the history of failure to secure legitimacy for these views since the end of the First World War at the various League of Nations conferences.

Despite the absence of accepted international norms, the US sought to get them accepted through bilateral commerce and friendship treaties (with the effort failing in the case of countries like India precisely over these supranational norms and the demand for international arbitration, and for placing rights of foreigners on a superior level to that of nationals).

The US also sought to use bilateral aid (and its control of multilateral aid through the World Bank and other international and regional financial institutions) to get Third World countries to accept these norms. But by and large these proved counter-productive and whatever their temporary success they did not have any long-term effects. Irrespective of their ideologies, Third World countries have developed a strongly nationalist attitude to foreign capital, to some extent due to their realization that the State has to play an important role in the economic transformation of their countries and also as a reaction to deep-seated historical memories of the way foreign capital came and established itself in their countries.

Foreigners, received with hospitality, invariably abused the privilege to acquire political control and enforce colonialism [4].

Reactions in most of the countries of Asia (with the exception of Japan) - irrespective of their political and economic ideologies - against the US efforts and the attempts of TNCs can be easily understood when seen against the background of their colonial past and memories. Even the reactions to Japan have to be seen in this context. Unlike the reaction of the rest of Asia to European powers and their forcible efforts to open up these economies for trade, Japan's reactions had been different, particularly after the Meiji restoration of 1868. Its attempt, through acquisition of scientific knowledge from Europe and America, was to convince the Great Powers of that time that "Japan was approaching their standards... and that in all except colour, Japanese were Europeans" [5]. In the 20th century, and after the First World War, Japan joined the Europeans in claiming extra-territorial rights in China and carving up that country into zones of influence, and occupying Manchuria and vast portions of China just before and during World War II [6].

In the post-war period, and in its role as the capitalist centre-country, the US could not enforce property rights of its nationals through open use of force and gunboat diplomacy (as the British did in the 19th century in Asia and Latin America and the US in the Caribbean and Central America). But the US sought to achieve the same purpose through covert actions - in Iran where the combined US CIA and British actions overthrew the Mossadegh government to restore the Shah; in Guatemala and Honduras in the 1950s when the military (under CIA instigation) intervened to overthrow democratic governments that were interfering with the interests of US TNCs with extensive banana and plantation holdings; and Chile in 1973 where Allende was overthrown in the CIA engineered military coup.

The idea of an investment regime in GATT had been advocated in the US in the 1970s. The proposal was made by Paul M Goldberg and Charles Kindleberger in "Towards a GATT for Investment: A Proposal for Supervision of the International Corporation" [7].

The US multilateral efforts on TRIMs in GATT have been preceded, in the 1980s, by bilateral efforts, particularly in the Third World, to reach bilateral Investment Treaties. The countries with which such accords have been sought or concluded include Argentina, Colombia, Costa Rica, Jamaica, Egypt, Morocco, Zaire, the People's Republic of China, Malaysia and the Philippines.

However, these treaties involve changes in policies of these countries towards inward foreign direct investment, and are seen in these countries as being made at the instance of the US, and have aroused anti-US backlashes in some of these countries. This explains the US constant threat to follow the 'bilateral approach' if it is unable to get a multilateral regime, and pushing at the same time for a multilateral regime since such a regime will reduce political opposition developing and centered against the US.

The 1984 Trade act had already empowered the Administration to deny benefits under its Generalised System of Preference scheme to Third World countries not providing investment rights and opportunities for US, or denying IPR protection. The 'super 301', and other provisions in the 1988 law carry things much further.

Before the US brought the issue before the 1982 GATT Ministerial, it had brought a complaint against Canada over the latter's Foreign Investment Review Act (FIRA), and the undertakings obtained by Canada from the US enterprises (before allowing them to establish and operate in Canada) about local content and export performance in the production facilities to be set up.

The GATT panel, whose report was adopted by the GATT

Council in February 1984, had ruled that GATT rules did not prevent countries from regulating foreign investments, in exercise of their sovereignty, but that Canada's domestic purchase requirements violated GATT obligations like national treatment as between domestic and imported equivalent products [8]. The panel however held that export performance requirements on foreign investment did not violate the GATT rules. A number of Third World countries had intervened before the panel as 'interested parties', and the panel had said that the GATT rules applicable to Third World countries, in respect of restrictions imposed by them for balance-of-payments and other reasons, were different and that its ruling on domestic purchase requirement should not be held as applicable to these cases also.

Third World's Measures to Regulate Investments

The moves on TRIMs by the US and other capital exporting ICs which are the home countries of the TNCs have to be seen against the background of the various measures that Third World countries have put in place in this area [9], and the reasoning and motivations behind them.

The Third World countries, whatever their ideologies and the mix in their economies, over the last two or three decades have brought to bear to their development an element of planning, and through incentives and regulations have sought to direct investments and projects in line with these overall objectives.

Generally they have two sets of 'investment measures' - those providing incentives to investors and those laying down conditions for investment. Since these countries need foreign investment, they feel impelled to provide incentives to attract the investor, particularly at a time of scarce capital in the world. But even while doing so, many countries also stipulate conditions for a number of reasons. The chief among these relate to their need and desire to ensure:

● That the investments are in accordance with their development needs and priorities,
● That the net outflows (on their current or capital accounts) whether by way of profit remittances or payments for goods and services etc do not cause strains on their balance of payments, that the restrictive business practices of the TNCs are kept under control and their adverse effects on their economies reduced, if not eliminated.

Table 1 lists some of the TNC practices, particularly restrictive business practices (RBP) and their effects, and the investment measures put in place by countries to deal with them.

The following is a brief explanation of some investment measures taken by Third World countries to regulate the behaviour of TNCs in their countries.

Export requirements: These oblige an investor to export a fixed percentage of production (in terms of minimum quantity or value or variations relating to the import balance of the investment or its servicing). Through this, countries try to stem the net outflow of foreign exchange. It also counters the common RBP of TNCs and international cartels that distort trade through allocation of global markets and by restraining or blocking exports from a given country. It also counters TNC efforts to allocate global markets within its subsidiaries, and trying to use the subsidiary's output to gain access to the domestic market of the subsidiary's host country.

Local content requirement: This obliges an investor to produce or purchase from local sources a percentage or value of the investor's production. Often these are used again to stem outflow of foreign exchange. TNCs, with their eye on maximisation of their global profits, often require the subsidiary to purchase inputs from the TNC or its subsidiary else-

Table 1
Restrictive business practices by TNCs in developing countries, their possible outcome and TRIMs designed to deal with them.

RBPs	Possible outcome	Associated TRIMs
A. Horizontal RBPs		
Market allocation	Export prohibitions; specific market allocation	Trade-balancing requirements; export requirement
Refusal to deal (boycott)	Refusal to supply	Manufacturing requirement
Price fixing	Excessive pricing for imports; low pricing for exports	Local content requirements; local equity requirement; joint venture with government participation
Collusive tendering	Excessive pricing for imports	Local content requirement; domestic sales requirement
B. Vertical RBPs		
Refusal to deal	Import refusal or prohibition	Local content requirement
Exclusive dealing	Export prohibition	Export requirement
Differential pricing	Excessive pricing for imports	Local content requirement; domestic sales requirement
Resale price maintenance	Excessive pricing for exports and imports	Export requirement; local equity requirement
Tied selling	Excessive conditions for imports	Domestic sales requirement; licensing and technology transfer requirement
Predatory pricing	Predatory pricing for imports	Manufacturing requirement
Transfer pricing	Predatory pricing for imports or excessive pricing which results in remittance evasion	Remittance and exchange restrictions; manufacturing requirement; domestic sales requirement

Source: UNCTAD, "Uruguay Round" (1989), p219

where. This can happen even if the inputs are locally available and without this external RBP, the free play of market
forces would have warranted purchase of the inputs locally. The local content requirement thus reduces the scope
for transfer pricing, and provides some countervailing force
on behalf of large numbers of domestic producers of the
inputs where the foreign investor and its subsidary enjoy
some monopsonic power or could resort to predatory
pricing to eliminate competitors.

Technology transfer or licensing requirements:
These typically strengthen the hands of domestic enterprises
in international contract negotiations with TNCs who have
monopoly power in the area of technology. Requiring a TNC
wishing to invest in a country to transfer and/or license
technology on reasonable terms in an area unrelated to the
TNC production in the country (but of value elsewhere in the
economy) is one way of providing domestic producers some
countervailing power in technology negotiations.

Domestic sale requirements: These are used to impose
an obligation on the investor to sell on the domestic markets
to ensure that products are available in sufficient quantity
and appropriate price for local industry. This is particularly
important where a TNC is producing an intermediate input
for a final product that competes on the global market with
that of the local producers, and through pricing policy or
denial of intermediate inputs the TNC could thwart competi-
titon on global markets from indigenous industry of the host
country.

Investment incentives: These are used to attract foreign investments in areas in accord with national development priorities. These are used not only by Third World
countries but a large number of ICs too, for attracting investment or persuading investors to open production in backward areas.

Limitations on remittances are used to reduce pressure

on balance of payments.

Manufacturing requirements: They are used to reserve certain markets to local firms and provide domestic firms with some countervailing power. They are used to counter international market allocations and predatory pricing policies and practices of TNCs to eliminate competition.

Product mandating: This requires an investor to export a specific product, and is a government imposed obligation to counter market allocations and other RBPs.

Local equity requirements: These specify the extent of equity in an enterprise created by foreign investors to be held by local capital and is intended to provide for a degree of local management and control over the subsidiary.

The Punta del Este mandate in TRIMs, and the proposals and stands of protagonists have to be seen in this light [10]. The Third World countries have taken a strict view of the mandate, while the US and Japan have sought an open-ended approach, namely, that any government actions on investment have effects on trade and should be dealt with under TRIMs.

In May 1987, the GATT Secretariat outlined the issues under the mandate thus: "The language of the Punta del Este Declaration on Trade-related Investment Measures would appear to represent a decision to focus on the direct trade effects of investment measures and the extent to which they are addressed by the GATT articles rather than on the broad relationship between investment, production and trade" [11].

Some 17 Articles of the General Agreement have been cited by the US, Japan and a few others as having a bearing on the mandate of the group, and needing examination with a view to changes or additions to the Articles or providing for new rules relating to the subject. But Third World countries have not agreed to these and, after two years of work, the negotiating group has still been unable to reach a common view either on the terms of the mandate or the GATT articles to be taken up for examination and review.

US, Japan & Europe Push For TRIMs

In tabling its proposals, the US has tried to relate them to individual GATT articles and provisions in an effort to relate them to the mandate.

Under local content requirements, it has tried to attack several production and sales arrangements, trade-balancing, equity shares, technology commercialisation practices, various licensing arrangements, incentive policies, balance of payments issues, remittance restrictions etc. The argument for all these has been that such requirements, directly or indirectly, or even potentially, can limit imported products being sold or used in a country and hence it is trade-restrictive and distortive.

The US has also sought to attack production and sales requirements which restrict ability of other countries to export to a host country of specific foreign investment and/ or technology undertakings. Requirements relating to trade, technology and licensing, various production, equity and remittance, as well as incentive policies of various countries on exports have also been sought to be attacked on the ground that they 'force' exports and distort trade.

While some of the US demands could be claimed to relate to existing GATT articles, others (such as those relating to equity holdings, remittance practices or licensing provisions) are very difficult to relate to the GATT provisions or said to be directly trade-related, except on the thesis that anything that results in production or investment has trade effects, and thus is 'trade-related'. While the US effort to relate its proposals to the existing GATT provisions gives every appearance of some convoluted logic, it is very logical in

terms of the attempt to set up an international investment
and foreign property protection regime.

While the US is pushing the interests of its TNCs in
outward investment, and in reducing the power of the
host states to bargain, there is also the growing concern
within the US about the takeover of industrial and other
sectors by foreign investors. Much of the debates and
media attention has been on Japanese investments. But in
actual fact European investments, and particularly British
and Dutch, are far ahead of Japanese investments in US. At
end of 1987, European investment in the US amounted to
$785 billion while that of Japan was only $194 billion
[12]. The administration has already powers to block any
particular takeover on grounds of 'national security'.

The Japanese proposals make clear that the intention is to create a new international investment regime centered in GATT. The proposals, under five categories - local
content, export performance, trade balancing, domestic
sales and technology transfer - are structured close to those
of the US. In its paper of June 12, 1987 [13], noting that
direct investments are increasing (both in volume and
number), while government measures on these investments,
with effects on trade, are 'multiplying', Japan says: "... It is
important to establish within the GATT a new system to
regulate these measures... to assure free flow of trade...
The Government of Japan thinks it necessary to prohibit
or limit these measures in principle and if necessary establish new international rules." Among the wide range of
measures it has sought are "assurances on transparency",
and on procedures and organs for consultations and dispute settlement.

As their statements and papers to the negotiating
group show, the US and Japan want to use the multilateral
negotiations as a starting point for putting into place an
international investment regime with rules and principles
that will restrict and limit host country policies and laws

and administrative measures in relations with foreign investors and technology suppliers. A broad range of issues are involved - social and development policy, financing, employment and industrial relations, regional development, fiscal policy, international capital flows, competition policy, control of Restrictive Business Practices, transfer of technology, regulation of conduct of TNCs etc. The intent clearly is to create rights for TNCs and make illegal restrictions or obligations imposed on them by host countries.

The issue of a code of conduct for TNCs, relating to their own conduct as well as that of host governments, has been sought to be dealt with at the UN Centre for Transnational Corporations (UNCTC) for more than a decade, and through multilateral negotiations under its auspices. They have been virtually blocked there by the US and other major home-countries of the TNCs. An international code for control of RBPs has been negotiated under UNCTAD auspices and adopted by the UN General Assembly, a voluntary code so far. But here again the home countries of the TNCs have resisted all efforts to make this a binding international instrument, with home countries assuming some obligations to enforce observance of the code by their TNCs.

As already noted, while the principal thrust on this issue at the GATT had come from the US, Japan had soon joined as an enthusiastic advocate. The attitude and stand of the European Communities appears to be conditioned by its considerable outward investments as well as its community-wide integration (with liberalisation of rules for all TNCs established already in the Community) to be achieved by 1992. It is thus interested in assuring its investors similar rights in other countries, including US and Japan.

At the same time, the EEC has also an interest, through outward investment, in Japan to gain access to that market and in US to obtain access to high technology. Foreign investors, EEC and Japanese, are attempting in the US to take over existing enterprises in high technology areas and thus gain access to the technology. The EEC members have also considerable overseas investment in extractive and manufacturing sectors in the Third World, and are interested in expanding them. In regard to inward foreign direct investment, and the Japanese efforts in this direction, the EEC and its states are trying to use their regulatory powers to ensure access to, and genuine transfers of, new technologies (as different from what are being called 'screw driver assembly plants') that would enable them to leapfrog and catch up with the US and Japan. These regulatory powers, which the EEC is trying to use, are no different in objective and purpose from those of Third World countries providing for local content and export performance requirements, as well as technology transfer conditions.

The EEC and Japan are trying to draw within the net of the TRIMs, not only measures at the level of national governments, but those of local governments and authorities. This is clearly aimed at the US and Canada, where restrictive policies are often at the state level. Japan does not refer to equity requirements - clearly related to its own policy of resisting foreign entry through wholly owned subsidiaries in core technological or financial business activities. The EEC has also steered clear so far of dealing with the globalisation of investment, raised by US and Japanese proposals. But the EEC references to foreign exchange restrictions is wide enough to cover invisibles and capital movements. It wants also to deal with TRIMs issues in terms of compatibility with existing or revised GATT disciplines, and then deal with any issues of 'exceptions', presumably development matters and perhaps its own internal market integration.

While there are these mutual conflicting interests, all ICs have also a common interest vis-a-vis the Third World. The positions and proposals of the US, Japan and the EEC have thus both North-North and North-South dimensions.

Third World Wants to Curb TNCs' Restrictive Practices

The proposals and ideas of all ICs seek to deal with trade-restrictive or distortive effects arising out of governmental actions and measures in the area of investments. But there are no references to any actions or policies of TNCs that have an effect on trade or business. In the discussions, Third world countries have raised this issue, but have elicited no real response. The Third World view has only been sought to be countered with the argument that the issue of RBPs had been raised at Punta del Este but there was no agreement to include it on the agenda, and hence the intention is not to tackle them, and that GATT is only intended to deal with government measures and bringing in the measures of private parties would alter the nature of GATT.

Thus while all governmental measures are sought to be curbed under the proposals of the ICs, TNCs will be left free to carry on with their own central planning and management decisions over the practices and affairs of various affiliates operating in multiple national spaces, and concentrate their corporate strategic activities - in terms of top management, technology development, control and monitoring of their worldwide affiliates etc - in the home country. Decisions on key trade, investment and production measures are to be internalized within the boundaries of the TNC in the home country - without any public accountability in any of the host countries. Also, while 'market' signals will operate in relations with the outside, within the TNC all issues (investment, performance, purchases and sales of inputs and outputs) will involve no obligations for arms length or competitive market decisions, but rather would be guided by centrally planned corporate decisions to maximise profits and global capital accumulation in the interests of the home countries of the TNCs.

It is difficult to envisage a more brazen effort to enrich the TNCs and their home countries, at the expense of the public abroad, particularly in the Third World.

As the South Commission has put it:

"A multilateral investment regime designed to promote
the interest of capital exporters in general and the TNCs
in particular would clearly have serious adverse effects
on development prospects of host countries.... In a situation characterised by vast imperfections in product
and factor markets, as is the case in most developing
countries, the volume and pattern of foreign investment
flows determined solely by corporate interests of foreign investors would not represent an efficient or opti-
mum outcome from the standpoint of capital-importing
countries... In their dealings with TNCs developing countries have to contend with market structures characterised by significant elements of market power and monopoly and a complete lack of transparency in the
behaviour of transnational actors. In such a setting, it is
a travesty of the facts to describe as trade distortions
measures adopted by the host countries to minimise the
harmful and maximise the favourable impact of foreign
investments on the national economy. In a world of monopolies, transfer pricing and internationalisation of economic processes represented by the TNCs, investment
regulatory measures are not trade distorting. Clearly all
countries need screening procedures to block un-
acceptable and counter-productive activities or projects
or to modify the terms of their operations to make them
consistent with their development objectives... If proper
balance is to be observed, preserving the integrity of the
development objective must also be given prime
consideration.... Equal attention must be paid to those
aspects of the behaviour of TNCs - restrictive business
practices, restrictions on freer flow of technology, market-sharing arrangements etc.... Any equitable multilateral arrangements must then also include acceptance
by TNCs and the governments of developed countries
of their own responsibilities to curb restrictive practices of TNCs and to facilitate the freer transfer of technology to the Third World" [14].

In their interventions and comments on the various proposals [15], Third World countries have said that not merely governmental investment measures, but non-governmental ones, including policies of TNCs, should be discussed. They have argued that without operationally effective rules to control TNCs and their conduct, they cannot dispense with their rights to impose restrictions on foreign investors. Some have attempted to approach the issue in terms of exceptions and special treatment for the Third World. In a statement in June 1988, Malaysia sought to counter the views and proposals of the ICs, and justify TRIMs of Third World countries in terms of the GATT provisions on BOP restrictions by the Third World countries and Part IV of the General Agreement. But over-reliance on these provisions could be counter-productive. A more worthwhile strategy and tactic could be to counter-attack and focus discussions on TRIMs of private parties and press for negotiations to deal with such matters as inter-corporate transactions, transfer pricing etc. Another aspect could be a demand to look at obligations of the foreign investors as well as of the home governments of these investors in policing the TNCs in their base countries. The development dimension, expressly mandated in the services negotiations should also be made a specific requirement in this area [16].

Notes on Chapter 7:

1. Developments in the negotiating process set out in this chapter have to be read along with the relevant portions in chapter 11 on the mid-term review accords in this area.

2. Charles Lipson, *op. cit*

3. American Law Institute, Restatement of the Law, Second: Foreign Relations Law of the United States, cited by Lipson *op.cit*. p 8.

4. K.M.Panikkar *op.cit.*

5. Panikkar *op.cit* pp 208-209.

6. *Ibid.* pp 276-277.

7. Cited by Lipson, *op.cit,* fn 27 to chapter 5, at page 298.

8. BISD/30S/140 and *GATT document* L/5504.

9. For a fuller understanding see Hardeep Puri and Philippe Brusick, 'Trade Related Investment Measures', *Uruguay Round,* pp 203-217.

10. For proposals and comments see *SUNS* 1689, 1734, 1797, 1816, 1884, 1966 and 2022.

11. *SUNS* 1797.

12. US Commerce Department data cited in *International Herald Tribune,* Paris of 28-29 Jan 1989, p 11.

13. For proposals of US, EEC and Japan, and reactions of Third World countries, including a Malaysian proposal, see *SUNS* Nos. 1816, 1884, 1966,and 2022.

14. *Statement on Uruguay Round,* Mexico 5-8 August, 1988, paras 62-68.

15. *SUNS* 1884 and 2022.

16. In March 1990, 14 Third World countries (Argentina, Bangladesh, Brazil, Cameroon, China, Colombia, Cuba, Egypt, India, Nigeria, Sri Lanka, Tanzania, Yugoslavia and Zimbabwe) tabled a paper (MTN. GNG/NG12/W/25) rejecting any moves to discipline 'Investment Measures', but deal only with 'direct and significant' adverse trade effects of investment measures, whether by governments or by corporations.

Chapter 8

AGRICULTURE

Bringing Agriculture into GATT

While successive GATT Rounds brought about substantial reductions of tariffs on manufactured goods and disciplined use of non-tariff barriers, Agriculture by and large escaped this process [1]. The General Agreement itself deals differently with Agriculture and Industry. Some of the Articles of GATT (about quantitative restrictions, subsidies for exports etc) have been so formulated that they do not apply to agricultural products, or only apply loosely to it.

But the US found even these provisions irksome and, in 1955, obtained a permanent waiver from GATT obligations in respect of the US Agricultural Adjustment Act. Japan and Switzerland got waivers for their agricultural policies as part of their protocols of accession to GATT. When the Rome Treaty was signed, bringing into being the European Community, a fundamental basis was the Common Agricultural Policy (CAP) and its variable levies. While the Rome Treaty was submitted to GATT and considered, it was never approved. But the EEC has functioned on the basis that it has not been disapproved either, and hence legal in GATT.

The net result has been that international trade in agriculture is virtually outside the jurisdiction of GATT. Domestic policy objectives and priorities have been asserted to enable agriculture being treated as an exception and left out of the application of any GATT disciplines. Though it figured on the Kennedy and Tokyo rounds, Agricultural trade was dealt with differently, and on the understanding that GATT disciplines could not be applied.

Very recently, the mounting budgetary costs [2] of the domestic agricultural support policies (mounting surpluses, storage costs, and subsidisation to dispose them in international markets) have induced governments to attempt to bring agricultural trade under greater GATT discipline. The ever increasing surplus stocks in the highly protected industrial countries are present alongside growing malnutrition and hunger in the Third World (due to under-production and lack of foreign exchange to import). Under the 1982 GATT Ministerial Work Programme, a Committee on Trade in Agriculture (CTA) was set up to tackle these issues. The CTA did a great deal of work to identify issues and begin a process of dialogue, but it could not move further. The Uruguay Round is the first time that a serious effort is being made to tackle issues in this area and bring this trade under GATT purview.

The Punta del Este declaration sets the mandate in this area in the following terms:

> Contracting Parties agree that there is an urgent need to bring more discipline and predictability to world agricultural trade by correcting and preventing restrictions and distortions including those related to structural surpluses so as to reduce the uncertainty, imbalances and instability in world agricultural markcts.

> Negotiations shall aim to achieve greater liberalisation of trade in agriculture and bring all measures affecting import access and export competition under strengthened and more operationally effective GATT rules and disciplines, taking into account the general principles governing the negotiations, by:

> (i)   improving market access through, *inter alia*, the

reduction of import barriers;
(ii) improving the competitive environment by increasing disciplines on the use of all direct and indirect subsidies and other measures affecting directly or indirectly agricultural trade, including the phased reduction of their negative effects and dealing with their causes;
(iii) minimising the adverse effects that sanitary and phytosanitary regulations and barriers can have on trade in agriculture, taking into account the relevant international agreements.

In order to achieve the above objectives, the negotiating group having primary responsibility for all aspects of agriculture will use the Recommendations adopted by the Contracting Parties at their Fortieth Session, which were developed in accordance with the GATT 1982 Ministerial Programme and take account of the approaches suggested in the work of the Committee on Trade in Agriculture without prejudice to other alternatives that might achieve the objectives of the Negotiations.

Though the term 'agriculture' has been used without any qualification, the products covered in the negotiations in this group are those not expressly dealt with elsewhere i.e. in the negotiations on Tropical Products and the negotiations on Natural Resource-based Products. However, any general principles and rules formulated for incorporation into GATT would perhaps have wider applicability. The major products falling under the purview of the agriculture negotiations are cereals, meat, dairy products, (non-tropical) oilseeds, vegetable oils, and sugar. In value terms, they account for the bulk of world trade in agricultural products.

The Third World Role in Agricultural Trade

Third World countries are highly dependent on production and export of agricultural products. In 1986, agriculture accounted for only three percent of the GDP of the OECD countries and seven percent of the labour force. But in the Third World it accounted for 19 percent of GDP and 60 percent of the labour force [3]. For the majority of the Third World countries agricultural products account for 50-100 percent of their total merchandise exports.

However, barring sugar, the ICs are the major exporters of food products - the major foci of negotiations in this group. Very few Third World countries are overall net exporters of food products. The vast majority are net importers and account for 40 percent of the world imports.

In wheat [4], the major exporters (the US, Canada, EEC/France, Australia, and Argentina) together account for 80 percent of world exports. Imports are spread around a large number of countries, though the Soviet Union is the predominant buyer. In coarse grains, the exporters are US, Argentina, EEC, China, Canada and Australia. The top importers are Japan, the USSR, Saudi Arabia, Taiwan and South Korea. In rice, the major long-term exporters are China and Thailand, and the US and Italy. Current major importers are Brazil, Iran, Iraq and Saudi Arabia.

The major oilseeds are palm, groundnut, soyabeans, rapeseed, sunflower and cottonseed. Export trade in oilseeds is dominated by US, Argentina, Canada, China, Brazil and recently France, while the major importers are EEC, Japan, USSR, Taiwan, Mexico, and South Korea. The EEC is the major importer of oilmeal (protein food for livestock), with East Europe as the other major importer. Exports of these are by Brazil, US, Argentina, the EEC, China, Chile and India. In vegetable oils, the EEC and India are the largest importers, with US, Pakistan, and Singapore closely behind them. Malaysia dominates the exports (with palm oil), with EEC, Argentina, Philippines, and US as significant exporters.

In dairy products (where trade is mainly in butter, cheese and non-fat dry milk, since milk cannot be stored),

Table 2
Net food imports of developing regions and selected countries [a] thereof, 1983-1985
(Annual average, in millions of dollars)

Region/country	Sugar	Live animals and meat	Cereals	Dairy products	Animal & veg.oils	Total Incl. sugar	Total Excl. sugar
AFRICA [b]	827.3	1484.2	5498.3	1440.3	1280.4	10530.5	9703.2
Algeria	150.1	96.6	786.2	429.4	218.7	1681.0	1530.9
Angola	16.8	55.0	75.4	42.4	24.9	214.5	197.7
Cameroon	-0.1	10.7	50.3	10.0	5.1	76.0	76.1
Cote d'Ivoire	-9.2	89.5	116.2	48.3	-57.8	187.0	196.2
Egypt	162.8	481.2	1607.4	260.8	410.1	2923.3	2760.5
Ethiopia	-3.4	-11.2	112.3	17.6	23.9	139.2	142.6
Ghana	6.9	8.7	52.0	6.1	10.6	84.3	77.4
Kenya	0.1	-14.8	57.1	5.9	56.5	104.8	104.7
Libyan Arab Jam.	41.1	286.3	244.4	128.2	77.2	777.2	736.1
Mali	13.7	-106.9	65.7	4.2	0.0	-23.3	-47.0
Mauritania	11.5	-33.7	54.5	25.1	5.2	62.2	51.1
Morocco	48.2	13.1	345.1	36.4	123.4	566.2	518.0
Mozambique	10.9	4.7	68.9	12.2	17.4	114.1	103.2
Nigeria	180.4	160.8	616.7	128.5	114.1	1200.5	1020.1
Senegal	4.8	21.1	105.2	21.1	-33.7	118.5	113.7
Somalia	11.2	-59.0	74.5	8.2	16.5	51.4	40.2
Sudan	17.0	-66.3	108.2	26.5	21.9	107.3	90.3
United Rep. of Tanzania	0.7	0.6	68.3	10.7	13.3	92.2	91.5

(continued)

Table 2 *(continued)*

Net food imports of developing regions and selected countries [a] thereof, 1983-1985

(Annual average, in millions of dollars)

Region/country	Sugar	Live animals and meat	Cereals	Dairy products	Animal & veg.oils	Total Incl. sugar	Total Excl. sugar
Tunisia	34.5	42.9	155.5	37.1	12.5	282.5	248.0
Zaire	4.8	50.8	76.0	19.2	-9.5	141.3	136.5
ASIA & THE PACIFIC [b]	1243.9	3688.0	7709.6	2332.4	2657.4	17631.3	16387.4
Bahrain	6.3	57.0	34.7	20.7	7.4	126.1	119.8
Bangladesh	23.8	- 6.9	343.1	48.1	151.7	559.8	536.0
Cyprus	4.9	9.3	61.0	1.7	9.4	86.3	81.4
Dem.Yemen	16.0	25.1	77.6	33.7	20.2	172.6	156.6
Hong Kong	54.8	620.6	246.3	137.1	67.6	1126.4	1071.6
India	17.1	-79.0	381.0	80.2	777.6	1176.9	1159.8
* Indonesia	23.9	12.6	454.6	75.2	-212.4	535.9	512.0
Iran (Islamic Rep. of)	114.7	424.6	926.1	358.5	334.0	2157.9	2043.2
Iraq	121.0	363.3	817.7	240.9	147.0	1689.9	1568.9
Jordan	19.3	90.4	143.2	56.5	34.2	343.6	324.3
Kuwait	32.5	231.0	114.7	88.5	19.2	485.9	453.4
Lebanon	27.1	114.5	87.2	43.0	33.1	304.9	277.8
* Malaysia	134.6	64.6	380.0	109.0	-1999.9	-1311.7	-1446.3
Oman	13.5	62.9	60.2	52.8	13.2	202.6	189.1

(continued)

Table 2 (continued)

Net food imports of developing regions and selected countries [a] thereof, 1983-1985

(Annual average, in millions of dollars)

Region/country	Sugar	Live animals and meat	Cereals	Dairy products	Animal & veg.oils	Total Incl. sugar	Total Excl. sugar
Pakistan	-24.9	- 6.6	-233.9	42.5	466.9	244.0	268.9
Papua New Guinea	0.8	55.1	42.0	9.3	-78.4	28.8	28.0
* Philippines	-275.6	8.0	248.3	87.5	-468.0	-399.8	-124.2
Qatar	6.0	59.1	30.4	21.7	8.5	125.7	119.7
Rep. of Korea	123.7	98.8	960.1	10.2	147.2	1340.0	1216.3
Saudi Arabia	142.6	886.1	1321.7	364.6	119.5	2834.5	2691.7
Singapore	50.0	128.0	115.4	69.7	-39.9	323.2	273.2
Sri Lanka	63.2	0.8	134.0	30.2	-10.1	218.1	154.9
Syrian Arab Rep.	108.0	4.2	327.1	69.5	40.8	549.6	441.6
United Arab Emirates	35.4	147.0	118.1	78.2	35.0	413.7	378.3
Yemen	54.6	79.9	127.3	66.1	24.5	352.4	297.8
LATIN AMERICA [b]	219.7	503.7	3740.7	770.7	854.8	6089.4	5869.9
Bolivia	-8.7	-2.5	70.6	8.2	8.8	81.4	90.1
* Brazil	-542.9	-804.1	918.2	21.4	-674.4	-1081.8	-538.9
* Chile	30.6	3.3	147.8	18.4	62.2	262.3	231.7
* Colombia	-52.6	- 6.7	161.6	8.9	77.3	188.5	241.1
Cuba	-4810.8	114.7	442.3	90.2	82.4	-4081.2	729.5
Dominican Rep.	-254.6	-1.9	62.6	14.2	40.0	136.9	117.7
Ecuador	10.3	5.9	75.5	5.4	38.3	135.5	125.2

(continued)

[handwritten annotations: "should be 114.9"; "typo: should be negative for a"; "* = net exporter of food"]

Table 2 *(continued)*

Net food imports of developing regions and selected countries [a] thereof, 1983-1985

(Annual average, in millions of dollars)

Region/country	Sugar	Live animals and meat	Cereals	Dairy products	Animal & veg.oils	Incl. sugar	Excl. sugar
Jamaica	- 40.0	22.5	85.8	23.0	15.9	107.2	147.2
Mexico	18.0	13.7	648.2	150.7	132.3	962.9	944.9
Peru	13.1	18.4	190.2	40.2	37.0	298.9	285.8
Trinidad & Tobago	- 9.4	51.2	75.7	61.2	19.5	198.2	207.6
Venezuela	111.7	30.0	476.0	131.2	193.3	942.2	830.5
Memo item:							
Other developing countries members of the Cairns Group: [c]							
Argentina	-131.7	-464.2	-2490.5	-22.8	-809.9	-3919.1	-3787.4
Fiji	-103.3	9.1	20.5	6.7	-3.5	-70.5	32.8
Thailand	-273.6	-53.5	-1306.5	77.4	17.8	-1538.4	-1264.8
Uruguay	-6.0	-192.8	-103.1	-24.3	1.0	-325.2	-319.2

Source: UNCTAD secretariat calculations

a The countries selected for each region had annual average net imports in 1983-1985 of at least $50 million for at least one of the product groups. A minus sign (-) indicates net exports.

b Regional totals cover, for each product group, all countries of the region except net exporters.

c Other than the developing countries members of the Group listed above.

* Member of the Cairns Group.

the major importers are from Latin America, India and the Soviet Union.

In meat the top five exporters are Australia, New Zealand, Brazil, France and Germany (the last three displacing traditional exporters Argentina, Uruguay and Ireland). The EEC has become a net exporter of beef, and the US and USSR are among the largest importers.

Sugar from cane is a tropical product, while that from beet is a temperate zone product. Cane sugar faces competition not only from beet-sugar (produced under high domestic protection and support in Europe and North America), but also from sugar substitutes (artificial sweeteners and corn syrup from maize). While previously the sugar trade was between low cost producers (Australia and Third World countries) and the ICs, high protection and domestic support in the industrial importing countries has changed all this. From a net importer, the EEC has emerged as the world's second largest exporter (through subsidised dumping of domestic beet sugar). US sugar imports have similarly been halved in this decade. The losers have been low cost cane sugar producers - in the Third World and in Australia.

While a few Third World countries are net exporters of these food products, and a few are significant exporters of individual products and derive substantial export earnings from them, the large majority are net importers. Excluding sugar, Third World imports averaged $36 billion annually according to UNCTAD data - $14.7 billion by major oil exporting countries, $5.9 billion by exporters of manufactures, and $2.5 billion for least developed countries.

On the export side, total Third World exports have averaged $15.5 billion. Only a few of these countries are overall net exporters in one of the four food categories and specially in all the groups. While some of the major food-importing countries are also exporters in some of the product groups, only a few are net exporters in all products combined - Brazil, Cuba, Malaysia, Mali and Philippines. If sugar is excluded, Cuba is a net importer. Among those who are overall net exporters (and do not import significantly any of the product groups) are Argentina, Fiji (net importer if sugar is excluded), Thailand and Uruguay. But only Argentina and perhaps Uruguay are net exporters in each of the categories.

Position of Different Country Groups

The negotiations in Agriculture, and the various groupings and viewpoints, can be understood only in this overall context of the limited nature of the products being focussed on, in terms of measures to improve access, and the varying interests of the exporters and importers, particularly within the Third World.

In the area of agriculture, importing countries use a variety of instruments for protection - tariffs and non-tariff measures (including the EEC's variable import levies), other charges and internal taxes, minimum import prices, 'voluntary' export restraint arrangements and sanitary and phyto-sanitary regulations and other technical standards.

At the broad conceptual level, there is widespread agreement that agricultural trade faces major problems due to actions of governments - supply/demand imbalances, depressed prices and large surplus stocks; protection which insulates domestic producers from world markets; lack of GATT rules and disciplines; sanitary and phyto-sanitary measures and barriers to trade.

But there are some major differences, among varying groups of countries, on the causes and solutions [5].

The EEC sees the supply/demand imbalance as caused by technological factors that have increased productivity, as in cereals, resulting in importing countries having become self-sufficient or even exporters. In this view demand will continue to stagnate or contract, while increased productivity, with or without domestic support, will continue to increase surpluses. From this perspective flows the EEC proposals for supply/demand management.

The US and the Cairns Group, on the other side, view the problems as due to domestic agricultural support policies. In this view, both argue for ending domestic agricultural support and intervention, and for free trade.

The net food importing countries argue that while there is excess production in a number of ICs, there is no excess production in the world. Domestic support policies in some ICs have created structural surpluses, making these countries net exporters. To this extent, the Third World competitive producers are being eased out of their traditional markets. But at global level in agricultural trade, there is inadequate purchasing power, and imbalances in production and consumption, in the importing Third World countries. A large number of them have structural deficits in agricultural trade, and the debt crisis and servicing difficulties have forced them to cut back on essential agricultural imports.

There are some large economies, with very large populations dependent on agriculture (like China and India), where through government support for increased domestic production, there is now food self-sufficiency and small surpluses. Yet there are large sections of under-nourished people due to low purchasing power. Satisfaction of these needs, provision of employment, the need to generate surpluses in agriculture for investment in industry and ensure availability of domestic wage goods - all this means there is a need for continued domestic support to increase production.

In this light, various protagonists have advanced various proposals relating to agricultural trade.

The US has called for a 'market-oriented' approach, and a complete phase-out, by year 2000 of all agricultural subsidies affecting trade - with exports based on subsidies to be frozen and subsidies phased out in the same period [6]. Only direct income or other payments decoupled from production and marketing are to be exempt. The US has also called for harmonisation of health and sanitary regulations.

The EEC has suggested that a better balance be brought about between supply and demand. Its proposals envisage exchange of concessions to improve market access, and phased reduction of agricultural support policies impinging on international markets. The reduction (not elimination) is to be in two stages - short term and emergency actions based on present policies and a second stage of concerted reduction in support policies and readjustment of external protection to stabilise world markets. The EEC proposes emergency measures (for cereals and cereal substitutes, sugar and dairy products) for a year, but renewable. This is to involve price disciplines and measures to reduce quantities put on the world markets. Other short-term undertakings (for cereals, rice, sugar, oilseeds, dairy products and beef/veal) would involve a freeze on support at levels of 1984 (when policy reforms were initiated in many countries) until final agreement. The EEC had envisaged agreement on these in 1988, and implementation from early 1989. Both dates have gone by without any agreement. In the second stage, the EEC envisaged concerted reductions in support and readjustment of external protection to stabilise world markets.

The Cairns Group proposals envisage measures to achieve full liberalisation of trade in agriculture by eliminating agricultural policies distorting trade and 'binding' necessary undertakings in GATT under strengthened rules and disciplines. The proposals on a long-term framework call for removal of restrictions on market access (with low or zero bound tariffs) and new GATT rules and disciplines on subsidies and government support measures affecting trade. The proposals also involve a reform programme for phasing down agricultural support using schedules of reduction for each country (based on measurement of agricultural support through a so-called producer subsidy equivalent or PSE). Priorities would be for phasing out export subsidies and systematic enlargement of import access. The Cairns group has also proposed early relief measures (but within the context of agreement in principle to the long term measures) - freeze on access levels and export and production subsidies, along with commitments on release of stocks, cuts in subsidies and increased market access - and transitional measures. Canada, a Cairns group member, has put forward some variations and departures from the overall Cairns proposals.

Among the importing countries, Japan has called for long-term stability in agricultural trade and for food security, and for each country excluding a limited range of products from the measures (which would be rice for Japan, but could be other products for other countries). Japan has also envisaged improved market access through reduced customs tariffs, improved criteria for waivers from elimination of quantitative restrictions. Switzerland has proposed a freeze on export subsidies. But unlike the US, which has said its own waiver is on the table for negotiations, the Swiss have given no indication that they are ready to negotiate away their GATT waiver obtained as part of their accession protocol.

Net importing Third World countries like Egypt, Jamaica, Mexico, Nigeria and Peru, have underscored the need for recognition of importance of agriculture for overall development in Third World economies - in terms of output, employment and export opportunities, linkages between agricultural policies and other socio-economic-political objectives, food security and need for government support to increase production.

The development dimension of agriculture has been specifically addressed by India in several interventions in the negotiating group. These have emphasised the very large proportion of population dependent on agriculture, and the need to increase production and productivity, and the important role of government, given the imperfect nature of the markets, in providing inputs at reasonable cost, research and development and extension services, provision of cheap credits and assurance of remunerative prices. Such essential measures for development taken by governments cannot be equated with the trade restrictive and distortive measures in the Industrialised countries.

The various proposals and papers do not indicate any common understanding of the product coverage under agriculture. The US wants all agricultural products (processed and unprocessed), as well as forestry and fishery products, to be covered. Thus its proposals include matters being dealt with under Tropical Products and Natural Resource-based Products, and it wants to include in the negotiations on agriculture all products where it is an important producer (rice, tobacco and groundnuts).

The EEC has also said it wants to cover all processed and unprocessed products, but its proposals involve really a commodity-by-commodity approach of products in over-supply and of export interest to industrialised countries. The EEC proposals also cover rice, sugar and oilseeds (falling within the Tropical Products group, but where the EEC offer excludes these).

The Cairns proposals talk of product coverage that is 'as comprehensive as possible', while Japan wants all agricultural, fishery and forestry products, and including tropical products where there are temperate zone substitutes (rice, vegetable oils, tea and tobacco). The Nordic's proposals call for coverage of all products in over-supply.

Another issue in the negotiations is over the application of the special and differential.treatment concept which under the Punta del Este mandate is to apply to every negotiating area. The US has envisaged this to mean a longer time frame, in proven cases, for Third World countries to comply. The

Cairns proposals envisage Third World countries being able to provide domestic government support, so long as it is not commodity specific and trade-related. But Third World countries have said the Special and Differential Treatment for Third World countries must go beyond the 'longer time-frame' concept for compliance. Development objectives, they emphasise, should form part of any new commitment or rules and disciplines relating to farm support or lowering of market access barriers or even subsidies for export to compensate for infrastructural handicaps.

An aspect of the EEC proposal is the view that commodity agreements (in areas of interest to it) should be negotiated in GATT. It should be noted that in other commodity negotiations (like tropical beverages or even some minerals and metals), some of the EEC member countries and hence the Community itself oppose supply/management and favour the free market. The position of other ICs in commodities where they are importers and consumers is no different.

Liberalisation: Effects on Third World

Whatever be the merits or claims of long-term benefits through free trade and liberalisation, it is also clear that any liberalisation would result in higher world prices and thus increased import prices of food for the net food importing Third World countries. Third World exports are concentrated in tropical products where, with the exception of sugar, improved market access will not result in higher world prices. For this class of countries, gains from trade liberalisation will be much smaller than losses in higher import costs.

A study by the Commonwealth Secretariat notes that in a world of 'freer' trade, most Third World countries would prove to have, or be able to develop, an international competitive advantage in producing and exporting staple agricultural products at present exported under subsidy by the major ICs. "Yet for most developing countries, liberalisation would be likely to cause or exacerbate balance of payments problems in the short and, may be, medium term, and substantial financial support would be needed to help them overcome these difficulties. For all these reasons, this paper attaches special importance to the concept of a 'development clause' which - particularly for countries of Africa and Asia - would recognise the distinctive role of small-scale farmers" [7].

Notes on Chapter 8:

1. Developments in the negotiating process set out in this chapter have to be read along with the relevant portions in chapter 12 on the mid-term review accords in this area.

2. According to UNCTAD estimates (TD/B/C.1/284), the US, EEC and Japan have been spending an annual $40 billion in budget support. This is over and above transfers from higher prices by consumers to producers. The OECD estimates (in Suivi et perspectives des politiques, des marches et des changes agricoles, Paris, 1988) the combined annual average consumer and tax-payer transfers to agriculture, during 1984-1986, to be about $177 billion dollars compared to about $88 billion during 1979-81. During the two periods overall costs rose by 40% in EEC, doubled in Japan, and more than doubled in North America, Australia and New Zealand.

3. World Bank, *World Development Report 1988*, tables 3 and 31.

4. Rankings and figures in all the product areas dealt with are UNCTAD calculations based on US Department of Agriculture data.

5. For details of viewpoints and proposals of protogonists and the evolving negotiating process see *SUNS* 1987 and 1988 and especially Morges group discussions 1636; initial views on the mandate and proposals 1658 and 1709; US proposals and discussions 1749, 1924, 1956, 1958; Cairns group proposals 1808 and on freeze on subsidies 1980; Switzerland 1810; EEC 1810, 1958, 2027; Canada 1811; Japan 2005; net food-importing countries 1811, 1882, 1877 and 1981 (Jamaica), 1924 (Nigeria), and 2005 (Egypt,Jamaica, Mexico and Peru); Development focus (India) 1841, 1882, 2027 and 2046.

6. After the December 1988 Montreal Ministerial mid-term review meeting, the US modified this zero option on subsidies and this enabled the US and EEC to reach the compromise on Agriculture at the April meeting of the TNC. see infra Ch 12.

7. 'Agricultural Trade Liberalisation and the Developing Countries. The Scope for action in the Uruguay Round', 1988, (*mimeo*) Commonwealth Secretariat, London.

PART III

TRADITIONAL AND SYSTEMIC ISSUES

Chapter 9

TRADITIONAL GATT ISSUES

When the new round, with new issues, was sought to be launched, and in the negotiations leading to it, Third World countries expressed their concern that the focus on new issues would result in some of their major trading problems and traditional GATT issues being pushed to the background [1]. Some, like the group of ten, had unsuccessfully sought to insist on solutions to old issues like safeguards etc, as a pre-condition for launching a new round of negotiations with new issues. But even those willing to go along with a new round and new issues, had laid stress on priority for the problems of Third World countries and early solutions for them. As noted earlier, the division among the Third World countries resulted in the ICs having their way in weakened language in the mandates on some of the traditional issues.

In the declaration, the only area of traditional GATT concern, and one of importance to Third World countries, which received some priority of sorts was 'tropical products' and, indirectly, the issue of a comprehensive 'safeguards' agreement.

But in the negotiations since then, the traditional issues have all been pushed to the background and little headway has been made on any of them. In several areas the actual mandates have been stood on their head, with leading industrial countries arguing that in these areas it is for the Third

World countries to take actions to liberalise their trade.

Some of these issues and problems, are discussed below.

Standstill and Rollback

Basic to the launching of the negotiations was the commitment for standstill and rollback of protection. When the idea of a new round had been broached in 1984, all the Third World countries were united in their demand for implementation of the 1982 Ministerial Declaration on this. In 1985 and 1986, Brazil, India and others sought to make this a pre-condition for the launching of the round through a legal commitment in the form of protocols. But the ICs declined to commit themselves. Ultimately what emerged, in the Ministerial Declaration, was only what was generally described as 'political commitment'.

The Ministerial Declaration on standstill had three commitments: not to take any trade restrictive or distorting measure inconsistent with the provisions of the General Agreement or *the Instruments negotiated within the framework of GATT or under its auspices* (emphasis added), an undertaking not to take even permissible measures beyond those absolutely necessary, and not to take any measures that would improve the negotiating position of the cp concerned [2].

The pledges were less than what the Third World countries originally sought as a pre-condition for launching the round. But more disquieting was the way the GATT provisions and obligations, and instruments like the MFA which were derogations from GATT, were put on the same footing in relation to the standstill. As repeated UNCTAD and GATT statements and documents make clear the standstill/rollback commitments have not been implemented; protection, particularly 'grey area' measures have proliferated [3]. In

discussions at the half-yearly special sessions of the GATT
Council, where developments in the trading system are reviewed, as well as in the Uruguay Round negotiating group
on Safeguards, and in the post-Montreal consultations on this
issue the US and EEC have been claiming that 'grey area'
measures are not illegal in GATT. S.1401 of the US Trade
and Omnibus Act 1988 has amended the provisions in existing law, Sections 201-204, to enable and facilitate voluntary
export restraints (VERs) and other such grey area measures,
and virtually mandates it in respect of Steel. The new US
Trade Representative, Mrs Carla Hills has also announced
she would be doing so [4].

The concept of standstill/rollback on the basis of
'GATT-inconsistency' has itself given rise to disputes, with
every-one concerned arguing that their actions are 'GATT-
consistent', and that any disputes are a matter for the GATT
dispute settlement machinery.

The monitoring and supervision of the standstill/roll-
back in the surveillance body has proved formalistic and
bureaucratic. The complaints are filed, complainants make
their case at periodic meetings, answers are given (often
on the basis that the measures complained of are GATT-con-
sistent), and the records are remitted to the Group of Negotiations on Goods (GNG) and the Trade Negotiations Committee. Nothing more happens. Since the Uruguay Round
commitment is said to be mainly political, unless someone
feels sufficiently aggrieved to use the TNC to bring the negotiations to a standstill across the board, nothing more than
'hot air' can be expected.

On rollback, there was a commitment to rollback all
measures inconsistent under GATT or instruments negotiated under it, and without seeking any concessions.
Additionally, the parties maintaining them had to notify and
table their plans for rollback to be completed in a phased
manner, and in any event before the conclusion of the
new round. Apart from the same arguments about GATT

consistency and inconsistency none of the industrial countries have filed any plans for rollback, though the deadline was December 1987. Some like the EEC are arguing that this is a political commitment and an autonomous one, and not negotiable. Some of the statements suggest that in any event 'grey area' measures would not be covered.

Tariffs

The negotiations in this area are to aim: "to reduce or, as appropriate, eliminate tariffs including the reduction or elimination of high tariffs and tariff escalation. Emphasis shall be given to the expansion of the scope of tariff concessions among all participants".

Successive GATT rounds, and particularly the Tokyo Round, have succeeded in lowering tariffs considerably in the industrial countries. The post-Tokyo weighted average MFN rates have fallen to 5.6, 5.5 and 4.8 percent respectively in the EEC, Japan, and the US [5]. In all these markets non-fuel exports of Third World countries face higher average MFN rates than exports of other ICs. Averages also blur substantial discrepencies and peaks. In the EEC, Japan and the US, tariffs above ten percent still account respectively for 21.5, 17.1 and 16.0 percent of all tariff lines. Most of these high percentages are concentrated in food and textile and clothing categories, items of main export interest to the Third World. Also, bound tariffs in agricultural items are small, which means industrial countries can raise them at will. There are also problems of tariff peaks and tariff escalation at every stage of processing [6].

In the first two years of negotiations, the negotiating group was not able to make much progress. A general tariff cutting formula to deal with the high tariffs and peaks in the OECD markets would benefit the Third World countries. But the US, EEC and Japan have all taken positions that imply that the major focus of negotiations should be the tariffs, admittedly high, of Third World countries and of others that did not participate in the general Tokyo Round tariff cutting formula, and that these countries should bind all their tariffs and reduce them over a period.

Non-Tariff Measures (NTMs)

"Negotiations shall aim to reduce or eliminate NTMs, including quantitative restrictions, without prejudice to any action to be taken in fulfilment of the rollback commitments."

Though previous GATT rounds tried to tackle them, NTMs in various forms, including discriminatory price-control or volume-control measures, have proliferated particularly after the Tokyo round tariff cuts. According to UNCTAD estimates, NTMs affecting imports into the OECD countries have increased between 1981-1988. In 1988, NTMs affected 21.4 percent of value of non-fuel imports into 17 developed market-economy countries as against 18.8 percent in 1981. There was some reduction in 1988 (compared to 1987) in intra-DMEC trade, but there was no relaxation of NTMs applied against imports from the Third World, and the trade coverage ratio of these NTMs was 25.6 percent [7].

There are multiplicity of NTMs, and they are pervasive and often have contradictory status vis-a-vis GATT. In the first two years of negotiations, there was not much progress in this group either.

Surprisingly, the US and EEC have sought to raise in the group as an NTM, the practice of many countries of Africa, Asia and Latin America, to engage inspection firms that conduct preshipment cargo inspection and advise the importing countries about the prices charged in invoices in comparison with prevailing world market prices. This system helps to combat the transfer-pricing practices of TNCs and prevent capital flight. But in an effort to end such inspections, the US TNCs have secured the support of their government to raise this in the NTM group. The EEC and Japan have supported this. There are also suggestions about dealing with this in the Negotiating Group on Tokyo Round codes.

As in other areas generally, the ICs are behaving as if the purpose of the negotiations is to reduce or eliminate import barriers in the Third World.

Tropical Products

"Negotiations shall aim at the fullest liberalisation of trade in tropical products, including in their processed and semi-processed forms and shall cover both tariff and all non-tariff measures affecting trade in these products.

"Contracting parties recognise the importance of trade in tropical products to a large number of less-developed contracting parties and agree that negotiations in this area shall receive special attention, including the timing of the negotiations and the implementation of the results as provided for in B (ii)".

This Clause B (ii) is the paragraph of the declaration which treats the entire GATT MTNs as one single undertaking, but enables early implementation of accords reached during the round. Tropical Products is the only area of negotiations where there is such a specific reference. Third World countries have been looking forward anxiously to progress in this area, but to their disappointment there has been little progress.

The term 'tropical products' has been used, for quite some time in GATT, for a group of products, selected and identified from the point of view of their particular export interest to the Third World countries. These products and product groups (though not accepted as a 'definition' or as an exhaustive listing, and could be added on during the course of negotiations) are: Tropical beverages; spices, flowers and plaiting products; certain oilseeds, vegetable oils and oilcakes; tobacco, rice and tropical roots; tropical fruits and nuts; natural rubber and tropical wood; jute and hard fibres.

The term includes agricultural commodities produced solely or mainly by the Third World and some without any natural substitutes - coffee, cocoa, tea, spices, bananas, natural rubber. In these products, the ICs use tariffs for protection of local processing industries, and levy internal consumption taxes and charges as revenue-raising measures (a hangover of immediate postwar period when these were considered luxuries). Tariffs are pretty high on processed cocoa, coffee or tea, processed beef and fish, fresh and preserved fruits and vegetables, sugar, processed cereals, manufactured tobacco, leather and products, yarn and woven fabrics. But not all these items figure in the list of tropical products. In some cases trade weighted averages are as high as 100 percent. There are also non-tariff measures weighing heavily on processed commodities.

This issue of liberalisation of trade in these products and improving market access to these Third World exports in the markets of ICs has been on the GATT agenda for over 25 years. Following the report of the Heberler Committee, at the GATT Ministerial meeting of 1963, twenty one Third World CPs presented a Programme of Action for the total liberalisation of trade in the Tropical Products [8].

Subject to some understanding and explanations, it was accepted by most industrialised countries, and an Action Committee was set up to carry out the Programme of Action. This called, among other things, for standstill on new protectionist measures against exports of the Third World, elimination of quantitative restrictions inconsistent with GATT provisions, duty free entry by 31 December 1963, elimination of tariffs on primary products and reduction and elimination of tariff barriers to exports of semi-processed and processed primary product exports of the Third World with at least a 50 percent reduction to be achieved by 1966, progressive reduction of internal fiscal charges and revenue duties. While all the Industrialised States accepted the Action Programme, the EEC countries entered reservations to the effect that the points in the Action Programme should be considered as objectives towards which concrete policies should be adopted, but that more positive measures were needed through organisation of international trade on products of interest to the Third World and by measures to increase exports at remunerative, equitable and stable prices [9].

The EEC 'understanding' and reservations were not that the Action Programme could not be implemented, but that it was not enough and more needed to be done! But ultimately, most of the programme and promises were never implemented.

The issue has figured on the agenda of several rounds but with no action or very limited results; there are many tariff and nontariff measures against imports of these products coming from the Third World countries, with high incidence of tariffs on semi-processed and processed items, due to the phenomenon of tariff escalation at every stage of processing. As a result raw materials (coffee or cocoa beans or jute fibres) may enter at zero or low tariff, but the processed product may face an effective protection of double-digit tariffs. There are also residual quantitative restrictions, and internal consumption taxes (as on coffee, tea and cocoa) in several of the EEC countries.

If industrial countries are really sincere about their commitments, as they profess, the appropriate approach would have been to remove all barriers, tariff and non-tariff, in the tropical products imported from the Third World countries, in their raw material, semi-processed and processed forms.

As already noted the products in this group were put together from the point of view of their export interest to Third World countries; and all along special efforts in successive rounds have been on the basis of liberalising access to these exports in markets of industrial countries to enable Third World countries to earn more. According to the negotiating plan several Third World countries tabled lists of specific tropical products of interest to them.

The Uruguay Round mandate talks of 'fullest liberalisation', which would mean tariff and non-tariff measures, including internal taxes which are significant barriers to trade. But ICs have been interpreting the mandate to mean 'widest' liberalisation, and have brought to the negotiating table their perspective that they are also exporters of these products. There is also the added complication of the EEC's preferences for ACP countries under the Lome agreement. On this basis, the EEC countries have built up a whole range of processing industries in these products, all in the hands of TNCs, and based on imports of raw materials in their primary or crude processed stages so that the value added remains in the EEC countries.

During the first two years of negotiations, the major ICs raised the issue of 'extended coverage', meaning negotiations should cover not only liberalisation by them, but also by Third World countries for the tropical products that these industrialised countries export (whether raw, semi-processed or processed). The US also linked progress in this group to progress in agricultural trade negotiations, while the EEC excluded those products that come under the purview of the agriculture negotiations or those for which there are temperate zone substitutes.

The positions of two sides on modalities for negotiations are also far apart. The US, Japan and others want a 'request/offer' basis for negotiations. The US and Japan are net importers. But the EEC is a major exporter, serving as a conduit for exports from ACP countries to the rest of the world, with the value added benefiting EEC enterprises. In the Nordic markets for example, the Third World share is said to be only five percent of the total imports of these products, and any liberalisation would only benefit the major suppliers, EEC countries and their enterprises.

The EEC has put forward proposals that appear to be slightly more forthcoming, but this is hedged in with conditions, the major ones being there should be a 'fair degree of burden sharing' by all participants, a 'satisfactory level of reciprocity' by the main beneficiary countries including more advanced Third World countries, and that those of them having a 'dominant supply position' for raw materials in the world market should have appropriate measures to reduce export restrictions [10]. All these are subjective elements and at the minimum would create confusion, and could have the net result of delaying or shelving the liberalisation prospects.

The supply assurances sought is also an issue raised by the EEC in the Natural Resource group. In effect it is an attempt to curb development policies and sovereignty of countries over the disposal of their natural resources, and ensure perpetuation of EEC enterprises based on raw material supplies from the Third World. The EEC demand is in conflict with Article 2 of the 'Charter of Rights and Duties of States' which specifically recognised that "Every State has and shall freely exercise full permanent sovereignty, including posession, use, and disposal, over all its wealth, natural resources and economic activities" [11].

The same principle is also found in Article 13 of the 1978 Vienna Convention on Succession of States in respect of Treaties which states: "Nothing in the present Convention shall affect the principle of International Law affirming the permanent sovereignty of every people and every State over its natural wealth and resources" [12]. Article 15:4 of the 1983 Convention on Succession of States in respect of State Property Archives and Debts reaffirms the same principle: "Agreements concluded between the predecessor State and the newly independent State to determine succession to State property of the predecessor State... shall not infringe the principle of permanent Sovereignty of every people over its wealth and Natural Resources" [13].

The talk of liberalisation by the Third World countries is also meaningless, because it has to be based on an effective capacity to pay. How could Third World countries liberalise their imports of tropical products, when they have no money to pay for essential imports?

All available data suggest that while Third World countries are the producers of primary tropical products, the trade is dominated by the TNCs, and is controlled by them. If liberalisation is to really benefit the Third World countries, an appropriate modality for liberalisation should be chosen that would ensure for them fullest market access and value added for their exports. Any other approach would only benefit the TNCs.

But it is not clear whether the Third World countries, particularly those which have been pushing this as a separate issue and which negotiated the mandate, have thought through these matters and taken account of the developments in terms of TNC domination of trade, since the issue was originally raised in GATT in the 1960s.

Other basic questions having a bearing on the strategy and tactics of the Third World countries arise out of the insistence of the ICs on 'reciprocity' and 'graduation', and refusal in practice to carry out any unilateral liberalisation or even implement earlier commitments of unilateral actions. In this context countries, and groups of them, have to carefully weigh the advantages and disadvantages of the sectoral negotiations (where their benefits are to be matched by reciprocal concessions), the payment of a price for initial and mid-term review and another at the end of the round. They also have to weigh the reciprocal concessions and commitments that might be sought in terms of removal of export restrictions and guarantees [14].

Natural Resource-based Products

"Negotiations shall aim to achieve the fullest liberalisation of trade in natural-resource based products, including in their processed and semi-processed forms. The negotiations shall aim to reduce or eliminate tariff and non-tariff measures, including tariff escalation".

This item was put on the agenda at the instance of Canada, Sweden and a few others. Though the NRPs have not been defined, and there are unresolved differences on what is or is not to be covered, it is generally accepted to involve (a) non-ferrous metals and minerals, (b) forestry products, and (c) fish and fisheries products. The last two are renewable resources (provided their exploitation is properly managed), while the first is a non-renewable one.

In 1985, world trade in mineral ores and metals was about $72 billion dollars, in fish and fisheries $17 billion, and in forestry products about $56 billion. The share of Third World countries in these trades were respectively 25, 41 and 18 percent [15]. Many Third World countries depend heavily on these exports, which are however largely confined to exports in unprocessed and semi-processed forms.

The idea of 'sectoral approach' to market access for some of these products (some ores, metals and metal manufactures and wood and wood products, at all stages of processing) was raised by Canada in the Tokyo Round, but failed to win approval. The issue was again brought up in the context of the 1982 GATT Ministerial meeting, and put on the Work Programme, resulting in the setting up in 1984 of a working party which did some exploratory work and made some recommendations for trade liberalisation for some of the products. In regard to fisheries no progress could be made because of issues raised by some parties over access to fishing grounds.

The negotiating plan in the Uruguay Round, approved in January 1987, provided for an initial phase (which was to have been completed by end of 1987, but had not been even by 1989). In this phase issues relevant to the negotiating objective and taking account of the report of the Working Party were to have been determined. A factual basis was to be established for negotiations, with elaboration of techniques and modalities, and establishment of a common negotiating basis. The subsequent phase involved tabling of requests and offers and negotiations on the common basis.

For Third World countries, the main interest is the phenomenon of escalation of nominal tariffs with processing, and the related effective rate of tariff protection. The ICs as a whole rarely import more than ten percent in processed or advanced fabricated forms.

In the two years of discussions in the group, some participants have sought an open-ended approach to product coverage, while others want coverage to be restricted to those considered in the working party and where work is already advanced enough to begin negotiations (fisheries, forestry and non-ferrous metals and minerals).

The EEC wants coverage to be extended to a few specifics - titanium sponge, metal scrap, phosphates, rattan, and hides and skins. The US wants the coverage to be broad and include energy-based products - in particular natural gas, petroleum, uranium, petrochemicals, construction materials, and oil and gas processing. Australia has sought extension of coverage to include problems of trade involving iron ore, primary steel, energy (including oil, coal, natural gas and uranium), salt, tungsten and mineral sands. While not opposed to addition of new product areas, the Nordics are against an open-ended definition or approach, and prefer a criteria based on significant world trade and facing access problems specific to the product.

Four African countries (Cameroon, Cote d'Ivoire, Senegal and Zaire - for whom these negotiations are of particular importance) in a joint proposal have said product coverage should be limited to products covered in the GATT Working Party, since the negotiations otherwise would be delayed. In support of this position, several others have said that before extending product coverage, negotiations should concentrate on products where sufficient technical work and study have already been done in the Working Party.

The ICs want other issues also to be addressed in these negotiations. The US wants negotiations on dual pricing of natural resources, export restrictions (including export taxes and charges, local processing requirements, embargoes), subsidies, and government ownership practices. The EEC wants negotiations on discriminatory public procurement, 'double pricing' (including what it calls 'reverse dumping'), pricing policies in transactions (of affiliated vs non-affiliated enterprises), restrictive business practices (RBPs), export restrictions, and access to supplies.

On the last, the EEC has focussed particularly on access to fishing in the 200-mile extended economic zone of countries and has made clear that unless this is tackled, no tariff concessions or liberalisation of NTMs need be expected. Japan also wants access to fisheries resources to be tackled. South Korea wants negotiations to deal with access to resources, export restrictions or prohibitions and trade distorting production, dual pricing and export subsidies.

The Nordic countries have said they are willing to discuss such issues as export restrictions, subsidies, dual pricing, and government ownership, but not the subject of fishing rights. Several Third World countries have said that most of these additional issues are outside the scope of the negotiations and covered by other international treaties - as in regard to access to fisheries which is governed by the UN Convention on Law of the Seas - or are issues which are not product specific and hence must be dealt with in other relevant negotiating groups. Interestingly, while the EEC in this context wants to discuss pricing policies of TNCs and RBPs, it is opposed to tackling RBPs as a general issue in GATT, or even in the limited areas of TRIPs and TRIMs where the Third World countries have raised this question.

For Third World countries seeking to increase their export earnings through value added, the basic policy issues are tariff barriers, tariff escalation and non-tariff barriers to the establishment and development of raw material process- ing industries. Tariff escalation which increases with every stage of processing and NTMs that are heavier on processed products are particularly important.

Broadening the issues for negotiations (as the US, EEC and others want) would slow down the progress on market access issues. As discovered earlier, issues of access to sup- plies raise questions of sovereignty and the long recognised right of a country to administer its natural resources the way it deems necessary.

In regard to energy and energy products, the major producers (USSR as well as most of the OPEC members) are not involved in the Uruguay Round negotiations.

Textiles and Clothing

"Negotiations in the area of Textiles and Clothing shall aim to formulate modalities that would permit the eventual integration of this sector into GATT on the basis of strength- ened GATT rules and disciplines, thereby also contributing to the objective of further liberalisation of trade".

This is perhaps the sector of greatest importance to the Third World countries, because of their major export interest in this trade. This is the first rung in the ladder of industriali- sation. It accounts for a large share of their manufactured exports, and the total share of this sector in total manufactur- ing value added and employment in the Third World is also substantial.

Trade in this sector has been governed by special arrangements for over 25 years - the Short-term arrangements for cotton textiles, followed by the Long-term Arrangement (LTA), and succeeded in turn by the Multifibre Arrangement (MFA). It is a major derogation from GATT rules and principles, enabling cps to escape some fundamental GATT obligations and to negotiate bilateral quantitative export restraints (and failing that impose unilateral discriminatory restrictons, applied primarily against exports from the Third World countries and some of the East Europeans). Successively extended by protocols, MFA-4 is due to run till July 1991. The signatory countries to the MFA account for 90 percent of the international trade in textiles and clothing.

In the weeks before the launching of the Uruguay Round, some of the Third World countries, like Pakistan, which had abated their objections to the new round and had joined the Colombian-Swiss effort to produce a compromise had hoped that in return for their cooperation the US and other ICs would agree to negotiate the phase-out of the MFA. But the MFA extension protocol, which was negotiated and concluded almost on the eve of the Punta del Este meeting was more restrictive than earlier ones, and extended the coverage to new fibres. At Punta del Este itself, the US did not agree to specific mention of the MFA, but diplomats from some of these countries gained the impression from the US negotiators that their tough stand was related to pending tougher legislative proposals in the Congress and the impending Congressional elections. After Punta del Este, the US negotiators privately tried to explain away their public position on the ground of the pending 'Jenkins Bill' (for textile import restrictions) in Congress and the politics of a Presidential election year. Only very recently, the MFA exporting Third World countries have begun to realise that the US and other ICs in this matter have been guilty of bad faith and have no intention whatsoever of doing away with the MFA.

When the negotiating plans were to be approved, there were efforts to de-emphasise the negotiations by creating a single negotiating group to deal with tariffs, non-tariff measures, natural resource-based products and textiles and clothing. Ultimately, separate groups were created with a common chairman. When the negotiations began, there were further efforts to delay the negotiations in this area, by suggesting that substantive negotiations should begin only in ·1989, with hints that these could be merged into the negotiations that would begin in July 1990 over the future of MFA. But from the beginning the US and the EEC were opposed to making the dismantling of the MFA as the process for integration of the trade into GATT. Throughout 1987 and 1988, none of the ICs made any serious effort at negotiating or putting forward their own ideas. The Third World members of the MFA, grouped in the International Textiles and Clothing Bureau, tried to engage them in dialogue and put forward their own proposals. Pakistan too put forward some proposals of its own. But none of these produced any response in the shape of negotiations [16].

In May 1988, the US made clear that it would not negotiate an end to the MFA and had no mandate to do so! The Omnibus Trade and Competiveness Act 1988, which gives the Administration the negotiating mandate, does not provide any authority to US negotiators in this area. This means any agreement negotiated by the administration would have to go before the US Senate for approval as a treaty, and later the enabling legislation before Congress, where any number of changes and amendments could be introduced. The Textiles issue would be effectively delinked from the other issues or agreements in the Uruguay Round, and when Congress wants some changes, the Third World countries would find themselves negotiating from the compromise position they had already reached, and very likely provide more concessions to the US.

As for the EEC, in effect it came out for managed trade in Textiles [17]. The EEC and others do make some noises about their willingness to negotiate, but it is clear they are not going to agree to remove their MFA restrictions unconditionally. The EEC has made clear that any moves towards phasing out the MFA and integration of this sector into GATT has to involve progress on 'safeguards', where it insists on 'selective safeguards' and on intellectual property protection in GATT. Only Sweden has now come out in favour of winding down the MFA and has said that at the expiry of the MFA-4, Sweden would not renew the trade restrictive arrangements.

Third World countries are aware of the unequal relationships, and the selective and discriminatory regime governing this trade. At the present time, the US remains the single largest market for their textiles and clothing exports. The US is also the major trading partner for the Third World countries. They want stricter GATT rules and disciplines to apply to this trade, and an end to the derogation from GATT rules and selective and discriminatory treatment for their exports. At the same time they don't want to jeopardise their relationships with the US either.

In September 1988, at the meeting of the ITCB in Geneva, its members were told, by no less a person than the GATT Director-General, that the MFA and its predecessors had served 'useful ends' such as permitting industry in the North 'to adjust to changing competition', and had 'permitted international trade to expand in an orderly manner..limited the recourse to unilateral measures of protection... (and)... allowed for entry of new comers' [18]. True, the GATT official also noted that the MFA had shown the way for circumvention of GATT rules in other sectors including automobiles, footwear, steel, machine tools, consumer electronics and high technology products like computer chips. The MFA, he further advised the ITCB members, had now become 'part and parcel of the international scene, and a system developed over so many years could not be dismantled abruptly or without due preparation' and that negotiators would have to select 'an appropriate modality' that would be 'feasible' and had to be 'politically acceptable' to all concerned [19].

Despite all this, the ITCB members stood firm and, much against the wishes of the US and EEC, got their proposals incorporated into the report of the GNG for the meeting at Montreal. Their seven-point recommendations involved: freeze on further restrictions under the MFA, agreement that the phase-out of MFA restrictions should begin upon expiry of the present MFA protocol (at end of July 1991) and that the time-frame within which the process of integration into GATT, which would be gradual and progressive, would be agreed upon during the Uruguay Round as also the modalities to achieve this [20].

Notes to Chapter 9

1. Developments in the negotiating process set out in this chapter have to be read along with the relevant portions in chapter 11 and 12 on the mid-term review accords.

2 See sec. C of Part I of Declaration in Annex 1.

3. See TD/B/1160, p 4-5 and footnotes; though in more guarded language, the GATT secretariat's reports to the semi-anual special GATT Council sessions also bring this out.

4. *Financial Times*, Jan 30, 1989.

5. TD/328/Add.4 Table IV,2.B, UNCTAD.

6. R.Ezran and J.Karsenty, UNCTAD Discussion Paper No.22

7. TD/B/1196, UNCTAD p 10.

8. BISD Twelfth Supplement pp 26-27.

9. *Ibid* pp 36-47.

10. Independent of the Uruguay Round, the EEC has already raised this as an issue vis-a-vis Indonesia and other Asean countries that are trying to develop their timber-based processing industries by restricting the exports of logs and other unprocessed timber.

11. *Collected Documents,* Vol V pp 567-572.

12. American Society of International Law, *International Legal Material,* Vol.16 No 6 (Nov 1978) p 1495.

13. *Ibid,* Vol 22 No 2 (Mar 1983) p 313.

14. For a full discussion of pros and cons and options see Patrick Low and Ramiro Guzman, 'Tropical Products in the Uruguay Round', *Uruguay Round,* UNCTAD/ITP/10 pp 329-368.

15. UNCTAD calculations, *Uruguay Round* pp 275, 263, and 270.

16. *SUNS* 1653, 1706, 1845, 1875 (proposals of Pakistan), 1934 (proposals on behalf of the ITCB).

17. *SUNS* 1935 and 1959. Also *SUNS* 1988, 2017 and 2041.

18. *SUNS* 2017.

19. *Ibid.*

20. MTN/GNG/13 and MTN.TNC/7(MIN).

Chapter 10

SYSTEMIC ISSUES

A number of issues on the agenda of the Uruguay Round do not relate to normal trade liberalisation issues of market access through reduction or elimination of tariff and non-tariff barriers [1]. They deal with 'systemic issues' which have a bearing, directly or indirectly, on the GATT trading system and its rules and principles. There are proposals for changes in GATT Articles, to the Tokyo Round codes or agreements under existing provisions or providing for their agreed interpretations (with benefits and obligations to signatories), for new understandings or agreements, and to deal with existing GATT practices, procedures and measures to improve and make them more effective.

These issues are: GATT Articles, MTN Codes and Agreements, Safeguards, Subsidies and Countervailing Measures, Dispute Settlement and Functioning of the GATT System.

The way these issues are dealt with and their outcome will change the nature of the GATT and its functions and will influence international economic relations well into the next century. The new themes, the traditional market access issues, and these systemic issues have to be seen together. Their overall effects will be greater than the sum of the parts.

Safeguards

The issue of 'safeguards' relates to GATT Article XIX, which is the principal 'escape clause' of the General Agreement. It enables a contracting party to 'escape' from its GATT obligations in respect of imports and take emergency actions to restrict imports of particular products or group of products.

(Other 'safeguard' provisions in the GATT are provisions of Article VI enabling imposition of anti-dumping and countervailing duties, Article XII enabling imposition of import restrictions for BOP reasons, Article XVIII which enables Third World cps to impose tariff and import restrictions for BOP reasons or for development, Article XX which enables cps to take any action to safeguard public health and safety, and Article XXVIII which enables renegotiation of concessions. There are also Article XXI which permits any actions contrary to GATT obligations on grounds of 'security', and Article XXXV which enables 'non-application' of the General Agreement between particular contracting parties.)

This issue of 'safeguards' under Article XIX was one of the items on the Tokyo Round agenda. The Ministerial declaration stipulated that negotiations should aim "to include an examination of the adequacy of the multilateral safeguard system, considering particularly the modalities of application of Article XIX, with a view to furthering trade liberalisation and preserving its results" [2].

This formulation must also be seen against the more general objective and promises made to the Third World that negotiations shall aim to "secure additional benefits for the international trade of developing countries so as to achieve a substantial increase in their foreign exchange earnings, the diversification of their exports, the acceleration of the rate of growth of their trade... a substantial improvement in the conditions of access for the products of interest to the developing countries and..." [3].

Soon after the launch of the Tokyo Round (and almost as a price for it), the ICs had pushed through the Multifibre Arrangement (MFA) in Textiles and Clothing, to replace the Long-term Cotton Textiles Agreement and extend the special regime that derogated from GATT principles to textiles and clothing made of synthetic fibre and wool also. The MFA incorporated in it the concepts of 'market disruption' and 'low-cost' imports which ran counter to theories of 'free trade' based on comparative advantage. Encouraged by this, other industries in the North - leather, footwear, cutlery and other miscellaneous goods - had begun their clamour for similar protection for themselves.

It was against this background that negotiations on safeguards were conducted in the Tokyo Round. All Third World countries , and many smaller ICs were opposed to any loosening of the strict standards and criteria of Article XIX. Actions under Article XIX of GATT have to be on the basis of the non-discrimination provisions of GATT in Article I, and applied against all sources of imports. ICs have been hesitant to invoke this provision, since such a general restriction would invite retaliation from their powerful trading partners. The EEC countries wanted to introduce the concept of 'selective safeguards' - the right to take emergency protective action against some but not all sources of imports - and the move was resisted by the Third World countries.

As a result, no agreement could be reached in the Tokyo Round, not even when the negotiations on this were continued in a Committee on Safeguards, with a mandate to submit a report by June 1980 [4]. The issue was given high priority in the subsequent work programme - as "an essential element" and to be carried out "as a matter of urgency". But with the EEC sticking to its demand for 'selectivity', there were no results. The subject figured in the 1982 Ministerial agenda and was put on the 1982 work programme, but again with no results. During the preparations for the launching of the new round Brazil, India and a few others sought to make this a pre-condition but failed. The issue is now on the agenda of the Uruguay Round.

The Punta del Este mandate on Safeguards reads: (i) A comprehensive agreement on safeguards is of particular importance to the strengthening of the GATT system and to progress in the MTNs. (ii) The agreement on safeguards:

(1) shall be based on the *basic principles* of the General Agreement (emphasis added);

(2) shall contain, *inter alia*, the following elements: transparency, coverage, objective criteria for action including the concept of serious injury or threat thereof, temporary nature, degressivity and structural adjustment, compensation and retaliation, notification, consultation, multilateral surveillance and dispute settlement; and

(3) shall clarify and reinforce the disciplines of the General Agreement and shall apply to all contracting parties.

The safeguards issue is perhaps the most important issue on the Uruguay Round agenda and the success of the Uruguay Round might well depend on the achievement of the comprehensive agreement on safeguards mandated by Ministers.

Few questions have brought the entire GATT and its system into such disrepute as the way its powerful trading blocs have evaded or ignored the GATT rules and principles and requirements of Article XIX while taking 'safeguard' actions. Often these actions to protect 'domestic industry' have been taken outside GATT and in violation of the spirit if not the letter of the GATT provisions, through so-called 'grey area' measures (voluntary export restraints, orderly marketing arrangements, price understandings, industry-to-industry arrangements and the like).

If the Uruguay Round ends, like the Tokyo Round, without an agreement on Safeguards or one providing for 'selective safeguards' or even one that does not specifically require application of the principle of non-discrimination, GATT will cease to be relevant or of benefit to the Third World, and their governments should seriously ponder whether continued association with GATT benefits them in any way and whether they would not be better off by collective or selective disassociation or neglect.

By their reference to the importance of a comprehensive agreement on safeguards, in terms of not only strengthening of the GATT system but "to progress in the MTNs", the Ministers in a sense have indirectly identified this (in addition to Tropical Products) as an issue where they envisaged an 'early agreement'.

However, in the first two years of the round, not only has there been no progress, but every sign of retrogression. At the time of the Tokyo Round, the EEC was the only one seeking the right to impose 'selective' safeguards. Now most of the major trading partners privately support this, knowing it will be used only against Third World countries.

The EEC has now also taken the position, which it began espousing during the preparatory stage, that even as it is safeguard actions that are contrary to Article I (MFN provision) are permitted. But a plain reading of the Article, which envisages suspension by a cp of its GATT obligations in specified circumstances provides no support for this view. Where the General Agreement has intended an 'exception' to prevail over all other provisions, for example the security exception provisions in Article XXI, this is made specific by the wording 'Nothing in this Agreement...' Article XIII relating to quantitative restrictions or prohibitions makes it clear that it has to be always on a non-discriminatory basis. Article XII, which enables such restrictions to be imposed for balance-of-payments reasons, is stipulated to be the exception to the general prohibition in Article XI.

Privately, the US [5] and other industrialised countries, and even senior GATT officials, have been advising the Third World countries to take note of 'political realities' and accept selectivity, but under conditions of transparency and multilateral surveillance etc. This will be no different from the MFA and such arrangements. Once in place, whether as a specific amendment to GATT or as a code, it would become permanent, and like the MFA restrictions will remain in perpetuity.

It appears 'reasonable', when the 'selectivity' argument is presented in terms of a country that faces a sudden upsurge of imports at low prices (which causes serious injury to its domestic producers) having to take limited measures against the source of the imports, rather than against all sources.

However, seen in practical terms, the risks of agreeing to 'selectivity' are clear: the weaker partners will be hit, there will be scope for actions based on political grounds, each one of the sources of supply will be tackled individually, and the net outcome will be injury for all. Unless a comprehensive safeguards agreement, based on non-discriminatory and other principles set out in the Punta del Este mandate, is concluded Third World countries will remain at the receiving end of discriminatory treatment in GATT in respect of all their exports, as is their experience under the MFA and its protocols.

Selective Safeguards Will Make GATT Itself A SUPER-MFA

All Third World exports will be subject to discriminatory import restrictions in the markets of the OECD countries, and the Third World countries would be competing with each other to get 'quotas' - in return for which in future they would

be forced to give away some benefit or other to the importing countries, and will find themselves subject to pressures
from   quota-holders in their own countries to retain the
benefits.

The EEC has also been taking the position that the 'grey
area' measures are not specifically prohibited and hence
legal, and thus not within the scope of the Safeguards Negotiations or Agreement. But given the general view that the
GATT Trading System has lost all credibility because of the
proliferation of such measures, which are clearly intended to
get around the GATT obligations and bend the rules for the
benefit of the stronger trading partners, such an interpretation
would be counter to the mandate's requirement that the
purpose of a safeguards agreement would be the strengthening of the GATT system.

The US has also now taken the view that 'grey area'
measures are legitimate and not illegal. The changes in US
law, relating to provisions for 'safeguard' actions - S.1401 of
the US Trade and Omnibus Act amending existing Sections
201-204 and S.405 (definition and determination of 'market
disruption') - now sanction VERs and other such measures
and strengthen the President's hand in negotiating such arrangements with US trade partners.

The US International Trade Commission (USITC), in
dealing with petitions from domestic industry for protection
and in its investigations, is mandated to look (as a sign of
injury entitling petitioners for relief) at the extent to which
the domestic firm is unable to generate adequate capital to
finance   modernisation of its plants or maintain levels of R
and D expenditure and the extent to which the US market
has become the focus for diversion of exports because of restraints in third country markets. Neither of these are under
the control of an exporting country, but that country will
nevertheless be penalised. The standards to assess whether
the imports are the 'substantial cause' of injury to the domestic producer are also changed. Apart from recommending

imposition of tariffs or quotas, the USITC can hereafter also recommend that the Administration initiate international negotiations to address the underlying causes for increase in imports or otherwise 'alleviate the injury or threat'. This is not a change from existing law, but does reiterate and strengthen existing tendencies for discriminatory relief options (through 'grey area' measures). The President's hand to negotiate such measures is also strengthened by the provision that "If the President takes action under this section other than the implementation of orderly marketing agreements, the President may, after such action takes effect, negotiate orderly marketing agreements with foreign countries, and may, after such agreements take effect, suspend or terminate in whole or in part, any action previously taken". The intent is very clear: the administration can impose some measures and, using that as a lever, negotiate and secure from weaker trading partners OMAs and other such arrangements.

MTN Agreements and Arrangements

The Punta del Este Mandate in this area provides that "Negotiations shall aim to improve, clarify, or expand, as appropriate, agreements and arrangements negotiated in the Tokyo Round of Multilateral Negotiations".

The Tokyo Round resulted in six agreements or arrangements on non-tariff issues, generally known as the Tokyo Round codes. These are: The Agreement on Technical Barriers to Trade, The Agreement on Government Procurement, The Agreement on Interpretations and Application of Articles VI, XVI and XXIII or the 'Subsidies Code', The Agreement on Implementation of Article VII or the 'Customs Valuation Code', The Agreement on Import Licensing Procedures, and The Agreement on Implementation of Article VI or the 'Anti-Dumping Code'. There were also three separate sectoral agreements: Arrangement Regarding Bovine Meat, The International Dairy Arrangements, and the Agreement on Trade in

Civil Aircraft [6].

These were essentially negotiated amongst the US, EEC and Japan, and placed before other participants, and particularly Third World countries on a 'take-it-or-leave-it' basis. The principle of special and differential treatment to Third World countries, promised in the Declaration launching the round, were largely ignored.

This imposition by the developed countries met with resistance from the Third World countries only in the case of the Customs Valuation Code. In this case, the Third World countries formulated their own code and tabled it. The major point of difference in the code of the Third World countries (apart from the longer time period sought for these countries to apply the code) related to the provision that the burden of proof to show that the relationship between buyer and seller had not influenced the price lay with the importer. At first both the codes were thrown open for signature - a procedure that was clearly in violation of the Vienna Law of Treaties. But the complications of GATT having to deal with two differing codes, with perhaps the code signed by the more numerous Third World signatories having an edge in terms of International Law, persuaded the major trading partners to negotiate and find a compromise. The hands of the Customs Authorities in dealing with 'related parties' and their claims about transaction value were slightly strengthened, by making clear that the provisions would not in any way restrict or call into question the right of customs administrations to satisfy themselves about the truth or otherwise of any statement, document or declaration presented for customs valuation purposes.

Signatories to the various codes undertook more obligations and got more benefits. But overall Third World countries saw little of additional benefits to them in the codes, and few joined. Adherence has ranged from two (to the Civil Aircraft and Government Procurement codes) to fifteen (for the code on Technical Barriers to Trade). All ICs adhere to the codes, but a large number of Third World countries have stayed out of them. This has resulted in a two-tier GATT, and the fragmentation of the entire GATT system [7].

Though negotiated under GATT auspices, and termed as part of the General Agreement and merely interpretations of the existing Articles, in fact all the codes are separate mechanisms. Unlike GATT, some of them are fully ratified treaties. The signatories have undertaken to strictly carry out the trade policies and obligations defined in the codes, and bring their legislations and administrative procedures in line with the provisions of the respective codes. In the case of GATT and its protocol of provisional application, they have only agreed to apply the provisions of Part II of the GATT relating to non-tariff measures "to the fullest extent not inconsistent with existing legislation" [8].

The relationship of the codes to the General Agreement is defined only in terms of the Decision of the Contracting Parties at their 35th Session. The Decision specifically reaffirmed "the intention of the CPs to ensure the unity and consistency of the GATT system", and also noted that "existing rights and benefits under the GATT, including those derived from Article I, are not affected by the new Agreements" [9]. This intention and promise appears to have largely fallen by the wayside in the ten years of the operation of the Codes. The GATT system has become largely fragmented, with separate sub-systems and their own rules applicable only to signatories.

As noted, the adherents to the code provide conditional application to signatories, with benefits to them. More serious, there are adverse effects to exports of non-signatories. This is justified on the ground that if some countries are willing to accept higher obligations they should get higher benefits. But it violates the specific affirmation of the CONTRACTING PARTIES in 1979, when the Tokyo Round agreements were incorporated into GATT, about the unity of the General Agreement. It is a reversion to the conditional MFN

concepts of the inter-war years, with all its disastrous consequences that led to the formation of the GATT and its unconditional MFN principle. Also, those who are parties to the
code demand their own price, apart from the obligations of
the code, before consenting to allow new members to come
in and enjoy the benefits.

Apart from this, the code approach has strengthened the
tendency inside GATT of not taking into account the views
and concerns of the smaller and less interesting countries
(from the viewpoint of their trade weight) and for the more
powerful to agree among themselves and present it to others
to accept it on pain of being excluded from the rights and
gradually marginalised from the system. There has even been
serious talk that GATT decisions and its 'consensus' approach
must reflect the trade weights. Even in practice now, in the
GATT bodies and in the Uruguay Round negotiating bodies,
when any of the three major trading partners say 'no', the
lack of consensus is quickly recognised. But when smaller
countries say 'no' it is ignored and sought to be brushed
aside. Even if such a country openly blocks the consensus,
the threat of others acting outside the GATT framework to
achieve the same purpose is being held out.

For example, in the case of the subsidies and countervailing measures code, the benefit of adherence is that the
US will apply to them the GATT 'injury' test, which it was ob-
ligated to do but had not been doing under the so-called
'grandfather clause' privilege. All the other major and minor
trading partners already do so. On a plain reading, the US
should extend the benefit of the 'injury' test it applies to the
signatories of the subsidies code to all contracting parties to
the GATT, whether they are signatories or not of the code.
This is an obligation under the MFN principle of Article I of
the GATT. But the US has declined to do this and none of the
Third World countries affected find themselves strong enough
to challenge the US. Even more serious is the US demand
that Third World countries wishing to adhere to the code,
which specifically enables them to adopt some subsidy prac-

tices they deem necessary from their 'trade and development needs', should enter into bilateral agreement with the US to phase-out these practices and undertake the higher level of commitments. None of the other signatories have even objected to this US demand.

The major challenge thus is how to ensure full application of the special and differential treatment principles, both of the General Agreement and in the codes, that would enable and encourage Third World countries to adhere to the codes, and also ensure that the codes function in a way that would ensure the unity of GATT. With few Third World countries actually members of the codes, and the revision of such codes viewed as an 'autonomous process' for code members, it is difficult to envisage how these problems will be tackled in the round, unless the Third World countries could take concerted steps.

Subsidies and Countervailing Measures

The mandate relating to the MTN codes (of which the Subsidies and Anti-Dumping code is a part) overlaps with that on Subsidies and Countervailing Measures where it is provided that "negotiations shall be based on a review of Article VI and XVI and the MTN agreement on subsidies and countervailing measures with the objective of improving GATT disciplines relating to all subsidies and countervailing mea-sures that affect international trade". A separate negotiating group has also been mandated to deal with this subject.

The codes relating to subsidies, and anti-dumping and countervailing measures, as also the GATT articles themselves raise some very important problems.

There is no general prohibition of subsidies as such in GATT. But there is a general obligation to notify and consult on any subsidies that directly or indirectly increase exports or reduce imports. In the event of 'serious prejudice' to any

other cp by such subsidisation, there   are provisions for
consultation, with a view to possible reduction of such subsidisation.

As far as 'export subsidies' are concerned, cps are to
'avoid' its use on export of 'primary products', or if used and
it increases the export of any primary product, the subsidy
should not be applied in a manner that results in the cp
concerned having more than an 'equitable share' of world
export trade in that product. The term 'primary product' in
GATT means the product of farm, forestry or fishery, or
any mineral, in its natural form or which has undergone
'such processing as is customarily required to prepare it for
marketing in substantial volume in international trade'. All
these have given rise to considerable controversies among
the ICs themselves because of the difficulties of interpretation, including the concept of 'equitable share'. A ruling in
a dispute between the US and EEC over pasta exports (where
domestic wheat in the community is available to pasta pro-
ducer/exporters at subsidised prices), which   probably is a
bad ruling, has resulted in the US pushing for changes on
the 'subsidy question' across the board. Whatever the compromises the ICs might ultimately reach, it would affect the
Third World countries.

As far as products 'other than primary products' are concerned, as of Jan 1, 1958, there is a complete ban on use of
export subsidies by the ICs. Thus, in terms of the General
Agreement, ICs are not supposed to give any subsidy for
manufactured or processed products. But the fact is that ICs
continue to provide subsidies in one form or another, and
this gives rise to problems of 'countervailing' which were
sought to be tackled by the Tokyo Round.

In the Tokyo Round Code, the subsidy practices which
the major partners agreed to eliminate were put into an
annex to the code. But those they could not agree upon, or
which they have been carrying out under the 'security exception' provisions (such as in military financed research and

development etc) were left alone. The net result is that while most of the practices of Third World countries (used by them to compensate for special disadvantages such as higher shipping freight for their exports or for market promotion to tackle the rigid market structures in export markets for new comers) are prohibited, such things as aid-credit mixes or non-trade benefits that the ICs can provide to promote their own exports are not.

As noted earlier, the subsidies code specifically recognises the right of Third World countries to subsidise their production and exports to meet development needs and compensate for their other disadvantages, making their phase-out an autonomous decision for the countries concerned. But the US made accession of Third World countries conditional on their bilateral agreement with the US to phase out such practices (even though sanctioned by the code).

This entire situation has enabled the ICs to use anti-dumping and countervailing duties against competitive imports, thus obviating the need for any 'safeguard actions'. While such actions affect all trading partners, the negative effects on Third World countries are greater. The number of cases initiated against Third World countries have also increased recently. Between 1980-1984, the number of cases targeted against the Third World as a proportion of total cases were in the 18 to 38 percent range. Between 1985-1988, they had gone up to the 45 to 53 percent range. Even the start of proceedings for such actions is a sufficient harassment and deterrent, and is the instrument used to 'persuade' the exporting Third World country concerned to accept voluntary export restraints, orderly marketing arrangements and other such 'grey area measures'.

Improving GATT disciplines in this area would clearly need clarifications and/or changes in the GATT provisions. It is their ambiguity that the powerful trading nations have used to further their own interests to the detriment of the smaller trading partners and the system itself.

In respect of primary products, the problems have re-lated to the provision that exporters should not resort to subsidies if it results in 'more than an equitable share'. This phrase has been responsible for many disputes. At the same time attempts to clarify them would necessarily lead to some 'market-sharing' arrangements to the detriment of new-com-ers. The real solution, but one that may elude negotiators, is to prohibit or substantially limit export subsidies on primary products by amending the relevant GATT Article and/or the relevant provision in the code.

Side by side the procedures for notification and multi-lateral surveillance would need to be strengthened. The sub-sidies code has already recognised the need for, and the right of, Third World countries to subsidise their exports in order to overcome various structural and other disadvantages faced by their exports. What is necessary is for major trading part-ners, and particularly the US, to recognise this (including their autonomous decision in phasing them out) and to ensure its implementation in practice. Their budgetary and economic situations alone will act as a curb on their subsidies. Also, the Third World countries account for so small a proportion of world trade that in practice their subsidies will have only marginal effects on world trade, though in specific areas and circumstances it could cause concern to their trading partners that could be tackled through consultation procedures.

Other major questions that would need to be tackled are those relating to laying down of agreed criteria in judging 'material injury' to domestic producers, which would entitle a country to impose countervailing duties against a subsidised export. Coupled to it would be remedies or compensation for exporters who are now subject to trade harassment through complaints. Even the starting of an investigation and lengthy hearing procedure could result in losses in trade opportunties, even if the complaints prove frivolous.

There is also a serious flaw in the negotiating process. The US is keen to introduce further disciplines on subsidies, including alteration of permissible subsidies for developing countries. The Tokyo Round code, for example, recognises that subsidies are an integral part of development programmes of these countries, and subject to some provisions for commitment to phase out when the country concerned finds such subsidies to be inconsistent with its development or competitive needs, developing country-members of the code have considerable leeway about assistance measures to their industry including the export sector. The US wants to discipline these and others. At the same time the US is not keen to accept any disciplines on its own capacity to take countervailing measures, which as several UNCTAD and GATT reports bring out are increasingly used by ICs to protect their industries. But it is not certain that the ICs would really tackle these problems and do so in a manner that would meet the legitimate concerns of the Third World countries.

GATT Articles

The mandate in this area provides: "Participants shall review existing GATT Articles, provisions and disciplines as requested by interested contracting parties, and, as appropriate, undertake negotiations".

The negotiating plan envisages interested cps submitting requests for review of specific articles, provisions and disciplines, for review of the articles on this basis, and determination of issues on which negotiations are appropriate.

About 15 articles have been suggested for review and for negotiations for changes. Most of the suggestions have come from the US, and some from the EEC. The latter has also suggested review of the protocol of provisional application, because of what it considers as abuse of the 'grandfather clause' privileges by the US. Some of the Third World countries too have suggested review of some articles and provisions, including Article XXIV which enables establishment of customs unions and free trade areas. Originally viewed as a step towards a world free of trade barriers, the provisions for customs unions and free trade areas have been abused to create large trading blocs with 'free' or preferential trade within them and with barriers to outsiders.

The Articles suggested for review include II, XI, XII, XIII, XV, XVII, XVIII, XXI, XXIV, XXV, XXVIII. Articles VI, XVI, XIX and XXIII, which fall within the ambit of other negotiating groups have also been mentioned.

In respect of Article XVII, dealing with State Trading Enterprises, there are proposals for expanding the rules and make them more stringent so that in a situation of substantially liberalised trade countries that use State Trading Enterprises are not in an unfair advantage.

Article XXVIII deals with situations where countries seek to re-negotiate their concessions. This is to be done currently with countries with whom the concessions were exchanged and those with 'principal supplying interest'. A number of smaller countries have sought changes in the definition of 'principal supplying interest' to safeguard the rights of 'small suppliers'. While the weight of their exports to a particular market may not be large, the exports themselves may have considerable weight in their domestic economy and any concessions affecting that trade could have serious consequences for them.

The review of Article XXIV and changes sought are to take account of the widespread growth of preferential regional arrangements, among ICs and between ICs and groups of Third World countries with adverse effect on those not beneficiaries. The suggestion is that the Article must be reviewed and changes introduced to ensure that the GATT's MFN principle is not undermined by such arrangements and no barriers are erected against the trade of third parties. The EEC's single market in 1992 makes this even more urgent.

The main issue in regard to the review of the protocol

of provisional application (sought by the EEC, but supported by others) is whether the 'grandfather clause' privilege should still persist after 41 years of the existence of the General Agreement.

While changes in some one or other of these articles are of interest to Third World countries too, the proposals that will affect them most are the proposals from the US for review and negotiations for amending Articles XII, XIV, XV and XVIII. Article XII deals with restrictions to safeguard Balance of Payments, Article XIV is a related article providing for Exceptions to the Rule of Non-discrimination, Article XV deals with Exchange Arrangements, and Article XVIII relates to Governmental Assistance to Economic Development. Though the four articles have been cited together, the real target is Part B of Article XVIII [10].

In conjunction with proposals in other negotiating areas, the proposals in this area, if effected, would change the nature of GATT as a multilateral trading system.

The US wants changes in the provisions in these articles that enable Third World countries to impose quantitative restrictions on grounds of balance of payments considerations. The basic thrust of the US and other ICs is to force Third World countries to take recourse to the provisions of Part C of that Article, where any actions to protect infant industry or promote development, would involve 'compensating' other cps for any impairment of their GATT rights or facing unilateral retaliations. The BOP restrictions themselves are sought to be made time-bound.

From the beginning Third World countries had consistently sought recognition of their special trade problems, and for its incorporation into the contractual framework of the GATT trading system. To meet their viewpoint, Article XVIII was amended in 1955 (and became effective in 1957). Part IV, providing for special and differential treatment to Third World countries, was incorporated into GATT in 1964; but these are only recommendatory provisions, and the industrial cps agreed to it on a best endeavour, and not contractual basis.

Till 1955, when the major review of GATT articles was undertaken, the BOP problems of Third World and other countries were dealt with under Article XII. These provisions are a kind of 'escape' clause, to enable countries to escape from the prohibitions against quantitative restrictions on imports (qrs), when they face BOP problems. This was a safeguard that Britain and other European countries insisted upon as a safety valve against their commitments to move towards currency convertibility. As Keynes put it: "I feel the gravest doubts whether we can accept convertibility if we are entirely cut off from using at our own discretion non-discriminatory quantitative regulation... To try and create an international system which excludes quantitative regulation is out of date and I should have thought impracticable... You must have some way of cutting off imports which you cannot afford. Of the various alternatives quantitative regulations is at the same time much the most effective and the most in tune with the modern world" [11].

The BOP situations envisaged under the Article are seen as of a cyclical nature. In 1955, the contention of the Third World countries about the structural nature of their problem was accepted, and Article XVIII was incorporated into GATT. Article XVIII:B enables them to impose tariff and quantitative restrictions on account of their balance of payments considerations, while XVIII:C permits introduction of restrictions to promote the establishment of an industry or (after the 1979 decision of the Contracting Parties) to develop, modify or extend production structures in accordance with their economic development.

XVIII:B recognised that Third World countries encountered BOP problems of a persistent and structural nature, mainly because on the one hand their demand for imports rises as a result of implementation of development plans, and on the other their export receipts do not increase because of the instability of their terms of trade.

Third World countries invoking Article XVIII:B rights undergo surveillance about their BOP situation and other criteria. Their situation is periodically examined by the BOP committee, where they have to satisfy the committee about their BOP situation and prospects, and justify their actions.

But in invoking this article, Third World countries have greater leeway than under Article XII (the general provision) that is available to all cps and used by ICs until their currencies became convertible, but invoked, if at all, very rarely now.

Restrictions imposed under Article XII are intended to be 'temporary' to meet the cyclical problems. By recognising that the BOP problems of the Third World are 'structural', Article XVIII enables the continuance of restrictions for longer periods, and as an autonomous decision.

Third World countries could impose restrictions when they consider their reserves are 'inadequate'. Even more, they can vary the incidence of their restrictions on different products or classes of products and give priority to importation of those considered essential on the basis of their development policies and objectives, and this is specifically affirmed to be an autonomous decision of theirs. In the review of their BOP restrictions, any challenge on the ground that adoption of other policies would obviate the BOP problems are precluded.

Several arguments have been advanced by the ICs to justify changes. Firstly, it is argued that the floating exchange rate system and the enhanced role of the IMF in the Third World have obviated the need for such actions. Even in respect of the ICs themselves, the persistence of glaring imbalances among the major trading partners (US, Japan and Germany) are proof that the floating exchange rate system is not the panacea that it has been made out to be. There is now enough evidence and recognition that the system has increased the instability for Third World countries, and the size of reserves that they have to maintain for normal trading purposes has increased, particularly because their access to short-term funds have become more difficult. In fact, as Frances Stewart points out, "the initial justification for Section B, which was phrased in terms of structural and persistent BOP problems arising from combination of development needs and external instability, has been reinforced and not weakened by changes in the world economy" [12].

Stewart adds: "The external environment facing developing countries in the 1980s is without question much more hostile than in any of the previous three decades... The references in Section B of Article XVIII to 'instability in their terms of trade' has not been invalidated by recent events - indeed there is good reason to extend the phrase to include adverse trends as well as fluctuations not only in terms of trade... but also in market access, and to fluctuations and adverse trends in the capital account. In any review... there would be a strong case for replacing the phrase 'instability in their terms of trade' by 'instability and adverse trends in their external environment'" [13].

There is also the neo-classical view of the IMF and the World Bank that qrs are more inefficient than devaluation in resource allocation between export and import sectors of an economy and that where imports have to be restricted tariffs are superior. Excepting as asserted self-evident truths there seems to be little proof of this. In most Third World countries with structural rigidities devaluation does not even achieve the purpose of switching from imports for domestic consumption to exports, and in fact it increases social and other inequalities, weighing heavily on the poor. QRs are also quick acting and can be imposed selectively [14]. Their inefficient administration or the corruption that they give rise to or the rentier incomes for quota holders are abuses that acknowledgedly have to be tackled by countries, but not by throwing the baby out with the bath water.

In fact the external environment facing Third World countries (rising debt burdens, less capital flows, protectionist barriers and terms of trade losses) is much more hostile and adverse than in the 50s and 60s. Their BOP problems, particularly in those many countries dependent on primary-product exports, have also become more persistent. Their case for special treatment is higher than ever before.

The US is trying to attack these rights, and restrict the ability to invoke these provisions. Among other things it wants the restrictions pro rata across the board, and not through QRs. But QRs are an essential need for the Third World countries for rationing available foreign exchange, and for promoting structural changes in their industrial sectors to make them conducive to development.

Third World countries have so far refused to take up for negotiations the BOP provisions applicable to them. In effect this group of issues is stuck at the initial negotiation phase. But while all Third World countries seem to be united, again few speak out. Unless more Third World countries speak out and take a stand, there is a serious danger of their agreeing by default to take up the articles for review and negotiations. The outcome will be serious jeopardy to their development prospects and programmes.

Dispute Settlement

Another negotiating issue of some general importance, and particularly for Third World countries and the smaller ICs, is the one relating to Dispute Settlement. The dispute settlement mechanism of GATT is an important part of its structure and had been intended by the framers to enable contracting parties to resolve trade conflicts and settle their disputes, without recourse to the pre-GATT practices of unilateral trade retaliations. The GATT provisions and procedures provide that when disputes arise, parties concerned first seek 'consultations' under Article XXII, and if they are

unable to settle them directly, refer the matter to the Contracting Parties (or the GATT Council in practice). Panels are
then named to hear the parties and give a ruling relating to
the GATT rights of the parties and recommend solutions to
the dispute. The reports are adopted and the concerned cp
is expected to carry out the recommendations and make the
necessary changes in its trade policy. Failing this, the complaining cp gets the permission or authorisation of the
CONTRACTING PARTIES to retaliate by withdrawing concessions equivalent to the damage it has been found to have
suffered. In the past trade disputes were few and far between. When panels gave a ruling, these were adopted by
the GATT Council and they were invariably carried out. In
very rare cases where the cp concerned had difficulties in
carrying out the recommendation, it negotiated with the
complainant and provided compensatory concessions in
some other area.

But in recent years, the smooth functioning of the
mechanism has been impaired by the rise in the number of
trade disputes, the difficulties in getting a panel appointed,
particularly when the party against whom there is a complaint is a major trading partner. Framing the terms of reference of the panels and agreeing upon panelists have also
been time-consuming and at the end of the process the
adoption of panel reports has also been blocked. In the dispute between Nicaragua and the US over the cut in its sugar
export quotas, the panel ruled against the US. The latter
allowed the report to be adopted but said it would not comply
and Nicaragua could retaliate by withdrawing equivalent
concessions, a remedy difficult enough for any major trading
partner to use but non-available for smaller trading partners.

It was against this background that the Punta del Este
declaration put this issue on the agenda and provided:

"In order to ensure prompt and effective resolution of
disputes to the benefit of all contracting parties, negotiations shall aim to improve and strengthen the rules

and the procedures of the dispute settlement process, while recognising the contribution that would be made by more effective and enforceable GATT rules and disciplines. Negotiations shall include the development of adequate arrangements for overseeing and monitoring of the procedures that would facilitate compliance with adopted recommendations".

There have been previous attempts to rectify the deficiencies of the dispute settlement mechanisms. It was discussed during the Tokyo Round, and resulted in the adoption of an "Understanding regarding notification, consultation, dispute settlement and surveillance" and in some technical and procedural modifications [15]. But these have not solved the problems and the number of unresolved problems has been increasing.

There have been a number of proposals for improvements: composition of panels (with reliance on roster of panelists and non-governmental experts), standard terms of reference for panels, improvement of positions of third parties before panels and in subsequent proceedings (currently if parties decide a dispute any time before the reports of the panel come up for adoption, third parties interested have no say), time limits for agreeing to set up panels (with establishment of panels to be treated as an unconditional right of the complainant) and agreeing to terms of reference and panelists, adoption of reports (with proposals for excluding the disputants in judging whether or not there is a consensus for adoption).

But the basic problem of securing compliance with panel reports, and for contracting parties committing themselves to abide by the panel rulings and recommendations of the CONTRACTING PARTIES remains. The US has flatly refused to undertake any commitment to adjust and/or administer its domestic trade laws and enforcement procedures in a manner ensuring conformity of all measures with GATT dispute settlement procedures. Unless this fundamental obligation is acknowledged and implemented, by the US and other major trading partners, all talk of strengthening and improving GATT's dispute settlement mechanisms and of the system will remain empty words and GATT itself will continue to lose credibility.

Functioning of the GATT System (FOGS)

The Punta del Este mandate provides that, while reviewing the functioning of the GATT system, contracting parties "shall aim to develop understandings and arrangements:

(i) to enhance the surveillance in the GATT to enable regular monitoring of trade policies and practices of contracting parties and their impact on the functioning of the multilateral trading system;

(ii) to improve the overall effectiveness and decision-making of the GATT as an institution, including *inter alia* through involvement of ministers;

(iii) to increase the contribution of the GATT to achieving greater coherence in global economic policy-making through strengthening its relationship with other international institutions responsible for monetary and financial matters."

The acronym for this group aptly sums up the veritable fog that has surrounded the discussions and negotiations in this area in the first two years of negotiations. From the outset the GATT Secretariat and the chairman of the Negotiating Group, Julian Katz, a former US State Department official (who has become in the Bush administration a deputy to the USTR) have been trying to push objectives, shared by the US, EEC and Japan, but which are not in the mandate, namely, creation of a GATT mechanism that could be used to bring the entire range of economic policies and objectives of Third World countries under review. This is also sought to be done, not in terms of their GATT obligations, but of some vague GATT/Fund/Bank economic philosophy. Another effort has been to create a small ministerial steering group in GATT, to manipulate and manage the trading system, just as the G3 or G5 are trying to do in the monetary and financial area. This is in practical implementation of the theory that the management of the trading system should be in the hands of the few who have the largest trade weight in the world.

The mandate in this area was framed by ministers essentially to find a response to the growing criticism of GATT in recent years, and examine its functioning in its entirety. The operation of the system has been of increasing concern to both industrial and Third World countries. A basic reason for GATT's increasing lack of credibility is the conduct of the major trading partners, who have been functioning in disregard of their GATT obligations and increasingly resorting to bilateralism and recourse to 'grey area' measures, and seeking modus vivendi among themselves to manage world trade.

Hence the mandate about enhancing the 'surveillance' to enable monitoring of trade policies and practices of cps and their impact on the functioning of the multilateral trading system. By any logic it is the policies and practices of the major cps, and not of the smaller ones, that impact on the trading system. The trade policies and practices of Third World countries are already subject to surveillance in GATT, because of their invoking BOP provisions, just as their monetary and economic policies are under IMF and World Bank review. The whole purpose of the Punta del Este mandate was to bring the policies and practices in the trade area of the ICs, and particularly of the major trading partners which have the greatest impact on the system, under 'surveillance'. But 'surveillance' is one thing that the US, EEC or Japan do not want. They do not want to have their 'grey area' measures and other instruments of managed trade to be questioned or subject to multilateral scrutiny.

In deference to these viewpoints, the chairman's discussion papers in the negotiating group even eschewed the use of the word 'surveillance', suggesting instead 'trade policy review' and using this terminology to achieve other objectives. There have been repeated and open complaints in the group that viewpoints of Third World countries have been ignored in the chairman's papers and that even the minutes prepared by the secretariat have been somewhat partisan. At the Montreal midterm review meeting in December 1988, when there was an attempt to achieve this objective, (through steamroller tactics, by pushing for visits to capitals by GATT visiting missions and the secretariat and inquisitorial examination of officials of countries by these missions), there was an open confrontation between the secretariat and the Swiss delegate who chaired the private negotiations and Brazilian and Indian delegates. The ensuing difficult situation was resolved only when the secretariat retreated and some of these ideas were given up or made 'voluntary' [16].

On the portion of the mandate (under the third indent) relating to GATT's contribution to global economic policy making by strengthening relationship with other international organisations responsible for monetary and financial affairs, the whole effort in the negotiations has been to center all these activities or efforts in a GATT/Fund/Bank mechanism. This ignores the fact that there are already UN fora dealing with these issues. The UN General Assembly and ECOSOC are supposed to help in bringing in overall coherence. UNCTAD is already preoccupied with, and discusses every year, the subject of interdependence of issues (trade, money, finance and development) and of economies.

If all these have not contributed to greater coherence in global economic policy-making, it has been because the US and other major industrial countries have prevented decisions or agreed conclusions in all these fora, even arguing against it on the ground that it would lead to 'management' of the global economy. But they now want to do it in the

GATT forum, and use trade to force GATT/Bank philoso-phies on the Third World. This would place Third World countries and their economies under the trusteeship of the Fund-Bank-GATT institution's and their secretariats.

Graduation

This issue is not specifically on the agenda, but is being brought forward under various heads, and in negotiating groups. The Punta del Este mandate specifically reaffirmed, as a general principle governing the negotiations the con-cepts of 'special and differential treatment' in Part IV and in the Enabling Clause of 1979 [17].

Despite these clear words, not only is there no trend towards providing special and differential treatment, but every effort to 'graduate' these countries out of the benefits of the special and differential treatment, leaving only the least developed countries in this category.

The US Omnibus Trade and Competitiveness Act, 1988, has in fact listed 'Third World countries' as one of the nego-tiating issues for the administration.

And while procedural ideas and even gimmicks are being trotted out to improve dispute settlement and the FOGS, there has been no attention paid to the basic problem of Third World countries, namely securing observance of their con-tractual rights by the powerful and a mechanism to ensure compliance by the powerful. In the final analysis, the only enforcement in GATT is the right of a contracting party to 'retaliate', after authorisation. Apart from the fact that in es-sence this is a jungle law concept, Third World countries have no capacity to retaliate. There is no real effort to have a dispute settled through payment of compensation, or joint action by the Contracting Parties against an offending con-tracting party to force compliance with panel rulings.

Notes on Chapter 10

1. Developments in the negotiating process set out in this Chapter have to be read along with the relevant portions in Chapter 12 on the mid-term review accords in this area.

2. Para 3 (d) of the Declaration adopted by the Ministerial Meeting Tokyo (12-14 Sept. 1973), *'The Tokyo Round of Multilateral Trade Negotiations'*, Report by the Director-General of GATT (1979), Appendix B.

3. *Ibid*, para 2 of the Declaration.

4. Decision of Contracting Parties of Nov. 28, 1979, *Basic Instruments and Selected Documents* (BISD), 26th supplement, p 202 .

5. The US Omnibus Trade and Competitiveness Act of 1988, in its mandate to US negotiators on this issue, does not mention 'non-discrimination' at all. The Act virtually mandates the administration to seek VERs in steel, a grey area measure that is clearly illegal in GATT but one that has been proliferating. President Bush in his election campaign, virtually promised to renew the steel VERS, and his USTR, Mrs Carla Hills has in effect committed herself to continue the steel VERs.

6. For text of codes see *BISD*, 26th Supplement (1979), GATT, pp 8 - 188.

7. Of the 70 or more Third World cps, only 15 are members of one or the other of the Tokyo Round codes. Only 10 signed the subsidies code, and eight each the antidumping and customs valuation codes.

8. Text of the General Agreement, *GATT* ISBN 92-870-1022-6 p77.

9. *BISD*, 26th Supplement, p 201.

10. For an analysis of the economic theory and justification of the article and use of QRs for BOP purposes, see, Frances Stewart, 'Proposals for a Review of GATT Article XVIII: An Assessment', Uruguay Round: Papers on Selected Issues, *op. cit.*

11. John Maynard Keynes in *Moggeridge* (ed) pp 325-326, quoted by Frances Steward p 3, p 18.

12. Frances Stewart pp 5 - 6.

13. *Ibid* p 9.

14. *Ibid* pp 18 - 34.

15. See 'Understanding Regarding Notification, Consultation, Dispute Settlement and Surveillance', adopted by CPs on November 28, 1979; *BISD* 26th Supplement, pp 210 -218.

16. *SUNS* 2065 pp 6 - 7, and Chakravarthi Raghavan, 'Uruguay Round After Montreal', *Mainstream*, New Delhi Vol. XXVII No. 21 p 23.

17. Punta del Este Ministerial declaration, Part 1 B. (iv), (v), (vi) and (vii), Annex I. For text of the Enabling Clause see 28 November 1979 Decision of GATT CPs, 'Differential and More Favourable Treatment, Reciprocity and Fuller Participation of Developing Countries', *BISD* 26th Supplement pp 203 - 205.

PART IV

THE MIDTERM REVIEW AND AFTER

Chapter 11

THE MIDTERM REVIEW, DEC. 1988

Preparations for the Review

During the preparations for launching the Uruguay Round, and at Punta del Este, the US had pressed for early agreements. While this was mainly focussed on Agriculture - there was frequent talk about an "early harvest" - in the background was the idea of some interim accords in new themes, particularly services. The European Communities flatly rejected any "early harvest", since it would involve agriculture, and refused to budge.

As a result, the Punta del Este Declaration did not provide for any "early harvest" or "mid-term review" - a term that came into vogue much later. The TNC was established to carry out the negotiations, and it was directed to meet before 31 October 1986. It was further provided that the TNC "shall meet as appropriate at Ministerial level". The only deadline envisaged was that the round "will be concluded within four years".

The declaration viewed the GATT MTNs in goods as a single undertaking, but envisaged the possibility of early agreements in individual negotiating areas and their implementation provisionally [1]. However it specifically mentioned for early accord only Tropical Products and, by implication, a comprehensive agreement on 'Safeguards'.

But soon after Punta del Este, and as soon as the negotiating plans were agreed to and the negotiating groups began meeting, the US and its friends began talking of a mid-term review and "early harvest". The Cairns group gave full support from the beginning, viewing the term as basically requiring some interim accords in agriculture. Slowly the US got the other ICs to fall in line, though the EEC was ambivalent because of agriculture. It was willing to have an early short-term accord in agriculture, but only on its terms.

At an informal meeting of some trade ministers at Lausanne (Switzerland) in November 1987, it was agreed, at the instance of the US, to hold a ministerial-level mid-term review meeting in December 1988. Canada offered to host the meeting. The timing was dictated by the US domestic political calendar of a Presidential election year. Of the countries present there, only France would appear to have expressed some doubts. The French suggested either holding the meeting much earlier in 1988 or sometime early in 1989, after the new administration had taken over.

But the EEC Commission and other EC member states did not agree with France. As Commission officials privately explained at that time (December 1987), they believed that by agreeing to the mid-term review meeting they were strengthening the hands of the administration in fighting a protectionist Congress and that, in any event, and irrespective of which party won the White House, (though they themselves preferred the Republicans to the "protectionist" Democrats), they would have locked the United States into an "irreversible process".

This was a phrase that GATT officials also were using, and did so right till the Montreal meeting itself, though it was never clear whom they expected to "lock in". As late as November 10,1988, at a press conference after securing a fourth three-year term, the GATT Director-General Arthur Dunkel spoke of "a non-reversible situation (to be) achieved" at Montreal by the Ministers in respect of the

Uruguay Round Negotiations [2].

At the TNC meeting in December 1987, Switzerland, which had hosted the Lausanne informal meeting, broached the idea and spoke of a "growing consensus" in favour of a "mid-term review". At that stage, a few like Brazil and India advised caution over a negotiating process run on the basis of "event planning", while Jamaica questioned how the consensus had been established when this was the first time the idea was being mentioned in the TNC! [3].

The TNC formally agreed to the mid-term review meeting in February 1988, though the agenda and other formalities were settled only in July. The talk about "early harvest" was again revived. In a reference to this, at the meeting of the GNG preceding the TNC, the EEC said that under the Punta del Este Declaration "1990 was the date set for 'reaping the harvest' and as far as it was concerned there was no other time-table"[5]. This EEC stand, even while supporting the "mid-term review", was really a caveat that the EEC could agree to early accords in other areas but not in agriculture. It was clear by then that the US and EEC positions on short-term measures in agriculture (with US insisting on linking it to long-term policy reforms and commitments for "elimination" of all government support to agriculture within a ten-year period) were irreconcilable.

At the Paris OECD Ministerial meeting in the summer of 1988, the US pressed for an endorsement of the idea of a framework agreement on Agriculture at the mid-term review. But the EEC was totally opposed, and a compromise was achieved by talking of a framework approach on all issues at Montreal.

But the informal agreement of the 'majors' at Lausanne in 1987 had been enough to set the GATT machinery moving - ignoring Third World viewpoints, the mandate for negotiations in individual areas set out in the Punta del Este Ministerial Declaration, the compromises forged in intense private negotiations (involving the US, EEC, Brazil and India) which had enabled the launching of the round and the Negotiating Plan adopted by consensus in January 1987.

From early 1988, the negotiating process and pace in individual negotiating areas were being manipulated with an eye on a package of early accords for the mid-term review.

Excepting in Agriculture, where as already pointed out there was a basic US-EEC clash, from early 1988 the US, EEC and other ICs, as also the GATT Secretariat and the chairmen of several of the individual negotiating groups, began manoeuvring to ensure pre-determined results in the areas of interest to them, while the major concerns of the South were ignored [6].

In the two years of negotiations, progress in the individual negotiating areas had been highly uneven. Issues of concern to the Third World like negotiations on liberalisation of trade in Tropical Products, comprehensive Safeguards agreement and phasing out the MFA governing trade in Textiles and Clothing had been blocked or relegated to the background. On Textiles, in fact, the ICs did not even engage in dialogue, often sending to meetings of this negotiating group local junior officials. But issues of interest to the major ICs had been pushed to the forefront.

Though there was always talk of a "balanced package" of results from Montreal, the US-led strategy was to narrow the agenda of issues to be decided by Ministers to a few areas - TRIPs, Services, Agriculture, and GATT institutional issues like FOGS and Dispute Settlement. All these were issues where the US had something to gain but was not called upon to give anything. Until August 1988, the administration did not even have a negotiating mandate, which meant that any concessions by the administration would have to be okayed by Congress and no one would have been ready to sign any mid-term accords on that basis. Instead of abandoning or postponing the review, the ICs all settled for agreements in areas where the administration would not have to seek any approval from the Congress. However, for any mid-term accord in Agriculture the EEC would have had to pay a price. With this in mind, the EEC made repeated references to its view that the only area specifically mentioned for early accords was Tropical Products and nothing else [7].

Given this last fact, and the clearly indicated priority of sorts in the Punta del Este Declaration, everyone mentioned Tropical Products as an item for early accords, but hedged it in with many ifs and buts. The US tied it to Agriculture, and the EEC to 'contribution' by all (meaning Third World countries) and the concept of 'burden-sharing' (meaning liberalisation by all ICs).

Against this background, it proved very difficult to produce any agreed report out of many of the negotiating groups, particularly on the traditional issues where the US and others favoured nothing more than procedural decisions to continue to negotiate.

In some areas this approach suited the Third World countries. In the area of Non-Tariff Measures and Natural Resource-based Products technical preparations had not been completed to enable negotiations to begin and hence no early agreements could be concluded anyway: on TRIMs, GATT Articles, MTN Codes and Agreements they were quite content to let things drag on without conclusions. But they were not willing to agree to mere procedural decisions to continue negotiations in such areas as Textiles and Clothing or Safeguards, or agree in the area of Tariffs to negotiate on what the North sought, namely to reduce and bind Third World tariffs, or in TRIPs where the US and others were really seeking to rewrite the mandate, or in Services where the US and others wanted a general framework agreement.

To get around these problems, there was an effort to ensure leeway for chairmen of individual negotiating groups to report to the Montreal meeting directly. This would have enabled the US to operate from behind the scenes, with the cooperation of the GATT Secretariat and some of the Chairmen, to face Ministers at Montreal with 'reports' and 'recommendations' that would meet the US objectives.

But these manoeuvres were partly foiled when, just before the Montreal meeting, Geneva negotiators from a number of Third World countries and the EEC (for its own reasons, including on agriculture) joined hands to insist that in all the areas   under   the jurisdiction of the GNG, the negotiating groups would report to the GNG which would then hold, if necessary, consultations on each of the subjects and formulate the report to the Montreal meeting. As in the weeks preceding Punta del Este, there was an effort, led by Canada, to gather together a group of countries to formulate some recommendations, but this failed.

The efforts of the Third World negotiators in Geneva ultimately resulted in the report of the GNG on all issues in goods, except Agriculture, with the viewpoints and recommendations of Third World countries being fully reflected in the contentious areas through formulations placed within square brackets. This was the case in regard to Tariffs, Textiles, Safeguards, TRIPs, Dispute Settlement and FOGS. In regard to Agriculture where consultations and negotiations continued, the chairman of that group, Aart de Zheew of Netherlands, was asked to formulate the report.

In   Services too, a number of Third World countries took a stand in the GNS. With the Chairman of the GNS unwilling to play a partisan role favouring the US, this ensured a report for the mid-term meeting, setting out clear options reflecting various viewpoints [8].

Reports for the Montreal Meeting

The preparatory process for the Mid-term review thus resulted in the Ministers at Montreal having before them sepa-

rate reports and recommendations from the Surveillance
Body (on observance of standstill and rollback), from the
GNG on the 14 items on trade in goods, and from the GNS
on the future orientation of work and issues for negotiations.

The report and recommendations to the Montreal
meeting from the Surveillance Body and from the GNG in six
areas (Non-Tariff Measures, Natural Resource-based Products,
GATT Articles, MTN Agreements and Codes, Subsidies and
Countervailing Measures, and TRIMs) were unanimous and,
apart from some declaratory statements of good intentions,
procedural. The Ministers were merely asked to endorse the
recommendations for continuing the negotiations, without
any decision or guidance on the procedural or substantive
issues blocking negotiations in each of these groups.

In all these areas, and two years after the negotiations
began and at the mid-point of the round, even the detailed
agenda of negotiations and the modalities and basis for
negotiations have not been settled. If this had happened in
any other international organisation (FAO, UNCTAD, UNESCO
etc), western governments and their media would have
revelled in castigating the organisations and their intergov-
ernmental mechanisms. In GATT not only has this failure
gone unnoticed, but the view of senior GATT officials, including the Director-General, about the enormous technical
progress, has been uncritically accepted in the media.

STANDSTILL AND ROLLBACK: The only decision, procedural, was that the TNC "at its meeting in July 1989 should
carry out a substantive evaluation of the implementation of
the stand-still and rollback commitments (including avoid-
ance of disruptive effects on the trade of less-developed
contracting parties) and its impact on the process of multilateral trade negotiations and in relation to the interests of
individual participants, with a view to taking such procedural
or other actions as may be appropriate".

The outcome could at best be described as technical

and politically weak. There has been a wealth of data about the violations of the standstill commitments undertaken at Punta del Este. There is not even a general condemnation of such violations. Under the negotiating plan adopted in February 1987, participants were to indicate their rollback intentions and programmes by end of that year. But no one had done so. Only a few, like Japan, had removed restrictions found illegal by GATT panels, and have claimed credit for it under Rollback and in Tropical Products. Against this background the Ministers could merely "affirm their determination to ensure that the standstill and rollback commitments are met... (and) *urge* participants... to *indicate* to the surveillance body how and when they *intend* to proceed to rollback measures covered by the commitment...."(emphasis added) [9].

NON-TARIFF MEASURES: The Ministers agreed that results from these negotiations "should" be substantial, and asked the Negotiating Group "to aim to establish" by June 1989, a framework for future negotiations, including procedures, taking account of principles and guidelines set out by them for the conduct of the negotiations. These would enable adoption of various approaches put forward in the group, but preferring those that would ensure "widest participation and broadest possible liberalisation". The other guidelines include transparency in negotiations to ensure application of results in accord with basic GATT principles (presumably a reference to the MFN provision), measures to ensure that concessions are not subsequently modified or withdrawn, immediate or staged implementation of results over agreed time-frame, transforming NTMs into tariffs where NTMs can't be removed, and "appropriate recognition" for measures already adopted [10].

The main problem in this area had been the procedure to be adopted to eliminate NTMs. In the course of negotiations various negotiating approaches have been put forward including multilateral approaches and 'request and offer' procedures. This issue has not been settled, though there is mention of the "formula approach" and preference for the approach that ensures "widest participation" and "fullest liberalisation". The text agreed does not help take the negotiations forward even procedurally.

NATURAL RESOURCE-BASED PRODUCTS: Participants are to provide as much relevant data as possible by 31 March 1989, and "effective negotiations should begin as soon as possible", it being recognised that work in three product areas - fisheries, forestry and non-ferrous metals is already well advanced [11].

The outcome was a fairly 'low profile' one, with the agreed text saying nothing. The only advance, in the light of efforts of the US and others to widen the subjects for negotiations, had been in the listing and recognition of three areas where effective negotiations could begin as soon as possible.

GATT ARTICLES: After recognising the importance for the GATT system of reaching "common views" on the large number of issues under consideration in the group, the Ministers directed work in the negotiating group to be pursued vigorously and urged the group to define the issues for negotiation "with precision and clarity", and to bring forward specific proposals as soon as possible, and "preferably" not later than 31 December 1989 [12].

All the disputed issues remained open, without any agreement on taking them up for negotiations: Articles XV, XVII, XVIII, XXIV and XXVIII.

MTN AGREEMENTS AND ARRANGEMENTS: The Group was urged to pursue negotiations vigorously, and participants were "encouraged" to expedite negotiations through early submission of specific texts. It was recognised that widened membership of agreements by more countries could contribute to improving further the unity and consistency of the GATT system, and that appropriate and effective use of the special and differential treatment provisions could facilitate membership of Third World countries [13].

In effect the text said nothing. All the unresolved points in the negotiations on various agreements and arrangements remained unresolved.

SUBSIDIES AND COUNTERVAILING MEASURES: The framework developed in the Negotiating Group to deal with various kinds of subsidies (prohibited subsidies, non-prohibited but countervailable or otherwise actionable, and non-countervailable and non-actionable subsidies - the so-called red, amber, green light approach), special and differential treatment, notifications and surveillance and dispute settlement, was noted and it was agreed that further progress in negotiations would depend on submission of specific drafting proposals [14].

While no substantive decisions had been taken, the points for negotiations have been narrowed down, and specific points had been spelt out. The issues had been systematically listed. From the viewpoint of Third World countries, the listing of the 'non-countervailable and non-actionable subsidies' in the framework for negotiations was perhaps a slight procedural advance, though much would depend on the contents of the list. However none of the basic issues bedevilling the GATT system in this area were resolved.

TRADE-RELATED INVESTMENT MEASURES: Drawing on the work of the Group so far, and on basis of proposals and submissions, the Negotiating Group was asked to integrate the following elements into the negotiating process:

(a) Further identification of the trade-restrictive and distorting effects of investment measures that are or may be covered by existing GATT Articles, specifying those Articles,

(b) Identification of other trade restrictive and distorting effects of investment measures that may not be covered adequately by existing GATT Articles but are relevant to the mandate of the Group,

(c) Development aspects that would require consideration,

(d) Means of avoiding the identified adverse trade effects of TRIMs including, as appropriate, new provisions to be elaborated where existing GATT Articles may not cover them adequately, and

(e) Other relevant issues, such as the modalities of implementation.

Participants were also asked to make detailed written submissions, as early as possible in 1989, which provide a description of the trade restrictive and distorting effects of investment measures and of operation and coverage of related GATT Articles [15].

The specific mention of "development aspects" as one of the elements to be integrated into the negotiating process was perhaps a small opening that the Third World could use to stem the major onslaught in this area by the US and other ICs to resuscitate the pre-World War I international property rules and regime that had lost their legitimacy over the last several decades [16]. Otherwise the accord did not take the process beyond that at Punta del Este.

Montreal Agreement on Tropical Products

The negotiations and consultations at Montreal in December 1988 were confined to Tariffs, Textiles and Clothing, Agriculture, Tropical Products, Safeguards, TRIPs, Dispute Settlement, and FOGS . The negotiations were on the basis of the texts (with many portions in square brackets) received from the GNG, and similarly on the text on Services from the GNS.

We now examine the results of the Mid-term Review Process in Montreal.

On Tropical Products, there had been agreement at Geneva, in the negotiating group, on the further course of negotiations. It had been agreed that negotiations should be pursued on the seven product groups (identified in the documents   before the negotiating group), and with due regard, *inter alia* to the following elements:

(a) elimination of duties on unprocessed products,
(b) elimination or substantial reduction of duties on semi-processed and processed products, including the objective of elimination or reduction of tariff escalation, and
(c) elimination or reduction of all non-tariff measures affecting trade in these products.

Also, in effect conceding the demands about "contributions" from everyone, the agreement provided that "all participants" would engage in the negotiations and make "appropriate contributions". The Negotiating Group at its next meeting was to make appropriate arrangements for continuation of   negotiations on the basis of these elements and understandings.

The real sticking point had been on "early results", and the insistence of EEC and some others on "contributions" to this by others, including Third World countries. In the negotiating group some Third World countries had indicated their willingness to contribute autonomously; but others had said that the ICs should implement their past pledges and undertake liberalisation to provide early results, and that in the light of these they would then consider their own contributions at the subsequent stage of negotiations.

At Montreal, those Third World countries that had agreed to make their own "contributions" to early accord and the ICs undertook their own intense consultations. Only these two groups of countries were involved, and all their "offers" were put on the table and, after some bargaining of sorts, were finalised and announced as a "X'mas package" (of gifts) for the Third World countries.

In briefing the press, the GATT Secretariat at Montreal suggested that the "package" agreed to at Montreal, coupled with the liberalisation achieved in earlier GATT Rounds, would mean "we have come a long way towards full liberalisation (of trade) in tropical products" (to which the ICs had committed themselves in 1963). The GATT Secretariat estimated the "trade coverage" of the products in the "X'mas package" as of the order of $25 billion [17]. Later, GATT officials privately said this was a rough estimate, based on figures of importing countries about their total imports of these products. Since Montreal the figure of trade coverage has been gradually brought down, and in March 1989, GATT officials privately put it as less than $20 billion.

All this is very different from "export earnings" or "windfall profits" (terms widely used in media and by some Third World officials) for the exporting countries. With trade data and directions of trade all expressed in CCCN system, and with offers etc according to the new Harmonised System (HS), the attempts to analyse and make independent estimates have been time-consuming. While the difficulties of the nomenclature change-over is given as the reason for inability to make an estimate or analysis of the impact of concessions, GATT officials have privately also said that until the end of the Round they would make no assessment, giving different reasons to different people.

This strengthens the preliminary estimations, done by analysts outside, which suggest that the claims of achievement are very exaggerated.

Simulations done in UNCTAD show that if all the tariff concessions are passed on to the consumer, there will be a nett trade creation effect annually of $333 million or two percent of value of such imports in 1986, of which only about $90 million will come from Third World countries or a 0.8 percent increase in their exports, while the balance of $243 million or a seven percent increase will accrue to the ICs. (See Tables 3 and 4).

Table 3
1986 Imports of Tropical Products from the World, Developing Countries and Industrialised Countries Covered in Uruguay Round Offers

(In US$ million and percentage of importer's value from world)

| MARKET | No. of IIS Lines in Offer | WORLD | | DEVELOPING COUNTRIES | | | | | | | | INDUSTRIALISED COUNTRIES | |
| | | VALUE | % | TOTAL | | AFRICA | | ASIA | | LATIN AMERICA | | | |
				Value	%	Value	%	Value	%	Value	%	Value	%
Australia	153	710	100	377	53.2	9	1.3	354	49.9	14	1.9	333	46.9
Austria	130	432	100	230	53.3	40	9.2	33	7.6	158	36.5	202	46.7
Canada	36	160	100	32	20.1	5	2.9	24	15.0	3	2.2	128	79.9
EEC	152	8,089	100	7,111	87.9	2,775	34.0	1,601	13.0	3,274	40.0	978	12.0
Finland	60	368	100	271	73.8	58	15.7	20	5.4	194	52.7	97	26.2
Japan	161	3,400	100	2,915	85.7	14	0.4	2,737	80.5	163	4.8	485	14.3
New Zealand	163	107	100	41	38.0	0	0.2	39	36.2	2	1.7	67	62.2
Norway	133	785	100	24	3.1	2	0.2	20	2.5	3	0.4	761	96.9
Sweden	20	87	100	27	31.4	2	2.8	19	22.1	6	6.5	58	68.6
Switzerland	124	519	100	370	71.3	66	12.8	47	9.0	257	49.5	149	28.8
United States	49	306	100	185	60.7	20	6.5	100	32.7	65	21.3	121	39.3
TOTAL		14,963	100	11,582	77.4	2,991	20.0	4,994	33.4	4,139	27.7	3,379	22.6

Source: UNCTAD/MTN/INT/CB.20

Note: The imports of each market refers to the 1986 c.i.f. imports of the tropical products covered in that market's offer of tariff concessions on tropical products.

Table 4

Estimated Direct Trade Effects of Uruguay Round Offers of Tariff Concession on Tropical Products

(In US$ million and percentage of exporter's value to the market)

EXPORTER / MARKET	WORLD VALUE	WORLD %	DEVELOPING COUNTRIES TOTAL Value	%	AFRICA Value	%	ASIA Value	%	LATIN AMERICA Value	%	INDUSTRIALISED COUNTRIES Value	%
Australia	169.94	24.0	47.43	12.6	0.46	5.0	45.86	12.9	1.12	8.2	122.51	36.9
Austria	1.89	0.4	1.20	0.5	0.01	0.0	1.09	3.4	0.10	0.1	0.69	0.3
Canada	9.65	6.0	2.57	8.0	-0.01	-0.2	2.49	10.4	0.08	2.7	7.08	5.5
EEC	27.84	0.3	0.74	0.0	-1.77	-0.2	2.27	0.2	0.23	0.0	27.10	2.8
Finland	5.94	1.6	4.80	1.8	-0.28	-0.5	0.18	0.9	4.90	2.5	-1.14	1.2
Japan	74.30	2.2	24.00	0.8	0.05	0.4	23.00	0.8	0.93	0.6	50.30	10.4
New Zealand	35.72	33.4	5.60	13.8	0.01	3.1	5.08	13.1	0.52	29.2	30.11	44.9
Norway	1.47	0.2	0.18	0.7	-0.01	-0.4	0.20	1.0	-0.01	-0.3	1.29	0.2
Sweden	2.84	3.3	0.27	1.0	0.02	1.0	0.11	0.6	1.35	2.4	2.57	4.4
Switzerland	2.48	0.5	2.57	0.7	0.48	0.7	0.45	1.0	1.64	0.6	-0.09	-0.0
United States	0.80	0.3	0.29	0.2	-0.02	-0.1	0.41	0.4	-0.10	-0.2	0.51	0.4
TOTAL	332.87	2.2	89.65	0.8	-1.06	-0.04	81.14	1.6	10.76	0.3	243.30	7.2

Source: UNCTAD/MTN/INT/CB.20

Note: *"Trade effects" refers to the estimated change in each market's imports, by regional origin, attributable to its offer on tropical products.*

Most of the concessions made are on products where Third World countries already enjoy benefits under the GSP schemes, and thus there had been no effective concessions. But given the nature of the GSP (as an autonomous scheme that could be varied or abrogated at any time), and given the efforts of the ICs to use GSP benefits to extract other concessions, the conversion of the GSP benefits into a Uruguay Round agreement would be beneficial, but only when the concessions are 'bound' at the end of the Round.

All the concessions are mostly at the stage of raw materials and do not extend to processed or semiprocessed products. None of the real issues in Tropical Products trade - such as tariff escalation at each stage of processing or internal consumption taxes - have been tackled. Nor has there been any guidance on how the negotiations on these are to be tackled. At best the accord could be described as carrying a 'political message'.

Japan made some non-tariff concessions. But most of these had been declared illegal by GATT panels. Japan made a virtue of necessity in offering these and one or two others as a concession. The EEC also provided some non-tariff concessions, but these were the residual quantitative restrictions in place which are anyhow illegal in GATT.

The US linked its 'offers' to the agreement on agriculture at Montreal (and no such agreement was reached). Then EEC without specifically saying so linked it to an overall package emerging at Montreal. But (as discussed below) when the Agriculture talks broke down, and the Latin American members of the Cairns Group did not agree to further negotiations on the other subjects, the TNC put the results obtained at Montreal, including on Tropical Products 'on hold' (as discussed below).

Agreements on Tariffs, Dispute Settlement and FOGS

The 'green room' consultations at Montreal resulted in some agreements on Tariffs, Dispute Settlement and on FOGS. In all these areas, the Third World countries did yield some ground to enable early agreements to be reached. In the area of tariffs, they agreed to negotiate the 'substantial reduction or elimination' of their own high tariffs and for a substantial increase in the scope of bindings.

In the area of Dispute Settlement, where the tentative accord mostly incorporated existing GATT practices, agreement became possible as a result of a concession by the Third World countries. They agreed to take up in the subsequent stage of negotiations the issue that, as part of the Dispute Settlement accord, CPs 'shall refrain from unilateral measures inconsistent with these GATT rules and procedures'. The US which has been using S.301 of its domestic law to take unilateral measures against trade partners, has flatly refused to provide any undertaking to abide by GATT rulings or abandon use of such unilateral measures. The USTR, Mrs Carla Hills, since Montreal, has told Congress that even if GATT rules against the US and holds S. 301 illegal, the US would continue to use it, as it has done against Brazil to impose unilateral discriminatory tariffs because Brazil would not agree to increase the level of protection for US drug companies [18].

On FOGS, the Third World countries compromised by agreeing to the proposed trade policy review mechanism (tprm); but the GATT Secretariat had to give up its pet idea (for expanding its own 'empire') of GATT teams (Secretariat officials and 'discussants') visiting capitals and of examination of countries' trade policies through use of 'independent discussants'. There is no provision for visiting teams and the provision for 'discussants', in the special meetings of the GATT council where trade policies are to be reviewed, is optional if the country concerned agrees to it.

TARIFFS: The agreement provided that 'all participants' (which implies Third World countries also) would negotiate reduction or elimination in their tariffs, including high tariffs, tariff peaks, tariff escalation and low tariffs, and a substantial increase in scope of tariff bindings. The tariff negotiations would begin from July 1, 1989. The only concession to the Third World was that participants would receive appropriate recognition for liberalisation measures adopted since June 1, 1986. Most of the Third World countries, either as part of their IMF-financed adjustment and stabilisation programmes or as part of the conditions for World Bank loans, have carried out unilateral tariff reduction exercises. They will now be able to take 'credit' for it in terms of GATT. But this would also require them to 'bind' these tariffs which means they can't raise them (which they could have done if there were no IMF/World Bank agreements in force).

DISPUTE SETTLEMENT: The agreement included several matters of procedure, setting among other things time-limits for the various stages of dispute settlement in GATT - from the stage when a dispute is sought to be raised through consultations to the establishment of a panel and its report. Replies to requests for consultations under Article XXII:1 or XXIII:1 are to be given in ten days, and 'good faith' consultations held within thirty days of request. If these are not done, any cp raising the dispute could ask the GATT Council directly to establish a panel. If the consultations do not yield results within 60 days, the complaining cp can request the establishment of a panel or a working party. In urgent cases, consultations should be held within ten days, and the establishment of panel sought if no settlement is reached within 30 days. There are also provisions for use of good offices, including that of the GATT Director-General, for arbitration if parties agree, for the establishment of the panel within specified timelimits (latest at the council meeting following the one at which the issue appeared on the regular agenda), for standard terms of reference (unless parties agree otherwise) within 20 days of the establishment of the panel, for appointment of panelists by the GATT Director-General within 20 days of setting up of the panel if there is no agreement among the parties on this, for multiple complaints on the same issue to be referred to a single panel or panels with same membership and for the rights of interested third cps to intervene before panels. A tight time-schedule was also set for the work of the panels and their reports - as a general rule not to exceed six months, and maximum of nine months. The time limit for the entire process, from the time of request to the adoption of the panel report, was also set at 15 months. All these were intended to prevent the delaying and blocking processes to which the major trading partners frequently resort to on complaints against them.

On the whole the decisions marked a positive step forward - in the recognition of 'arbitration', laying down of specific time-limits for various stages, standard terms of reference if no agreement on terms of reference are reached within specified time, and naming of panelists by GATT Director-General if there is no agreement. The provisions on adoption of panel reports could mark an advance, depending on how the Chairman of the GATT Council and the Secretariat act in the coming period when panel reports come up before the Council. If the parties to a dispute alone oppose adoption, as worded the Chairman could merely have their views recorded and declare the report adopted by consensus. But unless this is done in cases where the major trading nations are involved and try to block adoption, and until they accept the rulings and implement them in such a situation of the finding of a 'consensus' (which does not necessarily mean unanimity), it could prove illusory.

Before Montreal, there had been suggestions that the decision-making should be modified in dispute settlement, so as to prevent any party to a dispute using the consensus rule to block decisions, by providing that the consensus would be of the GATT council minus the two parties to a dispute. This could still come up in the further negotiations envisaged on this over the remainder of the Uruguay Round.

FOGS: The 'package of decisions' in this area relate to the tprm, greater Ministerial involvement and contribution of GATT to achieving greater coherence in global economic policy making.

The tprm is to contribute to improved adherence by all cps to GATT rules, disciplines and commitments, by achieving greater transparency and understanding of trade policies and practices of cps. It will enable regular collective appreciation and evaluation by CONTRACTING PARTIES of the full range of individual cps' trade policies and practices and their impact on the functioning of the multilateral trading system. But the tprm is not to be the basis for enforcement of specific GATT obligations or dispute settlement procedures or 'to impose new policy commitments' on cps. The assessment by the tprm to the extent relevant is 'to take place against the background of the wider economic and developmental needs, policies and objectives' of the cp concerned as well as of its 'external environment'. But the function of the tprm is to examine 'the impact' of a cp's trade policies and practices on the multilateral trading system. Each cp is expected to report regularly in the years when a cp's trade policy is to be reviewed, and on a format to be agreed upon by the GATT Council.

While trade policies of all cps are subject to periodic review, the periodicity is to vary depending on the share in world trade (and thus its impact on the trading system). The first four trading entities (US, EEC, Japan and Canada) will be reviewed once every two years, the next 16 every four years, and others every six years, with perhaps an even longer period for the least developed. The rhythm of review under tprm for Third World countries subject to 'full consultations' under GATT's BOP provisions are to be harmonised (but not postponed beyond a year) so as not to unduly burden them. But with the ICs trying to push for 'full consultations' on BOP every two years, even this concession could still result in GATT surveillance of Third World policies every three years in a four-year cycle. The reviews are to be carried out at periodic special meetings of the GATT Council based on a full report from the cp and a report by the secretariat on its own responsibility and based on information available to it. The secretariat is also enabled to seek clarifications from the cp concerned. The reports of the cp under review and that of the secretariat, and the summary record of the GATT council are to be published promptly.

At Punta del Este, the entire idea of 'surveillance' was put into the mandate in order to bring some symmetry into the system and bring under multilateral scrutiny the policies of the major trading partners which affect the system. Though several provisions have been put in to meet Third World viewpoints, the outcome could still be in practice another instrument against Third World autonomy.

The tprm is to be implemented on a provisional basis from the date the decision is adopted by the CONTRACTING PARTIES, and is to be reviewed (and if necessary modified) at the end of the Uruguay Round.

The two other decisions provide:

● for Ministerial meetings of GATT CONTRACTING PARTIES at least once every two years.

● for the GATT Director-General to explore with heads of IMF and World Bank on ways to achieve greater coherence in global economic policy making through strengthening relationship of GATT with other relevant international organisations and report by 1 September 1989.

On the whole the decision on the tprm could be considered 'positive' in that the efforts to load the scales against the Third World have been blocked. The decision to hold Ministerial level meetings of the Contracting Parties every two years could also be beneficial, though it has to be noted that so far at all previous Ministerial meetings the Third World has lost - since their Ministers seem to be not too familiar with technicalities and are amenable to pressures.

Agreement on Services

The consultations and negotiations at Montreal on these four issues (Tropical Products, Tariffs, Dispute Settlement and FOGS) had involved some tough negotiations, but were dealt with at the level of technical people and GATT negotiators.

The issue of Services, in the green room consultations, saw the US pushing for an understanding on the principles of a multilateral framework based (without defining them) on national treatment, right of establishment, transparency and progressive liberalisation. After some tough negotiations, the participants agreed on a compromise that in effect would enable all viewpoints to be addressed in the negotiations, over the next two years, without foreclosing or preferring any particular view.

But an important 'development' concept has been specifically excluded as a guideline or principle for the negotiations. The clause on 'development' had been promoted by Third World delegates but was eventually not included. It reads as follows: "Developing countries will not be expected to make contributions and shall not be required to make concessions which are inconsistent with their individual development, trade and financial needs; particular account shall be taken of the serious difficulty of the least developed countries in making concessions and contributions in view of their special economic situation and their development, trade and financial needs".

This is the same language as in the 1979 'Enabling Clause' decision of the GATT CONTRACTING PARTIES - and GATT does not even have 'development' as a fundamental objective, whereas the Punta del Este declaration mandates this as one of the objectives of the future multilateral framework for 'trade in services'.

The US stoutly opposed its inclusion - with USTR Clay-
ton Yeutter reportedly scoffing at the 'development'
concept as mere rhetoric. In the face of US opposition,
the Third World countries appear to have given way.

However, these and other elements, as well as new
ideas and concepts, could still be brought up under a provision in the mid-term accord which states (after mentioning
various concepts considered 'relevant'): "Other elements
mentioned in MTN.GNS/21 (the report of the GNS to the
Montreal meeting), as well as new ideas and concepts participants may wish to put forward, will also be considered".
Also, the language of the agreement at Montreal is such that
in effect nothing is foreclosed either. There are enough
ambiguities in the document to enable the issues being
raised in the negotiations over the next two years. But this
does not excuse the failure of the Third World Ministers to
stand firm and insist on its inclusion at Montreal.

Neither the 'right of establishment' for foreign capital
sought by the US and other industrial nations, nor movement of labour and labour-intensive services pressed by
Third World countries like India and Pakistan have been specifically included. That the US has not abandoned its efforts
to bring into the Services framework the issues of 'investment' and 'right of establishment' became clear at the first
meeting of the GNS (held after the April 1989 TNC meeting)
when Canada and the US insisted that these issues had not
been foreclosed and they could bring it up [19].

Work on 'definition' is to be on the basis that the proposed multilateral framework may include trade in services
involving 'cross-border movement' of services, of consumers,
and of 'factors of production' (which means both capital and
labour) where such movement is essential to suppliers, and
is to be further examined in the light of cross-border movement of service and payment, specificity of purpose, discrete-

ness of transactions, and limited duration.

The work is to proceed "without excluding any sector of trade in services on *a priori* basis" and coverage should permit "a balance of interests for all participants, that sectors of interest to developing countries should be included, that certain sectors could be excluded in whole or in part for certain overriding considerations, and that the framework should provide for the broadest possible coverage of sectors of interest to participants".

There was agreement that the negotiations on elaboration of a multilateral framework of principles and rules should proceed expeditiously. Various concepts, and principles and rules that the US and other ICs had been pushing were "considered relevant", but in effect they have been left wide open for negotiations. These include: transparency, progressive liberalisation, national treatment, mfn/ non-discrimination, market access, increased participation of Third World countries, safeguards and exceptions, regulatory situation. The main agreements on these issues are as follows:

- Transparency - provisions to be agreed to ensure availability of information regarding all laws, regulations and administrative guidelines, as well as international agreements on services trade to which signatories are parties.

- Progressive liberalisation - rules, modalities and procedures to be established to provide for progressive liberalisation of trade in services in this and future negotiations "with due respect" for national policy objectives including provisions for application of principles to sectors and measures, and taking "due account" of the level of development of individual signatories, and providing for reduction of the adverse effects of all laws, regulations and administrative guidelines as part of the process to provide effective market access. There is to be appropriate flexibility for individual Third World countries for opening fewer sectors or liberalising fewer types of transactions or in progressively extending market access in line with their development needs.

• National treatment - service exports and/or exporters of any signatory to be accorded treatment in market of any other signatory "no less favourable" treatment, in respect of all laws, regulations and administrative practices, than that provided to domestic services or service providers.

• Provision in the framework for MFN/non-discrimination.

• Market access - consistent with other provisions, foreign services may be supplied according to preferred mode of delivery.

• Increasing Third World participation - provisions for increased participation by these countries in world trade and in service exports, including through strengthening domestic services capacity and its efficiency and competitiveness; for effective market access for Third World service exports including access to distribution channels and information networks, and liberalisation of market access to sectors of export interest to these countries; autonomous liberalisation of market access in favour of Third World countries, and special provisions in respect of commitments by least developed countries.

• Provisions for safeguards for BOP reasons or exceptions for security and cultural policy objectives.

• Regulatory situation - governments regulate service sectors by granting exclusive rights in certain sectors or by attaching conditions to operations of enterprises within their markets for consumer protection and for macro-economic policies. Also there are asymmetries among countries on the degree of regulation of services. Hence countries, particularly Third World countries, have the right to introduce new regulations, but consistent with commitments under the framework.

These concepts have been spelt out as 'relevant' for negotiations, but do not necessarily mean acceptance. However, if negotiators do not keep this in mind, there could be problems in the further stages of negotiations.

In the orientation for future work, the GNS has been asked to endeavour by end of 1989 to assemble the necessary elements for a draft that would permit negotiations to take place for completion of all parts of the multilateral framework and its entry into force by the end of the Uruguay Round. This implies that the agreement will be concluded well before, so that States could sign and ratify. Unless it is viewed as merely a 'best endeavour' provision, it is difficult to see how this can be reconciled either with the globality concept of the entire negotiations or the decision at Punta del Este that at the conclusion of the negotiations the Ministers are to meet and decide on the international implementation of the respective results in the round.

The elements to be negotiated have been identified and specificity of parameters for negotiations have been provided. But on issues of interest to the Third World (like development) there is lack of specificity.

The four issues listed for negotiations in regard to 'definition' have been qualified by the stipulation that this should be examined further in the light of, *inter alia*, (a) cross-border movement of services and payment, (b) specificity of purpose, (c) discreteness of transactions, (d) limited duration.

Together these appear to rule out both permanent migration and general right of establishment. Cross-border movement of labour or capital to provide service must be for specific purposes, and for each transaction. A lawyer, doctor or other professional person or a worker 'crossing' borders to set himself up to provide service would not be covered, nor a bank wishing to open a branch. They would not satisfy the requirement about 'discreteness of transaction' or the 'limited duration' of the cross-border movement of service and payment. But a bank opening an office to carry out a particular transaction, or the setting up of a 'consultancy' office for a particular project could be. Only 'cross-border movement' of service and payment are to be covered, which implies that purely internal service trade is not to be covered through definition.

If the text in the Montreal accord on 'definitions' is faithfully observed, 'rights of establishment' and 'foreign direct investment' rights for service providers would be excluded. Otherwise, Third World countries would be worse off. In the very first meeting of the GNS, after the April 1989 meeting of the TNC, the US and its supporters had already begun to argue and push for 'right of establishment' and other rights for TNCs.

This underscores the crucial importance of 'definitions', and the need for Third World negotiators to be vigilant and insist upon an agreement on definitions before proceeding further to look at various concepts and principles. Otherwise they might find themselves agreeing to concepts and principles that would either defeat the intent of the mid-term accord on definitions or give a leverage to the powerful to interpret definitions as it would suit them.

The mandate that concepts, principles and rules are to be tested in terms of specific sectors and transactions is also perhaps an advance. This means that no general framework could be put in place without agreement on what sectors would be covered. When sectors are specified (and excluded or not specified), Third World countries might find a. wider area of joint interests. While considerable prominence is given to 'national treatment', 'transparency' and 'progressive liberalisation', there is no specificity in regard to 'development' and this last must be seen as a minus point.

No Agreement on Textiles, Safeguards, TRIPs and Agriculture

The consultations on four issues failed to produce any consensus at Montreal. These were the issues of Textiles and Clothing, Safeguards, Agriculture and TRIPs. While public attention was focussed on Agriculture, with the US and EEC publicly brawling on whether there should be a long-term commitment to "eliminate" all domestic support to agriculture or only to "substantially reduce" them, the other three issues were also the subject of some hard and difficult negotiations and confrontations. After some brief exchanges at Ministerial level, the Textiles and Safeguards issues were remitted to small drafting groups, while the TRIPs issue was handled by a ministerial group headed by Turkey.

On the textiles and clothing issue - a sector of international trade where Third World countries have been at the receiving end of discriminatory restrictions for 37 years now - there was a sharp North-South difference, reflected in the text received from Geneva. The only thing the ICs were agreeable to was a procedural decision for "commencing substantive negotiations early in 1989", and merely repeating the text of the mandate in this regard. This was sugar-coated with talk of "affirmation of political will" and "recognition" that negotiations in this area was "one of the key elements" of the round in view of the "importance of the sector for the economies of many countries and its particular importance for the economic and social development of many developing countries and for the expansion of their export earnings".

Given the nearly four decades of discriminatory and ever increasing restrictions on their exports, and consistent disregard of equally nice phraseology used in the MFA and its predecessors, the Third World countries were not ready to accept these in terms of any Montreal package. At their insistence, the GNG put in some formulations that would have provided a clear political message from the Ministers to the negotiators that a start should be made to wind down the discriminatory MFA regime. In this regard the Montreal meeting was asked to decide on a 'freeze' on further restrictions and agreement to begin the gradual phase-out of the restrictions under the Multifibre Arrangement from August 1991, when the current MFA-4 ends. The Ministers were also asked to direct the negotiating group to reach agreement in the Uruguay Round on modalities for integrating trade in this sector into GATT (as mandated at Punta del Este) and for the process of integration to be completed within a specified time-phase to be agreed upon during the Uruguay Round [20].

The positions of the US and EEC have been made clearer since Montreal. In a report to the European Parliament in Strasburg, on Dec 12-16, immediately after the Montreal meeting, EC Commissioner Willy de Clercq said "the Community was unwilling to accept an end to the Multifibre Arrangement" [21]. In testimony before Congress, USTR, Mrs Carla Hills, has said the "United States supports the negotiations that incorporate the *current system of global textile trade* (emphasis supplied) into the multilateral rules under the GATT" [22]. This implies that the US wants the integration of the trade into GATT, as mandated at Punta del Este, to be achieved by incorporating the MFA into GATT, instead of treating it as now as a derogation from GATT, sanctioned through protocols for extension of the MFA every three or four years.

The US, EEC and other industrial nations, which want the MFA to continue well into the 21st century and are opposed to any time-frame, did not agree to any compromise. In addition, the EEC linked the integration of the trade into GATT to acceptance of its demands on intellectual property and 'selective' safeguards. Only the Nordics seemed to be willing to discuss and agree on a time-frame to wind up the MFA, and starting this process with MFA-4. But there were differences even among them. On the eve of the Montreal meeting, the Swedish government had announced that it would not continue with the MFA at the end of the current protocol. However, the others, and particularly Finland, seemed to have some reservations. The drafting exercise was unable to solve these fundamental differences.

On 'Safeguards' (GATT-permitted emergency protective actions of countries), again there was no meeting ground. The text remitted to Montreal would have had the Ministers take a mere procedural decision that the "elements" of the agreement, specified in the mandate, were inter-related and no substantive agreement could be reached on individual elements in isolation; that the Chairman of the Negotiating Group should draw up a draft text (of the elements) as a basis for negotiations; that the work on a comprehensive agreement on safeguards should be pursued as expeditiously as possible; and that negotiations on the basis of the Chairman's text should begin by June 1989. At the instance of India, the GNG had remitted to Montreal, under square brackets, three additional points for Ministerial decision, namely that safeguard measures should be of limited duration, that they should be non-discriminatory and that 'grey-area' measures which resulted in selective application should be proscribed [23].

At Montreal, there was an attempt to brush this aside as just the view of one country, but it soon became clear that these ideas had wider backing. Brazil, India and several other Third World countries made clear that the safeguards agreement must incorporate the fundamental GATT principle of most-favoured-nation treatment and outlaw 'grey area' measures (like voluntary export restraints, minimum price agreements or orderly marketing arrangments) which were being used by the powerful trading blocs to circumvent the GATT obligations. The EEC (with tacit support from most of the industrial countries) insisted on the right to take discriminatory and selective safeguards actions against particular, but not all, sources of imports; it would not also agree to proscribing 'grey area' measures.

On TRIPs, the Geneva text had four different formulations, one provided by the Chairman of the Negotiating Group, another by the Third World countries, a third by the US and the fourth by Switzerland. The main difference between the text of the Third World and that of others was that all the other texts, though formulated in different language, clearly sought to provide for negotiations in the Uruguay Round of the substantive norms in intellectual property rights, and application of some of the GATT principles (as well as the use of GATT dispute settlement mechanisms) for settling at level of States disputes of foreign enterprises against a country about violation of their intellectual property rights in that country. The last would enable the ICs to have recourse to 'trade retaliation' as a way of enforcing the purported rights of their enterprises. The Third World countries refused to accept this.

In the negotiations in a working group, there was a sharp North-South divide. There was a draft prepared informally by Hong Kong and Australia, and mostly supporting the US views and presented as a non-paper by the chairman of the group, Turkey's Minister of State, Yusuf Ozal. It was countered by an Indian proposal for remitting the issue of establishing substantial or new norms, including dispute settlement, to WIPO, UNCTAD and UNESCO (where one or other aspect of these issues are already being handled), and for a report from them in 1990. In the discussions in the 'green room', the Indian paper was not even presented by Ozal or the secretariat but put on the table later at the instance of the Indian Minister. The paper had been informally circulated by India, and even before it spoke, to the surprise of most people in the 'green room', virtually every Third World representative came out against the Ozal compromise and supported the alternative. The whole issue was referred back to the Ozal group, but no compromise could be found between these two diametrically opposing viewpoints.

On Agriculture, the text [24] presented at Montreal by the Chairman of the Negotiating Group (Aart de Zheeew) posed, in clear terms, the basic issues avoided at Punta del Este and sought Ministerial guidance and directions. In terms of the long-term elements of a framework agreement on Agriculture, the Ministers were invited to decide whether the ultimate goal should be "elimination" or "substantial reduction" of trade-distortive support and protection, and whether these should be through specific policies and measures or through commitments on an aggregate measure of support to be negotiated or a combination of both. On the basis of a decision on this fundamental issue, the Ministers were asked to establish guidelines for a reform programme including on import access, export competition and internal support.

As short-term elements, the Ministers were asked to agree to implement "a freeze" on overall support and protection provided to their agricultural sectors at levels prevailing in (a specific year to be agreed) and refrain from initiating new programmes that would undermine this commitment; also, to realise the long-term objective to reduce overall support and protection by (x) percent by 1990. In this regard, special attention was to be given to the "possible negative effects" of short-term measures on the net food-importing Third World countries.

In terms of short-term elements, the Ministers were also asked to decide whether the freeze and reduction should be in terms of an aggregate measure of support or in terms of specific policies and measures or a combination of them.

In terms of the concept of special and differential treatment for Third World countries, mandated at Punta del Este to be an integral element of the negotiations, the Ministers were asked to recognise that: "Government measures to encourage agricultural and rural development are an integral part of the development programmes of developing countries. Such measures may involve direct or indirect government support." Also, in terms of short-term measures, the Ministers were asked to decide whether Third World countries should be exempt from such measures.

There were no real negotiations or consultations at Montreal, only bilateral talks between the US and EEC that got nowhere. The controversies between the two were over 'elimination' or 'substantial reduction' of government support to agriculture; none of the other issues were taken up. Most of the negotiations were conducted through public statements and press conferences. When the agriculture issue ultimately came up in the 'green room', and the TNC chairman, Uruguay's Ricardo Zerbino, asked for the views of the EEC on the de Zheew paper, EEC Commissioner Willy de Clercq reportedly asked Zerbino, in didactic tones, whether Zerbino had not been reading the papers or listening to the TV, since the EEC views had been made known clearly. A sharp rebuke from Zerbino that he at least was not going to negotiate through the media elicited an apology from de Clercq, but still there were no negotiations [25]. The US and EEC both reported their agreement to disagree, and said that the entire text (de Zheew paper) should be sent back to Geneva for further negotiations in the Agriculture negotiating group. This left little option to the others except to endorse the decision to send everything in Agriculture back to Geneva.

After the Montreal meeting collapsed, the western media portrayed the outcome as a failure - blaming the breakdown on US and EEC differences over the issue of subsidisation of agricultural exports. There was some truth to this. But in fact the US and EEC 'agreed to disagree' on agriculture, and wanted to move forward on the other three issues (textiles and clothing, safeguards, and trade-related intellectual property rights), where they had a common front against the Third World.

However, the five Latin American members of the Cairns Group (Argentina, Brazil, Chile, Colombia and Uruguay), concerned over the failure to agree on the agriculture issue, refused to proceed with further discussions. At that point, the meeting collapsed, though it continued for a day more to enable the fiasco to be masked through the procedural decision for high level consultations in Geneva.

The procedural decision called for:

- a TNC meeting at high official level in first week of April 1989;
- the results achieved at Montreal being put 'on hold' until that meeting;
- for Arthur Dunkel (GATT Director-General) in his capacity as chairman of the TNC at official level to hold high level consultations on Textiles, Agriculture, Safeguards and TRIPs; and
- the entire package of subjects, the results achieved at Montreal and other items to be reviewed at the TNC meeting in April 1989.

Notes on Chapter 11

1. Part I B (ii) of Declaration in Annex I.

2. *SUNS* 2045, 'Trade: Dunkel Upbeat on Uruguay Round and Montreal', press conference after securing a new term.

3. *SUNS* 1848.

4. *SUNS* 1881.

5. *SUNS* 1881.

6. See discussions in the GNG in *SUNS* 1881.

7. See speech of EEC's Commissioner for External Relations at European Management Forum in Geneva, *SUNS* 2047.

8. For reports on the pre-Montreal process see *SUNS* 2049, 2050,

2052, 2053, 2058 and 2060. for reports on Montreal and outcome see *SUNS* 2061, 2062, 2063, 2064, 2065, 2070, 2071 and 2074. Also, C. Raghavan 'Uruguay Round After Montreal', *Mainstream*, New Delhi, Vol xxvii no.21, pp 19-26.

9. MTN.TNC/11 pp 2-3.

10. *Ibid* pp 5-6.

11. *Ibid* p 7.

12. *Ibid* p 15.

13. *Ibid* p 16.

14. *Ibid.* pp 18-20.

15. *Ibid* p 25.

16. See chapter 5 on TRIMs.

17. *SUNS* 2062.

18. US Embassy daily bulletin of March 2, 1989 pp 7-8.

19. *SUNS* 2144.

20. MTN.TNC/7(MIN) pp 8-9.

21. *European Report,* No 1464 d. January 18, 1989.

22. US Mission, Geneva bulletin of March 2, 1989 pp 6-7.

23. MTN.GNG/13 and MTN.TNC/7/(MIN) p 17.

24. MTN.TNC/7(MIN) pp 10-13.

25. *SUNS* 2070 p 4.

Chapter 12

THE PROCESS
AFTER MONTREAL

Moves After Montreal

The outcome at Montreal heartened Third World countries and their Geneva negotiators, and over the next several weeks this unity appeared to grow. But on the eve of the crucial meeting of the TNC in April 1989, the Third World group was in disarray, thanks mainly to failure of their capitals to follow up on Montreal and on the work of their diplomats in Geneva. The Third World capitals continued to treat the Uruguay Round as just another trade issue, needing low political priority, either nationally or collectively.

In the aftermath of Montreal, Third World countries and their negotiators at Geneva were buoyed up and felt they had some unity and could make themselves felt. They made their presence and voice felt in the initial consultations undertaken by Dunkel, and successfully resisted the efforts of the US and other ICs to get the negotiating groups in the areas put 'on hold' to resume their work.

Dunkel agreed to hold 'green room type' consultations in each of the four areas at Geneva to promote agreements and, if needed, present a paper of his own. But it became quickly clear that he was opting for a 'power approach', rather than involve himself in a process that would permit a genuine process of give and take and solutions that would reflect the interest and concerns of everyone.

While holding initial rounds of consultations in each of the four areas and seeming to be responsive to Third World concerns, Dunkel also paid several visits to Washington and Brussels and impressed on the US and EEC the need for these two to arrive at a modus vivendi among themselves on Agriculture. His approach reflected the view that once the US and EEC agreed, it could be forced on others. Once the Agriculture issue was settled the broad front of Third World countries involving the Latin American Cairns group members (on the agriculture issue) which had combined with others at Montreal (over Textiles and TRIPs) would dissolve and agreements could be reached in all other areas.

Third World Joint Position on TRIPs

In February 1989, some of the Third World countries, representing a wide spectrum of views and interests, met at Tailloires, near Annecy in France, to discuss their course of action on the deadlocked issues. After the first meeting, devoted to 'safeguards', it was felt that the TRIPs issue was one where the developing countries had a common interest and where there was a broad unity among the ICs aimed against the Third World countries. A number of further meetings at Tailloires and then at Geneva resulted in a common position which received broad endorsement of the informal Third World group in GATT. It was presented to Dunkel as a contribution from developing countries, containing elements of an alternative approach aimed at promoting a consensus [1].

This provided that the negotiating group shall identify:

(a) circumstances in which measures 'necessary' [2] to secure compliance with laws and regulations relating to patents, trade marks, copyright or similar procedures shall be considered to constitute a means of arbitrary or unjustifiable discrimination and/or disguised restriction on international trade;

(b) practices in arrangements to license or assign IPRs which may result in distortions or impediments to international trade.

On the basis of this, the group was to determine appropriate rules and disciplines to deal with the problems identified.

The paper also provided for negotiations to develop a multilateral framework of principles, rules and disciplines to deal with international trade in counterfeit goods.

To meet the viewpoints of the ICs on the question of issues relating to substantive norms, their enforcement and dispute settlement, the Third World paper provided that the actions on TRIPs in the Uruguay Round would be complemented by time-bound "parallel actions in the competent international organisations such as WIPO, UNESCO, and UNCTAD". These complementary initiatives were to address such issues as:

(i) further specification of appropriate norms and standards covering the availability, scope and use of IPRs;
(ii) appropriate disciplines for preventing abuse of IPRs;
(iii) elaboration of procedures in WIPO for the settlement of disputes arising from the protection and exercise of IPRs; and
(iv) working out disciplines in UNCTAD on related corporate practices.
    Work on these was to proceed "with due regard to developmental, technological and public interests needs of countries in particular developing countries".

Dunkel's Consultations

Dunkel held between January and March 1989 three rounds of consultations devoted to each of the four subjects. In Agriculture, almost by common consent, the consultations marked time pending the on-going US-EEC bilateral talks, which ultimately yielded some acceptable compromises for the two on long-term measures, but not on short-term measures.

In Textiles, where the US and EEC are united in their stand against the Third World exporters and for continuing the current discriminatory regime, Dunkel did not even appear to be pushing the ICs to find compromises to meet the viewpoint of the Third World. On Safeguards, where the basic issue is one of explicit recognition of the applicability of the GATT's fundamental non-discriminatory principle in Article I, Dunkel identified it as the 'problem', and in effect suggested that Third World countries should have to agree to fudge the issue.

On TRIPS, he put forward 'ideas' that clearly reflected the US positions, and called for negotiations on any issue, without prejudice to the positions of participants on jurisdiction, and leaving the issue of implementation to the end. At the third round of consultations just before Easter he was faced with the Third World paper, which was expounded and presented by Egypt and supported by about 10-12 Third World countries. Both Dunkel and the US and other ICs were considerably upset over this mobilisation of Third World unity, and blamed UNCTAD for it. While Dunkel virtually ignored the paper and its ideas, considerable pressures were mounted in some key Third World capitals, through a disinformation campaign, to weaken the joint front on TRIPs that had emerged at Geneva. The failure of Third World countries to follow up on the recommendation of the South Commission (of holding a Ministerial meeting to coordinate positions) before Montreal, and after Montreal on the four deadlocked issues, helped this disinformation campaign.

GATT functions on a consensus basis, with every contracting party deemed equal, but in the consultation processes, GATT officials have always proceeded on the basis of 'trade-weights', and on the assumption that what is good for the US and EEC (and their TNCs) must be good for the rest of the world. This attitude was even more evident at the Trade Negotiations Committee (TNC).

Lack of Openness at Consultations

As pointed out in an earlier chapter, the GATT consultation and decision-making processes are 'non-transparent', with accords reached among a limited number of countries, 'invited' to these conclaves by the Director-General, being put to the rest of the membership for formal approval. At the TNC, this helped the US and other ICs and the GATT secretariat to divide and weaken Third World opposition.

The consultations (beginning March 31), before and at the high-official level TNC meeting, were even less transparent than normal. On April 5, when the high official level TNC meeting formally opened, a number of participants complained about the lack of 'transparency' in the processes for consultations and negotiations. Among these was Tanzania, whose permanent delegate, Amir Jamal, was the Chairman of the Contracting Parties for 1989 and a Third World country normally invited to all the GATT 'green room' consultations, both because of the personality of Jamal (he had held the posts of Finance Minister and Planning under President Nyerere and was very widely respected), and Tanzania's political weight in the Non-Aligned movement, in the African Group and the Group of 77. Another complainant was Colombia, whose permanent delegate, Felipe Jaramillo, is the Chairman of the GNS. The only result of the complaints was an announcement that the TNC would meet in the morning every day informally at the level of heads of delegations to receive information about the progress. But this did not change or influence the decision-making in a small group and facing the membership with it.

The consultations at the TNC were first focussed on Agriculture, and once the US and EEC reached accords, and forced the others to agree to it, the attention was turned to TRIPs where the US and EEC (with Japan and other ICs) had a common position against the Third World. After agreements satisfactory to the US and EEC, and involving the rewriting of the mandate (however much the Third World negotiators might be explaining it away otherwise domestically) the consultations then took up textiles and safeguards, and the Third World negotiators again compromised.

The Battle Over TRIPs

In the intense consultations and negotiations on TRIPs at the TNC (which were taken up after the accord on Agriculture), Dunkel   produced a new text (ignoring once again completely the viewpoints of the Third World and the amendments   to his original text by Brazil, which had received large support at the meeting of the informal Third World group). This new text swung even further towards the views of the US and EEC, who were now united against the Third World countries. But when it became clear that a large number of Third World countries were even more opposed to the new Dunkel text and even the normal 'green room' process would bring this up, the invited participants in the consultations were further restricted, with some of smaller Third World countries (like Tanzania) which are normally invited and likely to take a strong stand kept out.

The TRIPs negotiations became largely a US-EEC vs Brazil and India affair. A number of other Third World representatives appeared to float in and out of these restricted consultations (on the night of April 7). But the delegates of these very same countries that spoke out against the US-EEC demands and the Dunkel texts at the informal Third World group meetings, apparently did not actively participate, giving the negotiators from Brazil and India a feeling that they were alone against the coercive power of the two major trading blocs, and would have to bear the brunt of the responsibility for any breakdown.

Unlike their mutual coordination before Montreal, and thanks to the change in the personalities of the Indian negotiating team [3] and the diplomatic disinformation campaign (of the US and the Secretariat), each of the two seemed less sure at Geneva of the other's position. Some of the Cairns Group members from Latin America had also privately said that unlike in Montreal (where they could take advantage of the US-EEC differences to block an imbalanced package) it would be difficult for them to do so in Geneva and block the Uruguay Round process, if the US and EEC reached an agreement on agriculture, with commitments for long-term reforms.

US Uses 301 to Weaken Third World

It is also clear, at least in retrospect, that sections within the governments in Brazil, India, and the other Third World countries, had been against taking a firm stand at the April TNC meeting, hoping that by this they could manage to avoid the threatened US actions against them under 'Special 301' in respect of their domestic intellectual property regimes. It is known that some of the countries were at that time holding bilateral talks with the representatives of the USTR in Washington and Geneva, and with US officials in their own capitals, trying to ensure that their names would not figure in the US hit list of 'priority' countries for S. 301 actions on their domestic intellectual property regimes.

In the fact sheet put out on 25 May 1989 at Washington (in announcing the Special 301 actions) the USTR claimed that the enactment of the Omnibus Trade and Competitiveness Act's Special 301 provisions and its implementation had already contributed positively to US efforts to ensure adequate and effective intellectual property rights protection, and listed among these the "positive Uruguay Round midterm review decision on intellectual property (April)".

In any event, the countries concerned failed even in their objective of avoiding Special 301 actions. After securing

all the advantages in the TRIPs group at the TNC, the USTR
still went ahead and took the 'Special 301' actions, though
the US tried to present it for public image purposes (in the
countries affected) as something different, whilst clarifying
(for domestic purposes) that though the countries had not
been designated as 'priority' countries, the actual actions taken
are no different. The USTR has identified 25 countries -
putting eight of them on a so-called 'priority watch list' (Brazil,
India, Mexico, China, South Korea, Saudi Arabia, Taiwan
and Thailand) and 17 on a 'watch list' (Argentina, Canada,
Chile, Colombia, Egypt, Greece, Indonesia, Italy, Japan,
Malaysia, Pakistan, Philippines, Portugal, Spain, Turkey,
Venezuela and Yugoslavia). The USTR has also made clear
that as far as the US and its demands in the area of intellectual property protection (and the US legislation in this regard) are concerned, "no foreign country currently meets
every standard for adequate and effective intellectual property protection" as set forth in the US proposals tabled in the
Uruguay Round on intellectual property and "all countries
are eligible for potential priority designation" based on the
standards of the US Uruguay Round proposals. By these
actions, the USTR has also sought to make sure that all the
Third World countries (those on the priority watch list,
watch list and not on either) would remain aware that they
could all be hit, under an accelerated deadline, any time
during the Uruguay Round negotiations, if they did not
behave themselves or as the USTR has put it, 'participate con-
structively' in the Uruguay Round TRIPs negotiations.

As the proceedings [4] at the June meetings of the GATT
Council (both in the Special session for reviewing developments in the trading system, and at the ordinary meeting on
specific complaints by Brazil and India (over the Super 301
and Special 301) actions against them) have brought out, the
US is isolated on this issue. Nevertheless the Third World
countries are not united enough to force the US to retreat.
And while the EEC and other Industrialised Countries are
equally opposed to the US actions and have given verbal
support to the countries against whom actions have been

initiated, they also want to derive advantage from the pressures generated against the Third World. On the new themes, all the ICs have a common interest with the US, and against the Third World, and want to make sure that the Uruguay Round negotiations are not disrupted and agreements are reached in the new areas. But unless the Uruguay Round negotiations are disrupted, the US will not abandon its '301' weapon - of bilateral consultations and threat of retaliation and retaliation - to achieve its neo-mercantilist economic aims and objectives. Also, while at present strongly opposed to the US 301 (because of its potential and actual uses against them), the EEC and others are fashioning their own similar instruments against the Third World.

Accords Reflect Third World Compromises

Overall, the package of accords [5] reached at Geneva (on Agriculture, Textiles, Safeguards and TRIPs) has perhaps made the entire 'mid-term' package even more imbalanced, and is going to complicate the tasks of Third World negotiators in the remaining period of the negotiations. In the midterm package as a whole, in areas where the North has a common interest against the South, and where differences in interpreting the mandate have blocked negotiations (as in Services or TRIPs), the accord now provides clear guidelines for the future course of negotiations. But in areas of interest to the South (but where there is again a basic unity of the North) as in Textiles or Safeguards, none of the problems holding up negotiations have been resolved.

In the four areas where agreements were reached at the Geneva meeting of the TNC, Third World countries may perhaps have gained something in the way of commitments for long-term reform in Agriculture, but have given way in the other three areas.

In TRIPs, the compromises agreed to may have some serious medium to long-term implications in terms of industrialisation and development goals and objectives.

In Textiles and Safeguards, the decisions are essentially procedural, without specific directions on substantive issues that have bedevilled negotiations in the first two years of the Uruguay Round.

Textiles: No·Phasing Out of MFA

In Textiles, the·accord provides that "substantive negotiations (which was to have begun in 1988 under the negotiating plan) will begin in April 1989 in order to reach agreement within the time-frame of the Uruguay Round on modalities for integration of this sector into GATT in accordance with the negotiating objective".

A minor gain perhaps has been the omission of the word 'eventual' before 'integration', which is found in the mandate and which has been repeatedly cited by the US and EEC to mean that the phasing out of the MFA is a long-term objective and no time-frame or even starting point could be fixed. At the first meeting of the Textiles negotiating group (on April 20), the US continued to take this position.

The accord provides that modalities for integration into GATT "on the basis of strengthened GATT rules and disciplines should *inter alia* cover the phasing out of restrictions under the MFA and other restrictions on textiles and clothing not consistent with GATT rules and disciplines and the time span for such a process, and the progressive character of this process should commence following conclusion of the negotiations in 1990." [6]

While this does not meet the Third World demand for commitment to phase-out the MFA, starting from the expiry of MFA-4 in July 1991, and within a timeframe to be agreed upon in the Round, the accord does mention that the modalities should cover the phasing out of the MFA, but weakens it by use of "*inter alia*", which could leave the door open for other proposals.

As already pointed out earlier, the US Trade Representative, Mrs. Carla Hills, is on record as having told Congress that the US .wants the present 'global system' of trade in this sector, presumably meaning the MFA, to be incorporated into GATT. The then EEC Commissioner, Willy de Clercq told the European Parliament, after Montreal, that the EEC envisaged MFA-4 to be replaced by an MFA-5.

The Third World did not get the provision for 'freeze' on new restrictions (under the MFA and its bilateral accords) to their exports. The US flatly refused this in the consultations, citing a Presidential guarantee to Congress to enforce the MFA vigorously. The EEC went one better and demanded language to provide for 'contributions' by all participants. The agreed formulation on this says: "To provide a positive climate for these negotiations, and without prejudice to the existing rights and obligations, and reaffirming the commitments (on standstill and rollback) embodied in Part I.C of the Punta del Este Declaration, all participants shall endeavour to improve the trade situation paving the way for integration of the textiles and clothing sector into GATT".

Agriculture

In agriculture, the text [7] commits participants to negotiate principles and rules to achieve the long-term objective of 'substantial progressive reductions' in agricultural support and protection sustained over an agreed period of time. The goal is to be achieved through agreed policies and measures and commitments to be negotiated on an aggregate measurement of support or a combination of them. Credit is to be given for measures implemented since Punta del Este and which contribute positively to the reform programme.

These strengthened GATT rules and disciplines are to

apply to all contracting parties, and encompass all measures directly or indirectly affecting import access and export competition.

The measures under import access will include those maintained under waivers (as that of the US), protocols of accession (as that of Switzerland) and other derogations and exceptions (as claimed by the EEC for its common agricultural policy as a part of the Rome Treaty that was notified and discussed in GATT, but neither approved nor disapproved, with the EEC citing the latter as amounting to GATT sanction as a Customs Union).

Other areas to be covered are subsidies and export competition, and export prohibitions and restrictions. On all but the last the specific issues to be negotiated are also spelt out. Measures maintained under agricultural policies due to "factors other than trade policy", such as food security, are to be taken into account.

However, there is agreement that special and differential treatment to Third World countries is an integral element of the negotiations, that "government measures on assistance, whether direct or indirect, to encourage agricultural and rural development are an integral part of the development programmes of developing countries", and that ways should be developed "to take into account the possible negative effects of reform process on net food importing developing countries."

The modalities for all these are to be developed over the following 20 months of negotiations as part of the work programme of the negotiating group.

The implementation of the first tranche of agreed commitments on long-term reform programme are to take place in 1991. Not later than end of 1990, participants are to agree on the long-term reform programme and the time-period for its implementation.

The short-term measures agreed to in effect call for a standstill in the area of agricultural protection. It is to commence from 8 April 1989 (when the decision was adopted) and will continue till formal completion of the negotiations in Dec 1990. Third World countries are exempted from this.

Participants have undertaken 'to ensure' that current domestic and export support and protection levels in the agricultural sector are not exceeded, and that tariff and non-tariff market access barriers in force at the time of adoption of the decision are not subsequently intensified in relation to imports of agricultural products nor extended to additional products, including processed products.

Support prices to producers, expressed in national currencies (in ECU for the EEC), are also not to be raised above the level prevailing at the date of the decision. Actions are also not to be otherwise taken that would increase the current levels of support for the commodity concerned.

The issue of export subsidies and the US set-aside programmes have been omitted. As worded, it could mean that while the EEC, for example, cannot raise its overall levels of budgetary outlay and support for export subsidies or domestic support, it could reduce it for some commodities and increase it for others, as the EEC claims it could do, and intends to in respect of soya. But some Cairns members already have challenged this interpretation.

There will be a work programme to develop harmonization of sanitary and phytosanitary regulations and measures, and for strengthening Article XX of GATT (the general exception article with provisions for trade restrictions on among others health grounds) so that measures taken are consistent with 'sound scientific evidence' and use suitable principles of equivalence. This last has been an issue in the US-EEC dispute over hormone treated beef imports into the Community from the US.

Safeguards

On safeguards, the agreement is mainly procedural and, operationally, provides for the chairman of the negotiating group to draw up a draft text of a comprehensive safeguards agreement as a basis for negotiations and for negotiations to begin on this basis by June 1989 at the latest.

None of the basic problems that have blocked such an agreement in the Tokyo Round, and in the subsequent GATT work programme or the two years of negotiations, have been tackled or guidelines given to negotiators. The major issue of non-discriminatory safeguard actions have not been tackled, but postponed. The accord merely reiterates the Punta del Este mandate about the agreement being based on the 'basic principles' of GATT, and that it should "aim" at reestablishing multilateral control over safeguards "*inter alia* by eliminating measures which escape such control".

Both the use of "aim" rather than a direction to "reestablish" and the use of "*inter alia*" leaves the door open for attempts to legitimise 'grey area' measures.

TRIPs: Third World Backs Down

In TRIPs, the text:

- recognises the importance of successful conclusion of the MTNs in TRIPs,

- recalls the objectives in the Punta del Este mandate about strengthening the role of GATT and bringing about a wider coverage of world trade under multilateral disciplines as well as the provisions about special and differential treatment in the general principles governing negotiations, and

- agrees that the outcome of negotiations is not pre-

judged, and that these negotiations are without prejudice to the views of participants concerning the institutional aspects of the international implementation of the
results of the negotiations in this area, which is to be
decided by ministers meeting on the occasion of a Special
Session of the GATT CONTRACTING PARTIES at the
conclusion of the round.

The text then provides that the negotiations "shall continue in the Uruguay Round and shall encompass:

- the applicability of basic principles of GATT and of
relevant international intellectual property agreements
or conventions,

- provision of adequate standards and principles concerning the availability, scope and use of TRIPs,

- provision of effective and appropriate means for enforcement of TRIPs, taking into account differences in
national legal systems,

- provision of effective and expeditious procedures for
multilateral prevention and settlement of disputes between governments, including applicability of GATT procedures, and

- transitional arrangements aiming at fullest participation
in the results of negotiations."

Taken together, these are intended to enable the US to
raise as a GATT dispute the 'adequacy' of patents and other
rights provided by Third World countries and enable the US
to undertake cross-retaliation. In effect this would internationalise and multilateralise its S. 301 powers.

But the formulations are in language that could also
create new controversies as to what they mean. They probably will, when policy-makers in Third World capitals, in more

substantive ministries as well as domestic industries, realise what their negotiators have done and look for ways to get out of the difficulties.

There is also agreement that in the negotiations "consideration will be given to concerns expressed by participants relating to underlying public policy objectives of their national systems for protection of intellectual property, including developmental and technological objectives". But this is weaker than the formulation about the issues to be negotiated.

The importance of reducing tensions in this area by reaching strengthened commitments to resolve disputes on TRIPs issues through multilateral procedures is also emphasised, a somewhat weaker formulation than in the Dunkel text in a reference to the need for the US to refrain from use of S. 301.

Other provisions call for negotiations to develop multilateral framework of principles and rules to deal with international trade in counterfeit goods.

There is a final provision that the TRIPs negotiations should be conducive to a mutually supportive relationship between GATT and WIPO as well as other relevant international organisations.

Whatever the post-facto rationalisation that some of the Third World negotiators have been providing for the compromise, and about what or what has not been agreed to, the failure of the Third World countries to join together and block this rewriting of the Punta del Este mandate, with senior officials over-riding the Decision of their Ministers taken at a Special Session of the CONTRACTING PARTIES, puts a greater burden on their negotiators to safeguard national interests. The earlier Third World countries recognise this, and concert with each other, the easier would be the path to preserving domestic space and national autonomy.

Much would depend on whether Third World countries would at least now concert and stand together to make sure that their own concerns are fully reflected and provided for (including for example compulsory licensing in public interest and right to decide whether processes or products or none should be protected in any particular area, and for what periods and under what conditions, and for the right balance between rights and obligations of those who secure from a country intellectual property protection).

Notes on Chapter 12:

1. *SUNS* 2125.

2. The term used in Article XX (d) of the GATT, which enables trade policy measures against imports, among others, for enforcement of patents and other rights.

3. India's GATT negotiator (from 1984-1988), S.P.Shukla, who had played an important role in the formulation of the Indian stand on new themes and in mobilising support for it among like-minded Third World countries, had been reassigned to India to take up a post as Secretary to Government in the Ministry of Health and put in charge of family planning. His post in Geneva had not been filled (at the time of the April TNC meeting), and the permanent Secretary of the Commerce Ministry, who came from New Delhi to negotiate, did not manage to establish that personal rapport and confidence among other Third World countries that negotiators on the spot establish over a long period.

4. See *SUNS* 2181, 2182 and 2183 for discussions in the Council.

5. For texts of the accords see MTN.TNC/11, GATT.

6. MTN/TNC.9 p 2.

7. MTN.TNC/11 pp 9-13.

Chapter 13

THE SITUATION
IN JANUARY 1990

Third World Position Worse Off

The negotiating processes after the mid-term review decisions have made the outlook even more asymmetric and skewed than before.

In January 1990, as the Uruguay Round negotiations moved into the final year, overall the situation of the Third World was worse off than after the mid-term review accords in April 1989.

In December 1989, when negotiators adjourned for Xmas holidays, in several of the negotiating areas of priority and interest for the Third World there had been no progress: the major ICs, who are the Third World's interlocutors, had not even put forward any counter-proposals or engaged in any serious dialogue.

It was also becoming clearer that while the US and the EEC continued to spar and fight each other in areas like Agriculture, they were working in parallel, if not jointly, in extracting the maximum from the Third World, through OECD processes in Paris and various other ad hoc arrangements at Geneva and elsewhere.

There are also continued and concerted efforts on their part to prevent the Third World countries from coalescing.

The Third World countries continue to be in disarray and most of them have even failed so far to identify their individual and collective strategic interests and tactical options.

During the first three years of negotiations, some Third World delegations viewed the Round in terms of their gaining access to markets of Industrial Countries (through the latter fulfilling their past commitments), in return for which the Third World may have to make concessions in other areas (new themes), but gain some flexibility through the 'special and differential (more favorable) treatment' provisions of GATT and the Punta del Este mandate.

But this view of some Third World countries appears to have been based on a false promise: in every negotiating area now the 'demanders' are the major ICs and the 'yielders' are to be the Third World nations.

At the end of December 1989, while (with cooperation of the Third World) some mid-term accord deadlines had been fulfilled (e.g. in assembling elements for negotiating a multilateral framework on services and tabling proposals on standards etc. in TRIPs), other deadlines such as on Textiles and Clothing or Tariffs and other 'market access issues' had been allowed to go by without any progress.

Traditional and Systemic Issues

In **Tariffs**, according to the midterm accord, agreement on the tariff cutting approach was to have been completed and substantive negotiations for tariff cuts, including on tariff peaks and tariff escalations, was to have begun in July 1989. But no agreement was reached, even by December end, on the modalities.

Giving the deadlock in Tariffs as an excuse, ICs had neither put forward serious proposals nor allowed negotiations and discussions to move forward in other areas of Third

World priority, including Non-Tariff measures, Natural Re-source-based products, and Tropical Products.

In January 1990, the deadlock on modalities (between US insistence on traditional requests/offer approach and EEC's general formula reduction approach) in Tariffs was bypassed by agreeing on 'procedures'. This can best be described as providing for 'offer/request' procedures: each participant notifying by 15 March its proposals for tariff-cut on each tariff-line of its customs schedule and explain how it would be in line with the mid-term accord - which is now being interpreted to mean that every participant should reduce its weighted average tariff by at least 40 percent and 'bind' them. Requests for adjustments of these offers are to be put in by 30 April, and negotiations would only commence thereafter!

Even though there are still references to the 'special and more favourable treatment' concepts included in the Punta del Este mandate, meaning Third World countries would not be called upon to make concessions 'inconsistent with their individual development, financial and trade needs', it would appear that the main effort is going to be to force Third World countries to reduce and bind their tariffs or use their failure to do so as an excuse to maintain the high peaks and tariff escalations against imports from the Third World countries.

For most of the Third World countries, and many of the leading economies among them, tariffs are not merely protective devices as in the North but also a source of revenue for the State. The procedures agreed to, if implemented, would not only have trade policy implications but fiscal implications in countries where governments have already had to cut social expenditures to balance their budgets under adjustment programmes.

In **Tropical Products,** it is now clear, from simulations done in UNCTAD, that the much-advertised December 1988

Montreal 'Xmas gift' to the Third World Tropical Products
exporting countries (through offers of tariff concessions) was
a gift-wrapped package with little inside, and would result
in no more than a two percent trade creating effect. The
EEC's concessions have been found to be a case of 'rob-
bing Peter (Africa) to pay Paul (ASEAN and some Latins)',
while concessions of Japan and Australia and others have
benefited Europe more than the Third World countries
themselves [1].

In the area of **Textiles and Clothing**, accounting for
a major proportion of Third World manufactured exports,
the US ideas formulated in January 1990, show that the US
wants to continue MFA-type restrictions into the next century, gradually replacing the present country-wise product-
specific quotas by so-called global quotas that would create
competition among exporters but would insulate the US
industry itself from competition. The EEC approach, while
favouring a gradual phaseout of MFA restrictions over the
decade, is contingent on other conditions and disciplines in
other negotiating areas like TRIPs, subsidies, etc. It is clear
that there is a broad convergence of views, and evidence of concerted attempts, among ICs to maintain at least
until the end of the century, the current status quo: discriminatory quotas on Third World exports of Textiles and Clothing. These restrictions, maintained as a derogation from the
normal GATT provisions for free trade, are sought to be
continued under 'transitionary' arrangements.

In the **Non-tariff** area, there has so far been no move
by the ICs to discuss and deal with their proliferation of 'grey
area' measures - those that may not be strictly illegal but are
not also sanctioned by the General Agreement. The EEC, in
its proposals on safeguards , has even sought to get GATT
legitimisation for such measures.

In the related area of implementation of the **rollback**
commitments there has been no progress since Punta del
Este. On the other hand, the ICs are trying to get credit in the

Round, as autonomous implementation of 'rollback', for the measures they have had to take to implement GATT panel rulings.

The subject of **Natural Resource-based Products** (NRBPs) had been put on the Uruguay Round agenda by some of the resource-rich nations of the North and South in an effort to put together a database of various types of restrictions on their exports and negotiate them down. Instead, the negotiations have turned into an exercise in which the US, EEC and Japan want assured access to the natural resources of other countries. They thus seek to discipline measures taken by producing countries to encourage local processing and value-added before exports.

In the negotiations on **GATT Articles,** those provisions that provide an element of flexibility to Third World Nations, such as BOP provisions, are being targeted for changes. Even practices which have sound basis in neo-classical economic theory, such as state subsidies to correct market imperfections, are sought to be attacked; and the limited GATT prohibitions against export subsidies are being sought to be expanded to outlaw a wide range of Third World domestic policies of economic organisations and production.

In the important area of **Safeguards**, where everyone had agreed to take a draft text of elements prepared by the Chairman (in accordance with the mid-term accord) as a basis for discussion and negotiations, a mere footnote reference noting the view of some favouring 'selective safeguards' now looks like advancing from the footnote to the main text.

The European Community has put forward a proposal that would enable 'selective safeguard' measures to be taken and in effect legitimise 'grey area' measures (like voluntary export restraints etc, that might be agreed to by exporting countries to avoid 'selective safeguards') and make them enforceable through a supervisory body of the GATT! The

US has made statements that suggest it is in sympathy with such a move.

Position of the New Themes

As for the new themes, in **TRIPs** the ICs are inexorably pushing towards GATT agreements on higher standards of protection in various areas of intellectual/industrial property rights, extending such protection to virtually all areas of inventive activity - a sweep so wide that a few ICs themselves have found it expedient to specifically seek to exclude patentability of human beings!

These negotiations are going on side-by-side with bilateral pressures by the US on Third World countries to change their patent laws and provide patent protection for pharmaceutical processes and products for long periods.

In **TRIMs**, the ICs seem likely to succeed not only in disciplining, through new rules and new GATT provisions, 'local content' requirements which are per se illegal in GATT (except when Third World countries justify their import restrictions on grounds of their BOP situation), but also prohibit such things as export performance requirements (held to be legal by a GATT panel), manufacturing requirements, domestic sales requirements, product mandating requirements and trade balancing requirement - investment measures which Third World nations impose to counter transnational corporate practices 'restricting' and 'distorting' trade.

The US has tabled a draft agreement for a full-fledged investment regime spelling out a wide range of rights and freedoms for investors whilst placing great restrictions on governments. The scope of the US proposals go beyond anything it had sought at the Havana Charter negotiations, and even beyond the claimed rights that prevailed in the colonial era, with the difference now is that instead of gunboat diplomacy and military occupation or other interventions, the rights of foreigners would now be backed by trade sanctions applied by their governments.

In the area of **Services**, a draft text was drawn up in December 1989 by the Group of Negotiations on Services (GNS) to form the basis for negotiations in 1990. A programme of work and timetable agreed for the GNS until end of July 1990 would suggest that work on a draft framework agreement would be completed by then. GATT officials have in fact claimed that the programme meant there was now 'a definite commitment' on the part of everyone to conclude a draft framework, perhaps leaving a few square brackets to be tackled, by then.

The present draft text which is the basis for negotiations bristles with some 160 square brackets and Third World delegations claim that all their interests have been included in the square bracketed texts, thus keeping them on the table for negotiations in 1990. But if past GATT and Uruguay Round 'green room' consultations, including the mid-term one at Montreal in December and at Geneva in April, provide any guidance to the future, in the next phase of negotiations and green room consultations square brackets around formulations of ICs (because of reservations of Third World Nations) are likely to be resolved by removal of square brackets, while those around formulations of Third World Nation would be cleaned up by knocking out the formulations.

Moves to Expand GATT's Powers

There are also behind the scenes efforts to *institutionalise the GATT and its secretariat* by the backdoor and ensure implementation by all the GATT contracting parties of the results of the Uruguay Round in the new areas. The aim is to overcome difficulties that would arise if the new agreements envisaged in TRIPs, TRIMs and Services are sought to be incorporated into GATT in the normal way and also provide the secretariat a role, power and function to enable it to act, in tandem with the secretariats of the IMF and the

World Bank, as a trade policeman of sorts over the Third World.

Any straightforward effort to incorporate the Uruguay Round agreements through Article XXV of the General Agreement (by CONTRACTING PARTIES acting jointly) or through protocols to amend the General Agreement pose problems. The Article XXV route, where contracting parties meeting from time to time take joint action, by a majority of the votes cast, to give effect to the provisions of the General Agreement, cannot be used to impose new obligations in areas not covered by GATT (TRIPs, TRIMs and Services). Amendments to the Agreement through protocols would need the affirmative votes of a two-thirds majority of the contracting parties, and would be binding only on those who accept the amendments. It is also doubtful whether the amendment procedure could be used to incorporate into GATT obligations in areas which, it could be argued, fall outside the scope of GATT. Also, any amendment if it involves changes in Article I (most-favoured-nation treatment provision) would need unanimity.

An idea being canvassed informally and sought to be pushed through is to create an international trade organisation - not through the normal process for adoption of a treaty or convention, namely, summoning an International Conference by a few sponsoring States or a UN Conference summoned by the UN General Assembly, to negotiate and adopt the new treaty and throw it open for signatures and ratification - but through the non-transparent GATT Uruguay Round processes. The intention appears to be to get Ministers, at the final meeting in Brussels in December 1990, to agree to this as part of the overall package of Uruguay Round agreements and open the agreement for signature. The new institution, though it might evoke the image of the Havana Charter and its International Trade Organisation which was aborted by the US refusal to ratify, would be nothing of that sort. It would not, for example, deal with the restrictive business practices and other anti-competition activities of the TNCs, nor deal with commodity policies and stabilisation of markets and earnings, nor provide for development.

It would in fact be an organisation guaranteeing the rights of TNCs and spelling out the obligations of governments and providing for trade sanctions to enforce these TNC rights.

In sum total, the overall implications of the Uruguay Round negotiating process will be more severe and adverse to the development aspirations of the Third World than the sum of the outcome of its 15 individual parts.

In the market access cluster, Third World countries have to make 'offers' and thus pay an entry fee merely to sit in on the negotiations; otherwise they will be shut out from the very process itself. The ostensible liberalisation of trade that could be achieved in the market access cluster pales into insignificance when compared to the costs of what will emerge in the three new areas.

Shorn of technical verbiage, the package in the three new areas will result in creating further barriers to the Third World's access to technology, capital and capacity to establish a modern infrastructure, through development of producer services. Third World countries will find the price of development will be that much higher: the ground rules, and the terms and conditions will make the external environment more restrictive and hostile, rather than supportive.

A GATT agreement on TRIPs, possibly on TRIMs, and certainly a multilateral framework on Services, are being negotiated to provide enhanced protection and rights for TNCs. Even elementary countervailing obligations, such as disciplines on corporate entities and their practices, have been ruled out of court.

The real immediate challenge before Third World countries is to ensure at least 'damage-minimisation' and preserve their political and economic independence and right of autonomous development.

Notes for Chapter 13

1. See Tables 3 and 4 of Chapter 11 of this book (Source: UNCTAD/MTN/INT/CB.20).

PART V

EPILOGUE

Chapter 14

WHAT NEEDS TO BE DONE

The Need for Third World Unity

Anyone making an objective and frank assessment of the South and its situation at the present juncture cannot but be struck by the disarray and disunity among its different countries. It is an irony that the South which has to seek equity and justice in the current iniquitous and unjust international economic system is now not united and organised whereas the North, which already enjoys a vastly disproportionate part of world wealth and income and is now striving to get more, has become increasingly united and coordinated.

Thanks to this basic unity of the North against the South, and the aggressive neo-mercantilist policies of the major ICs, on the whole the developing countries are now worse off in the Uruguay Round than when it was launched. If there is no high-level political effort in the South to confront and reverse these tendencies, the possibility has to be faced that the dominant ICs would succeed in putting in place a New International Economic Order more unjust and more inequitable to the peoples of the South than even the present order.

In 1961 the Non-Aligned Movement at its first summit in Belgrade initiated steps that led three years later to the founding of UNCTAD and to the formation of the Group of

77. Thereafter for two decades the South strove with unity for equity and justice and even made some limited gains. But now the countries of the South face some major threats to their independence of action and hopes of securing the economic well-being of their peoples. At this juncture, there can be no higher priority for the South and its movements, governmental and non-governmental, than to understand this and take remedial measures through unity and with determination.

In the arena of governmental actions, the first priority must be to rediscover the unity and solidarity of the South and forge a united front, and achieve this without any further delay. Enough time has already been lost. This too is a priority for non-governmental forces in the South: they should persuade and lobby their governments to take the necessary steps.

In the 15 areas of negotiations in the Round, there may be some areas, and some issues within them, where developing countries or groups of them may have some differing (but not necessarily conflicting) interests. But in a number of others they share fundamental common interests. The existence of diversified sets of negotiating interests in a few areas should not hence be allowed to come in the way of a common stand on the more important issues.

But achieving such a unity needs political involvement of the capitals, and an approach that brings to bear on this effort a wider vision than mere immediate expansion of exports or curbing of imports. Only such an approach among the countries of the South would enable the creation of mechanisms for political concertation and coordination at periodic intervals over the remaining part of the Round. If such an effort is not mounted at this stage, and unity and solidarity are not achieved, all the medium to long-term aims and objectives of the NAM, the Group of 77 and of leading economies and powers among them, will be brought to naught and the South will receive a major setback.

Such an effort would not be an attempt to form a bloc and cut the South off from the North, but rather an attempt to deal with the North in a way where the South and its interests will be heeded. As already noted, the ICs concert among themselves, while discouraging any such moves on the part of the Third World countries. Only periodic and political level consultations within the South could help in maximising their commonality of interests and present a credible countervailing force. Any effort by any of the countries, big or small, to deal singly or in small sub-regional groups would fail to safeguard legitimate interests of these countries and their future generations.

A related issue is the grouping of some developing and developed countries into special interest groups, for example, the Cairns Group. The rationale has been that as against the giant three (US, EEC and Japan), these special interest groups, bringing together the medium and small countries of the North and the South and having a common interest, could exercise some influence and ensure the interests of these countries are advanced.

However, the mid-term review process at Montreal and Geneva have brought out the limitations of and the price for such combinations. At Montreal when the US and EEC tried to put agriculture aside and move on to other negotiations, and Argentina and other Latin American Cairns members sought to persuade their group as a whole to block the process, Australia and New Zealand made clear that they could not join. When anyhow the Latin American Cairns members acted to block the process at Montreal, they received the 'understanding' of other Third World countries. Subsequently, at Geneva, the entire Agriculture negotiations was bilateral between the US and EEC, and once they reached their own agreement, the Cairns group had no influence to change anything to get their concerns accommodated. On the contrary, the agreement on Agriculture between the US and EEC was used to extract a price from the Third World Cairns members (as other Third World countries) on Textiles, Safeguards and TRIPs, and prevent the developing countries as a group (which had a common interest on all these) to coalesce and influence the outcome.

In all probability, the final outcome too would not be very different. Third World members of the Cairns group have thus to weigh whether in fact they are getting any benefit or whether they are merely being asked to pay a price for an accord which the US and EEC will in any event reach in their own mutual interest.

In reality, in the economic arena, the Third World is facing the same dilemma that the States of Europe faced in the inter-war years over their security and demands from Hitler, and where each tried to buy peace at the expense of the other. The lessons of that period have been hammered into the postwar political relationships in the community of Nations, but its lessons have not been grasped in the area of international economic relations, particularly when the concepts and consensus about international economic cooperation have now given way to greed and aggrandisement. Appeasement is as useless an exercise in the economic and trade spheres as in the political and security spheres. It only whets appetites. The more countries yield now, the more they will be asked to yield in the future.

Any attempts by policy-makers in the Third World to seek compromises in the economic arena now, in the expectation of short-term gains, will only make the situation worse in the medium-term, and over the long-term foreclose other development options and result in mortgaging the future of the next generation well into the next century.

In the present situation the South cannot afford to fight its battles on the ground chosen by the North or according to rules formulated by the North. The South need not fight trade actions only on the trade or economic front. The South should evolve its own 'globality', not only within the Uruguay Round but other issues too on the North's political, cultural and economic agenda, including the North's versions of the 'Environment' agenda.

The efforts at political-level concertation and harmonisation of the South on these issues will never get off the ground if it has to await unanimity in the South. As many of those as are concerned about the future autonomous development processes of their countries should begin to get together and act together, keeping the door always open to others from the South.

A welcome move in this connection is the formation of a 15-country 'Summit level group for South-South consultation and cooperation', as a result of an initiative taken on the occasion of the ninth Non-Aligned Summit at Belgrade in September 1989. The 15 countries (Algeria, Argentina, Brazil, Egypt, India, Indonesia, Jamaica, Malaysia, Mexico, Nigeria, Peru, Senegal, Venezuela, Yugoslavia and Zimbabwe) represent a broad spectrum of politically or economically significant countries of the South. One of the tasks that the group has set for itself is to "review periodically the world economic situation and the state of international economic relations affecting developing countries and suggest strategies for developing countries for coping with the emerging challenges, including initiatives to be proposed in North-South forums."

In March 1990, senior trade officials from Brazil, China, Colombia, Cuba, Egypt, India, Indonesia, Jamaica, Kenya, Malaysia, Mexico, Nigeria, Pakistan, Peru, Singapore, Tanzania, Yugoslavia and Zimbabwe met in New Delhi and called for coordinated action on the part of Third World countries in the Round. They also agreed to continue the process of consultation and coordination among themselves at senior officials level.

In the context of such a broad united front of the South,

a few key issues need urgent and clear political agreement and directions to negotiators.

Negotiation Strategy

1. The negotiating process: This is a basic and critical issue. The GATT processes of consultations and decision-making, typified in the so-called 'green-room consultations', are intended to isolate and intimidate Third World negotiators, with the 'invitees' to this process 'selected' in a non-transparent way by GATT officials and the major ICs.

It is important to put an end to this process, and ensure transparency and more open participation. Any country that has an interest on any issue (and it is for the country concerned to determine this), and whatever its 'trade weight', should be able to participate. Otherwise Third World countries will continue to face the 'power' approach favored by the major trading blocs and the GATT secretariat, whereby a few Third World countries are forced to involve themselves in hard bargaining in an intimidatory atmosphere, and facing individually the responsibility of breakdown and trade retaliation, apart from orchestrated and insidious campaigns in their capitals to change the negotiators and replace them by those more amenable to the North.

Agreement with the North is not even needed to end the asymmetric processes of 'consultation' and decision-making in GATT. Only a political decision in a few capitals is needed. If enough countries, not involved in the 'green room' process, refuse to accept "chairman's texts" sprung on them as a result of the 'green room' process and insist on full discussion and negotiations, this practice will come to an end. It is undoubtedly difficult to negotiate with 92 participants. In practice not all would in fact participate. But there is no reason why consultations and negotiations, as in other UN fora, cannot be open-ended, and open to any country that has an interest. This is particularly necessary on new themes and systemic issues that have far-reaching effects on the future.

It is also essential that the countries of the South speak up loudly and clearly in the GATT. It is not enough if they speak in their own informal group meetings. They must do so in the GATT meetings. Often they are diffident and hesitant because of the hush-hush atmosphere there and the aura of GATT being a contract. But developing countries must shed their hesitation and clearly spell out what they will accept and what they will not accept. Even if 10-15 of them speak out clearly in open meetings (open to delegates, though not to observers or the media), it is likely that decisions detrimental to these countries would be avoided. Considering the differing perceptions and specific interests of the countries of the South, it is not possible that all of them will speak uniformly on all the subjects. However, a system of mutual support needs to be built up.

On issues where the interests of all coincide, they should together issue and present a common statement, with as many of them as possible speaking up individually in support on that occasion.

On issues of interest only to some of them, those who are interested should issue their common statement and those among the others whose interests are not opposed should provide open support even if they do not have a direct interest in the subject.

On such issues where there are differing interests, the various interest groups among the countries of the South should hold consultations in order to understand each other with the objective of achieving agreements through appropriate mutual concessions, and then meeting the North with this modified position which should then have the open support of all in the South.

It can be said that these are suggestions advocating only elementary principles of solidarity. But the countries of the South inside GATT are in such disarray that their leaders should consider commiting themselves to such a code of solidarity, in order to facilitate a degree of cohesive unity at the GATT forum.

Traditional Issues

2. Textiles and Clothing: The developing countries must ensure full return of this trade to GATT rules and disciplines, and the phase-out of the discriminatory MFA regime, even though the phase-out has to be gradual. Otherwise they will encourage the current tendencies to extend such special and discriminatory regimes to every area of activity where the Third World is emerging as competitors.

They must also stand together and condemn and reject any attempt to extract a price from them for the phasing out of the MFA and the discriminatory regime. For the last 25 years they have already paid a price to the North by the agreement to restrain the exports of the Third World. If anything the Third World countries have to be compensated for this past injury to their exports.

3. Agriculture: This is an area where Third World countries have some differing interests: those exporting temperate zone products and competing with the ICs and deriving their export earnings mainly from these, others exporting one or two major agricultural products competing with similar or other IC exports, some who are major exporters in one or two products but are net importers in the sector as a whole, the net food importing countries, and the relatively self-sufficient and continental economies where agriculture is an important area for development.

It is necessary for all these countries to think through

their interests and differences and come to a common position that would be mutually supportive. This is particularly essential in relation to the efforts at drawing up new rules and principles and/or strengthening existing disciplines.

They should particularly take care that their 'development' interests are not sacrificed in favour of a 'market-sharing' arrangement between the US and Europe, with perhaps a few crumbs thrown in for some of the agricultural exporters and for which they and others would be called upon to pay a price in this or other areas.

Systemic Issues

4. GATT Articles: Third World countries should refuse to agree to any tinkering or modification of their existing GATT rights, and in particular those in Article XVIII enabling them to impose trade policy restrictions for reasons of BOP and to take autonomous decisions on their imports based on their development policies, goals and objectives.

5. Safeguards: This is a basic fundamental question of primary importance for the current and future trade prospects of developing countries. The Third World countries must unite themselves and ensure a clear agreement in the Round to specifically outlaw any 'selective' or discriminatory safeguard actions or 'grey area' measures.

It is not enough that no agreement permitting 'selective safeguards' is concluded. It is imperative to secure an agreement that prohibits such 'selective' safeguards, given the practice and assertion of legitimacy for selectivity by major trading nations over the last two decades.

It is better to end the Round in failure than to conclude it without a comprehensive safeguards agreement based on non-discrimination.

There should also be provision for effective multilateral surveillance of any safeguard action by any country, and requirement for multilateral approval.

Without such an agreement, any concessions to Third World countries in any of the traditional areas of market access will be illusory and will be easily negated.

Even more, a safeguards agreement which does not outlaw but legitimises in any way 'selective' safeguards will enable the major ICs to impose trade restrictions for political ends (without invoking the current requirement of 'security exceptions' and thus attracting political opprobrium), and/or enable the powerful trading partner to take actions against their weaker partners.

Any country taking a non-discriminatory safeguard action is doing so to adjust its economy. The costs of this adjustment cannot be allowed to fall on the exporting countries. Hence, the country taking safeguard actions should provide compensation for the countries affected by its measures, either in the form of concessions in export sectors of interest to the country affected and/or even financial compensation. This is particularly important for Third World countries, and those with very few export sectors.

6. Subsidies and MTN Agreements: There should be explicit provisions that the 'non-exclusion' clause cannot be used to extract concessions not in consonance with the provisions of the agreements. The US has been using this provision to exclude application of the code to Third World countries unless they give up their privileges under the codes for special and differential treatment.

Third World countries should also refuse to agree to new disciplines or changes in the GATT rules relating to subsidies that would prohibit a whole range of their domestic subsidies and policy measures aimed at correcting at their structural deficiencies and market distortions or restrict their right to use export subsidies to correct market imperfections.

7. Special and Differential Treatment: This is a fundamental principle underlying the negotiations and the current
GATT framework. Provisions for this in Part IV of GATT and
in the Enabling Clause have to be made operational, and
specified as an obligation for the ICs rather than a 'best
endeavor' effort as has been interpreted by the ICs so far.

8. Enforcement of Rights and Obligations: This is an
important issue relating to two areas of negotiations - Dispute Settlement and the Functioning of the GATT System.

At present in the GATT system, enforcement of rights
and obligations rests on 'retaliation'. All the mechanisms for
settlement of disputes boil down to this. When any cp,
against whom a ruling is given, does not implement it, the
only remedy provided is for the GATT CPs, acting together,
authorising an aggrieved CP (whose rights were violated and
had brought up the complaint) to 'retaliate' by withdrawing
'equivalent concessions'. But this is a remedy available only
to the most powerful, and is of no use to the weaker trading
partners and developing countries. There should be provision in the General Agreement that where the rights of a
developing contracting party has been breached, and when
everything else fails, the CPs in the final analysis would act
jointly and retaliate against the offending cp by withdrawing
concessions.

It is also important to insist that any package of agreements in the Uruguay Round must include a specific obligation to abide by GATT rules and principles and bring
domestic legislations and administrative rules and practices
fully in line. There can be no place in an international system
based on rules and principles for any member to assert the
right of 'unilateral' interpretations or retaliations as the US
has been doing on 'Super S.301' and the EEC is gradually
beginning to do in its own way.

New Themes

In all the three areas of 'Services', 'TRIPs' and 'TRIMs' they should make sure that corporate policies and practices are explicitly covered and disciplines on governments are matched by disciplines on private operators in the market. Any disciplines covering government actions, without covering the actions of the private firms, would make the system even more asymmetrical. Third World countries must work for and ensure new rules and disciplines on the exercise of economic power and privileges by firms, including obligations on 'home' countries to enforce the rules and disciplines on their enterprises.

9. Services: Whatever agreement might emerge in this area, developing countries must make sure that they would be free to enact or implement laws, regulations and practices in respect of services which they consider 'appropriate' for the development purposes. 'Development' should have the same status as 'Security' in Article XXI.

They also have to make sure that they do not end up with an exemption or special treatment as a result of which while they are not compelled to accept obligations they are also excluded from benefits that accrue only to those who accept obligations. Any kind of conditional MFN must not be given the imprimateur of the Uruguay Round agreement or an international agreement.

The framework of rules and disciplines under services should also ensure access of Third World countries to such services (including technology, etc.) which are now denied to them by enterprises or through regulations of countries purporting to be acting under 'security' exceptions or the restrictive practices of dominant suppliers.

All institutional and other arrangements should be kept outside the GATT, and there should be no linkages nor any umbrella secretariat to coordinate goods and services.

10. TRIPs: Now that developing countries have agreed to negotiate issues of substantive norms and standards and their enforcement and settlement of disputes in the Round, they should bring to the negotiating table the full range of issues and proposals for reforms in this area that they have put forward in the various UN fora and insist on agreements satisfactory to them.

At the minimum they should ensure that intellectual (industrial) property protection laws and regimes in Third World countries - introduced, maintained or changed in the context of their development objectives and public policy and public interest - are not made the subject of international scrutiny or subject for settlement of disputes.

They should also make sure that any regime that might emerge is not institutionalized in GATT or in any way tied to it and its general trade policy regimes.

11. TRIMs: Third World countries must ensure that the outcome in this area in no way circumscribes their capacity to attract foreign direct investment or channel it according to their national priorities. Investment measures, employed by countries in the broader context of social and economic policy objectives and in furtherance of industrialisation and development or to safeguard their balance-of-payments, cannot be negotiated away by them in trade negotiations in the GATT. Third World countries should insist on tackling only the 'trade-related' aspects of such measures, and that too of those which have a direct and significant adverse effects on trade. Where such effects can be demonstrated, such adverse effects could be reduced or eliminated by addressing them through available remedies of rights and obligations within the GATT framework.

As in Services and TRIPs, the policies and practices of

private operators on the market which have trade-restrictive or distorting effects would also need to be disciplined simultaneously.

Time Now For Action

On the wide range of technical issues and details of
concern to the Third World, referred to above or not touched
at all, there is need for broad political guidance from the
countries to their negotiators to undertake coordination and
harmonisation of positions.

Over the past two decades, governments of the South
have missed many opportunities where with some unity
among themselves, they could have influenced the course of
events and ensured better equity and justice. If in the
1970s, the OPEC members and the capital surplus countries
among them, had not put their wealth at the disposal of the
Northern controlled international institutions and private
banks, but had joined hands with the other Third World
countries to reform the system, not only the South but the
OPEC members too would have been better off now. If the
Third World countries had not, for the short-term gains of
the Trust Fund (through sales of IMF gold owned by them),
accepted the Jamaica agreement, the current disorders and
high interest rates and a financial and monetary system run
for the benefit of the private banks, would not have been
possible. If the debtor countries of the South, and particularly those with private bank debts had concerted together
and had forged a common front (and they are yet to do this
despite all the rhetoric that comes out of their periodic
meetings), the debt crisis would not have ravaged the South
as it has and continues to do now.

If in 1982, the Third World governments had joined to
block the new GATT agenda and work programme on new
themes, they would have blocked the United States and its
efforts to rollback the South and might even have prevented

the solidification of the North against the South. If in 1986, they had stood together, or at least had not undercut each other, and subsequently if they had refused to negotiate so long as the threat of unilateral retaliation was being held out, they could have ensured that the economic issues of interest to the US and not related strictly to Trade is kept out of the GATT agenda and made part of a global agenda for change (in universal fora) that the South has been striving for. If they had concerted together at a political level in relation to the Uruguay Round mid-term review (before Montreal, at Montreal and at Geneva), they could have prevented the further worsening of their situation.

The South and its peoples cannot afford many more ifs. The non-governmental organisations and peoples' movements in the South, which began their efforts for change at micro-level, have begun to relate the underdevelopment of their countries and communities to the macro problems of the global system. A broad united front of such groups and organisations of the South is emerging, and refusing to be manipulated by the North and its institutions or be co-opted by them. While striving for change these peoples and their organisations have to prevent their governments from making things worse by accommodating to the North for short-term gains. In the countries of the South the present GATT (and the one that would emerge out of the Uruguay Round if the North has its way) must be seen and identified as an instrument for oppression and enslavement of the South and its poor, as much as the IMF and the World Bank have been. The NGOs of the South should put these fundamental issues on the agenda of cooperation with NGOs and other institutions in the North.

The public of the South need not sit as helpless spectators. What is now taking place at the GATT may seem remote and intangible. But this development is of crucial significance to the economic independence, sovereignty and well-being of Third World peoples who only decades ago fought for political independence. Mahatma Gandhi in India realised the relationship between the conditions of the peasants in Champaran, and later in the whole of India, to colonial rule and its economics and began the Swadeshi movement that made India ungovernable and unprofitable to the British, thus forcing them to quit. In the process he also formulated development ideas that were ecologically sound.

The peoples and their movements of the South can take a few lessons from this and begin actions to safeguard their own future and destinies.

THE PUNTA DEL ESTE DECLARATION

[Meeting in Punta del Este (Uruguay), 15-20 September 1986, on the occasion of the Special Session of GATT Contracting Parties, ministers of member-countries of GATT adopted the declaration launching a new round of multilateral trade negotiations. The Declaration itself is in two parts:

First, meeting as contracting parties, the ministers adopted Part I of the Declaration, a decision to launch Multilateral Trade Negotiations on trade in goods. Second, as representatives of governments meeting on the occasion of the Special Session, the ministers adopted a declaration to launch negotiations on trade in services. Third, the ministers then adopted the Declaration as a whole.]

Ministers, meeting on the occasion of the Special Session of CONTRACTING PARTIES at Punta del Este, have decided to launch Multilateral Trade Negotiations (The Uruguay Round). To this end,they have adopted the following Declaration. The Multilateral Trade Negotiation (MTN) will be open to the participation of countries indicated in Parts I and II of this Declaration. A Trade Negotiations Committee (TNC) is established to carry out the Negotiations. The Trade Negotiations Committee shall hold its first meeting not later than 31 October 1986. It shall meet as appropriate at Ministerial level. The Multilateral Trade Negotiations will be concluded within four years.

PART I

NEGOTIATIONS ON TRADE IN GOODS

The CONTRACTING PARTIES meeting at Ministerial level

Determined to halt and reverse protectionism and to remove distortions to trade;

Determined also to preserve the basic principles and to further the objectives of the GATT;

Convinced that such action would promote growth and development;

Mindful of the negative effects of prolonged financial and monetary instability in the world economy, the indebtedness of a large number of less developed contracting parties, and considering the linkage between trade, money, finance and development;

Decide to enter into Multilateral Trade Negotiation on trade in goods within the framework and under the aegis of the General Agreement on Tariffs and Trade.

A. OBJECTIVES

Negotiations shall aim to:

(i) bring about further liberalisation and expansion of world trade to the benefit of all countries, especially less-developed contracting parties, including improvement of access to markets by the reduction and elimination of tariffs, quantitative restrictions and other non-tariff measures and obstacles;

(ii) strengthen the role of GATT, improve the multilateral trading system based on the principles and rules of the GATT and bring about a wider coverage of world trade under agreed, effective and enforceable multilateral disciplines;

(iii) increase the responsiveness of the GATT system to the evolving international economic environment, through facilitating necessary structural adjustment, enhancing the relationship of the GATT with the relevant international organisations and taking account of changes in trade patterns and prospects, including the growing importance of trade in high technology products, serious difficulties in commodity markets and the importance of an improved trading environment providing, *inter alia,* for the ability of indebted countries to meet their financial obligations;

(iv) foster concurrent cooperative action at the national and international levels to strengthen the interrelationship between trade policies and other economic policies affecting growth and development, and to contribute towards continued, effective and determined efforts to improve the functioning of the international monetary system and the flow of financial and real investment resources to developing countries.

B. GENERAL PRINCIPLES GOVERNING NEGOTIATIONS

(i) Negotiations shall be conducted in a transparent manner, and consistent with the objectives and commitments agreed in this Declaration and with the principles of the General Agreement in order to ensure mutual advantage and increased benefits to all participants.

(ii) The launching, the conduct and the implementation of the outcome of the negotiations shall be treated as parts of a single undertaking. However, agreements reached at an early stage may be implemented on a provisional or a definitive basis by agreement prior to the formal conclusion of the negotiations. Early agreements shall be taken into account in assessing the overall balance of the negotiations.

(iii) Balanced concessions should be sought within broad trading areas and subjects to be negotiated in order to avoid unwarranted cross-sectoral demands.

(iv) The CONTRACTING PARTIES agree that the principle of differential and more favourable treatment embodied in Part IV and other relevant provisions of the General Agreement and in the Decision of the CONTRACTING PARTIES of 28 November 1979 on Differential and More Favourable Treatment, Reciprocity and Fuller Participation of Developing Countries applies to the negotiations. In the implementation of standstill and rollback, particular care should be given to avoiding disruptive effects on the trade of less-developed contracting parties.

(v) The developed countries do not expect reciprocity for commitments made by them in trade negotiations to reduce or remove tariffs and other barriers to the trade of developing countries, i.e. the developed countries do not expect the developing countries, in the course of trade negotiations, to make contributions which are inconsistent with their individual development, financial and trade needs. Developed contracting parties shall therefore not seek, neither less-developed contracting parties be required to make concessions that are inconsistent with the latter's development, financial and trade needs.

(vi) Less-developed contracting parties expect that their capacity to make contributions or negotiated concessions or take other mutually agreed action under the provisions and procedures of the General Agreement would improve with the progressive development of their economies and improvement in their trade situation and they would accordingly expect to participate more fully in the framework of rights and obligations under the General Agreement.

(vii) Special attention shall be given to the particular situation and· problems of the least-developed countries and to the need to encourage positive measures to facilitate expansion of their trading opportunities. Expeditious implementation of the relevant provisions of the 1982 Ministerial Declaration concerning the least-developed countries shall also be given appropriate attention.

C. STANDSTILL AND ROLLBACK

Commencing immediately and continuing until the formal completion of the Negotiations, each participant agrees to apply the following commitments:

Standstill

(i) not to take any trade restrictive or distorting measures inconsistent with the provisions of the General Agreement or the Instruments negotiated within the framework of GATT or under its auspices;

(ii) not to take any trade restrictive or distorting measure in the legitimate exercise of its GATT rights, that would go beyond that which is necessary to remedy specific situations, as provided for in the General Agreement and the Instruments referred to in (i) above;

(iii) not to take any trade measures in such a manner as to improve its negotiating positions.

Rollback

(i) that all trade restrictive or distorting measures inconsistent with the provisions of the General Agreement or instruments negotiated within the framework of GATT or under its auspices, shall be phased out or brought into conformity within an agreed timeframe not later than by the date of the formal completion of the negotiations, taking into account multilateral agreements, undertakings and understandings, including strengthened rules and disciplines, reached in pursuance of the Objectives of the Negotiations;

(ii) there shall be progressive implementation of this com-

mitment on an equitable basis in consultations among participants concerned, including all affected participants. This commitment shall take account of the concerns expressed   by any
participant about measures directly affecting its trade interests;
(iii) there shall be no GATT concessions requested for the
elimination of these measures.

Surveillance of standstill and rollback
Each participant agrees that the implementation of these
commitments on standstill and rollback shall be subject to multilateral surveillance so as to ensure that these commitments are
being met. The Trade Negotiations Committee shall   decide on
the appropriate mechanism to carry out the surveillance, including periodic reviews and evaluations. Any participant may bring
to the attention of the appropriate surveillance mechanism any
actions or omissions it believes to be relevant to the fulfillment
of these commitments. These notifications should be addressed
to the GATT secretariat   which may also provide further relevant
information.

D. SUBJECTS FOR NEGOTIATIONS

Tariffs
Negotiations shall aim, by appropriate methods, to   reduce
or, as appropriate, eliminate tariffs including the reduction or
elimination of high tariffs and tariff escalation. Emphasis shall be
given to the expansion of the scope of tariff concessions among
all participants.

Non-tariff measures
Negotiations shall aim to reduce or eliminate non-tariff measures, including quantitative restrictions, without prejudice to any
action to be taken in fulfillment of the rollback commitments.

Tropical Products
Negotiations shall aim at the fullest liberalisation of trade
in tropical products, including in their processed and semi-processed forms and shall cover both tariff and all non-tariff measures affecting trade in these products.
The CONTRACTING PARTIES recognise the importance of
trade in tropical products to a large number of less-developed
contracting parties and agree that negotiations in this area shall
receive special attention,including the timing of the negotiations
and the implementation of the results as provided for in B (ii).

Natural Resource-based products
Negotiations shall aim to achieve the fullest liberalisation of trade in natural resource-based products, including in their processed and semi-processed forms. The negotiations shall aim to reduce or eliminate tariff and non-tariff measures, including tariff escalation.

Textiles and Clothing
Negotiations in the area of textiles and clothing shall aim to formulate modalities that would permit the eventual integration of this sector into GATT on the basis of strengthened GATT rules and disciplines thereby also contributing to the objectives of further liberalisation of trade.

Agriculture
The CONTRACTING PARTIES agree that there is an urgent need to bring more discipline and predictability to world agricultural trade by correcting and preventing restrictions and distortions including those related to structural surpluses so as to reduce the uncertainty, imbalances and instability in world agricultural markets.

Negotiations shall aim to achieve greater liberalisation of trade in agriculture and bring all measures affecting import access and export competition under strengthened and more operationally effective GATT rules and disciplines, taking into account the general principles governing the negotiations, by:

(i) improving market access through, *inter alia*, the reduction of import barriers;

(ii) improving the competitive environment by increasing disciplines on the use of all direct and indirect subsidies and other measures affecting directly or indirectly agricultural trade, including the phased reduction of their negative effects and dealing with their causes;

(iii) minimizing the adverse effects that sanitary and phytosanitary regulations and barriers can have on trade in agriculture, taking into account the relevant international agreements.

In order to achieve the above objectives, the negotiating group having primary responsibility for all aspects of agriculture will use the Recommendations adopted by the CONTRACTING PARTIES at their Fortieth Session, which were developed in accordance with the GATT 1982 Ministerial Programme and take account of the approaches suggested in the work of the Committee on Trade in Agriculture without prejudice to other alternatives that might achieve the objectives of the negotiations.

GATT Articles
Participants shall review existing GATT articles, provisions and disciplines as requested by interested contracting parties, and, as appropriate, undertake negotiations.

Safeguards
(i) A comprehensive agreement on safeguards is of particular importance to the strengthening of the GATT system and to progress in the MTNs.
(ii) The agreement on safeguards:
- shall be based on the basic principles of the General Agreement;
- shall contain, *inter alia,* the following elements: transparency, coverage, objective criteria for action including the concept of serious injury or threat thereof,temporary nature, degressivity, and structural adjustment, compensation and retaliation, notifications, consultation, multilateral surveillance and dispute settlement; and
- shall clarify and reinforce the disciplines of the General Agreement and should apply to all contracting parties.

MTN Agreements and Arrangements
Negotiations shall aim to improve, clarify, or expand, as appropriate, agreements and   arrangements negotiated in the Tokyo Round of Multilateral Negotiations.

Subsidies and countervailing measures
Negotiations on subsidies and countervailing measures shall be based on a review of Articles VI and XVI and the MTN agreement on subsidies and countervailing measures with the objective of improving GATT disciplines relating to all subsidies and countervailing measures that affect international trade. A negotiating group will be established to deal with these issues.

Dispute settlement
In order to ensure prompt and effective resolution of disputes to the benefit of all contracting parties,negotiations shall aim to improve and strengthen the rules and the procedures of the dispute settlement process, while recognising the contribution that would be made by more effective and enforceable GATT rules and disciplines. Negotiations shall include the development of adequate arrangements for overseeing and monitoring of the procedures that would facilitate compliance with adopted recommendations.

Trade-related aspects of intellectual property rights, including trade in counterfeit goods
In order to reduce the distortions and impediments to international trade, and taking into account the need to promote effective and adequate   protection of intellectual property rights, and to ensure that measures and procedures to enforce intellectual property rights do not themselves become barriers to legitimate trade, the negotiations shall aim to clarify GATT provisions and elaborate as appropriate new rules and disciplines.

Negotiations shall aim to develop a multilateral framework of principles, rules and disciplines dealing with international trade in counterfeit goods, taking into account work already undertaken in GATT.

These negotiations shall be without prejudice to other complementary initiatives that may be taken in the World Intellectual Property Organisation and elsewhere to deal with these matters.

Trade-related investment measures
Following an examination of the operation of GATT Articles related to the trade restrictive and distorting effects of investment measures, negotiations should elaborate, as appropriate, further provisions that may be necessary to avoid such adverse effects   on trade.

E. FUNCTIONING OF THE GATT SYSTEM

Negotiations shall aim to develop understandings and arrangements:

(i) to enhance the surveillance in the GATT to enable regular monitoring of trade policies and practices of contracting parties and their impact on the functioning of the multilateral trading system;

(ii) to improve the overall effectiveness and decision-making of the GATT as an institution, including, *inter alia*, through involvement of Ministers;

(iii) to increase the contribution of the GATT to achieving greater coherence in global economic policy-making through strengthening its relationship with other international organisations responsible for monetary and financial matters.

F. PARTICIPATION

(a) Negotiations will be open to:
(i)   all contracting parties,

(ii)   countries having acceded provisionally,

(iii)   countries applying the GATT on a *de facto* basis having announced, not later than 30 April 1987, their intention to accede to the GATT and to participate in the negotiations,

(iv) countries that have already informed the CONTRACTING   PARTIES, at a regular meeting of the Council of Representatives, of their intention to negotiate the terms of their membership as a contracting party, and

(v) developing countries that have, by 30 April 1987, initiated procedures for accession to the GATT, with   the intention of negotiating the terms of their accession during the course of the negotiations.

(b)   Participation in negotiations relating to the amendment   or application of GATT provisions or   the negotiations of new provisions will, however, be open only to contracting parties.

G. ORGANISATION OF THE NEGOTIATIONS

A Group of Negotiations on Goods (GNG) is established to carry out the programme of negotiations contained in this Part of the Declaration. The GNG shall, *inter alia*:

(i)   elaborate and put into effect detailed trade negotiating plans prior to 19 December 1986;

(ii) designate   the appropriate   mechanism   for   surveillance   of commitments to standstill and rollback;

(iii) establish negotiating groups as required. Because   of the interrelationship of some issues and taking fully into account the general principles governing the negotiations as stated in B(iii) above it is recognised that aspects of one issue may be discussed in more than one negotiating group. Therefore each negotiating group should as required take into account relevant aspects emerging in other groups;

(iv) also decide upon inclusion of additional subject matters in the negotiations;

(v) coordinate the work of the negotiating groups and supervise the progress of the negotiations. As a guideline not more than two negotiating   groups should meet at the same time;

(vi) the GNG shall report to the Trade Negotiations Committee.

In order to ensure effective application of differential and more favourable treatment the GNG shall, before the formal completion of the negotiations, conduct an evaluation of the results attained   therein   in   terms of the Objectives and the General Principles Governing Negotiations as set out in the Declaration, taking into account all issues of interest to less-developed contracting parties.

PART II

NEGOTIATIONS ON TRADE IN SERVICES

Ministers also decided as part of the Multilateral Trade Negotiations, to launch negotiations on trade in services.

Negotiations in this area shall aim to establish a multilateral framework of principles and rules for trade in services, including elaboration of possible disciplines for individual sectors, with a view to expansion of such trade under conditions of transparency and progressive liberalisation and as a means of promoting economic growth of all trading partners and the development of developing countries. Such framework shall respect the policy objectives of national laws and regulations applying to services and shall take into account the work of relevant international organisations.

GATT procedures and practices shall apply to these negotiations. A Group on Negotiations on Services is established to deal with these matters. Participation in the negotiations under this Part of the Declaration will be open to the same countries as under Part I. GATT secretariat support will be provided, with technical support from other organisations as decided by the Group of Negotiations on Services.

The Group of Negotiations on Services shall report to the Trade Negotiations Committee.

IMPLEMENTATION OF RESULTS
UNDER PARTS I AND II

When the results of the Multilateral Trade Negotiations in all areas have been established, Ministers meeting also on the occasion of a Special Session of CONTRACTING PARTIES shall decide regarding the international implementation of the respective results.